THE
COTTAGE GARDEN

month-by-month

THE
COTTAGE GARDEN

month-by-month

JACKIE BENNETT

David & Charles

A DAVID & CHARLES BOOK

Book design by Diana Knapp
Illustrations by Eva Melhuish
Additional illustrations by Michael Lye (pp28, 29, 32, 72–3); Coral Mula (p114); Avis
Murray (pp 33, 40, 64, 122); Maggie Raynor (pp21, 52, 56, 57(bottom), 58) and
Maggie Redfern (pp20, 49, 65, 115(bottom), 118(centre), 119 (centre), 131(top))
Photographs: Clive Nichols: pp2 (designer Stephen Woodhams), 62–3, 120–1, 128–9
(photographed at White Windows, Hampshire);
S.&O. Mathews: pp3, 9, 50–1, 88–9; Neil Campbell-Sharp: pp6–7;
Jerry Harpur: pp9 (designer Christopher Grey-Wilson),
38–9 (photographed at Eastgrove Cottage Garden)
Garden Picture Library: pp10–11 (photographer Howard Rice), 18–19 (John Glover),
26–7 (Lamontagne), 100–1 (Juliette Wade), 108–9 (Brigitte Thomas)

First published in the UK in 1996

A catalogue record for this book is available from the British Library.

ISBN 0 7153 0388 0

Typeset by ABM Typographics Ltd, Hull
and printed in Italy by New Interlitho SpA
for David & Charles
Brunel House   Newton Abbot   Devon

CONTENTS

INTRODUCTION

'With marjoram knots, sweetbrier and ribbon grass,
And lavender, the choice of every lass,
And sprigs of lad's love, all familiar names
Which every garden through the village claims'

JOHN CLARE: THE SHEPHERD'S CALENDAR (1821–24)

 In poet John Clare's day, every village home was a cottage, and every cottage had a garden. Honeysuckle and climbing roses covered old stone walls, lavender and marjoram scented the pathways – these cottage garden flowers were as familiar as old friends. Over the past century, there have been great changes to our houses and gardens: many of us have moved to towns, to terraced streets and new housing developments, and few people actually live in cottages anymore. Cottage gardens should have died out with the industrial revolution; perhaps they did, but cottage gardening did not it lived on in the hearts and minds of ordinary people.

Cottage gardening does not belong to any particular type of house – it is an approach to gardening, not a fixed regime. Today's cottage gardeners can choose to follow history slavishly, growing only plants that were available several centuries ago, maintaining a vegetable patch and keeping bees, chickens or even a pig, as pre-nineteenth century cottage gardeners would have done. Or take inspiration from the intellectuals of the late Victorian age who turned cottage gardening from a purely practical activity, developed through necessity, into an art form – a style of gardening. By doing the latter, we allow ourselves to use both traditional *and* improved varieties of plants and to create a garden in which the best of the past and the present is combined.

WHAT IS A COTTAGE GARDEN?

So, what is a cottage garden? Does it have vegetables and fruit? Are herbs and flowers all mixed together? Is there a lawn or a patio? There are a few generally held principles about the overall style of cottage gardens: they have a relaxed, easy, informal planting, which is instantly recognizable, and the borders are full-to-capacity, while lawns and hard landscaping are kept to a minimum.

The intention is to create a garden that looks unplanned and to which nature has lent a helping hand. Of course, the subtle combination of herbs, flowering shrubs, perennials and fruit *is* planned and it is the aim of this book to help readers to create this seemingly artless effect.

COTTAGE GARDEN HISTORY

Historically, the garden had to provide a family with food for the table, flavouring for the kitchen, medicinal cures, and cleaning agents for the house. Today, with supermarkets, cars and busy working lives, few people rely on it to provide for their needs. The garden is now a source of leisure and pleasure and most of us are content if it looks attractive, is not too time consuming and, as a bonus, provides a few herbs and salad ingredients for the table.

The medieval cottage garden was, in truth, not one we would want to recreate. It probably had a single apple tree, a pig sty, a muck heap and a patch of herbs, selected for their medicinal qualities rather than their beauty. The principle was always utility above decoration – plants had to earn their keep. But, somehow, imperceptibly over the years, plants with prettier flowers were gleaned from hedgerows and fields, seed of successful strains was saved and swapped, and gradually more and more colour crept into the cottager's plot. By the eighteenth century, the cottage garden had become something wonderful to behold, full of ornamental and productive plants, all jostling for

Punctuated by a white fence and a terracotta urn,
this informal planting includes hardy geraniums,
polemonium *and an unusual deep red astrantia*

SEASONS AND MONTHS

The seasons used in the book correspond to the months below. Obviously spring will come later in some areas and the weather varies from year to year, but in average conditions these can be used as a guide:

SPRING
Early: March
Mid: April
Late: May

SUMMER
Early: June
Mid: July
Late: August

AUTUMN
Early: September
Mid: October
Late: November

WINTER
Early: December
Mid: January
Late: February

space, and buzzing with bees. This change perhaps owes something more to the humble honey bee than we might imagine, for by planting nectar-rich plants for their bees, cottagers were inadvertently introducing more colourful and attractive plants.

Reformers of the nineteenth century saw gardens as a way of improving the health and conditions of poor labourers. Cottagers were encouraged to grow a variety of foodstuffs, and plans were devised for the 'ideal' plot. Some commentators said it should be a rood (a quarter of an acre); John Claudius Loudon, a well-known Victorian garden writer, suggested twenty perches or rods (an eighth of an acre) filled with potatoes, cabbages, parsnips, beans, onions and carrots.

In the Victorian era, when a craze for annual bedding plants hit the gardens of the wealthy merchants, industrialists and landed gentry, the small village gardens became the unwitting conservators of many old-fashioned perennials. Cottagers had neither the time, the space, nor the financial resources to cultivate bedding schemes.

By necessity, cottage gardeners over the years had selected the hardiest, the most attractive and the most wildlife-friendly plants for their gardens – foxgloves, marigolds, snapdragons, mignonette, thyme and borage. They had raised gardening to the level of a technical craft, setting up florist's societies and organizing competitive flower shows. Today, in villages all over Britain, remnants of this passion remain in gardens that appear to have been unchanged for centuries. In fact, cottage gardens are constantly evolving and new recruits to the style create flowery havens in the most unlikely places – on the balconies of apartment blocks, in the back yards of terraced houses and in the front gardens of modern housing estates. Architecture may be moving away from the cottage style, but in gardens the spirit of the old cottagers is very much alive and well.

HOW TO USE THIS BOOK

The aim of this book is to make the essential gardening information accessible at any time of year. So, whether you pick it up in summer or in the depths of winter, you will find details of jobs to do and planting suggestions and tips. In the past, the traditional planting times were autumn and spring: this is when

the plants are dormant and less likely to be disturbed by being moved. However, more and more nurseries and garden centres are selling container-grown plants throughout the year. Because these plants have not been lifted from the ground, they have had less disturbance and can be planted at any time – as long as the ground is workable (that is, not frozen, waterlogged, or baked hard with heat). One of the key aims of this book is to ensure that the garden looks good all through the year, so even in the winter months there are ideas for plants and work to be done.

Each monthly chapter is divided into four sections: an introduction, a checklist of tasks and instructions on how to carry them out, profiles of plants which are at their peak, and one or more practical projects designed to enable you to extend your range of planting techniques and skills.

Within the space of this book it has only been possible to suggest a small range of plants for each month and the selection has been made on the basis that these are the flowers and shrubs that no cottage gardener would want to be without – plants like honeysuckle, pinks, lilies, lavender, primroses and roses. Although more experienced cottage gardeners might find the selection a little limited, it is intended to be a foundation on which a more adventurous plant collection can be built. Those plants that it was not possible to include, such as verbenas, phlox and penstemons, should be assumed to be welcome in the cottage garden.

WARNING

Throughout this book, reference is made to the medicinal use of plants and herbs – particularly in previous centuries. These are mentioned for historical interest and are not recommended as remedies. Although many people do use herbs in this way today, they should never be taken internally or applied to the body without advice from a qualified herbalist or doctor.

Left: The key to cottage garden success is full-to-capacity borders where bare earth and weeds are nowhere to be seen
Right: Rosa 'Alchymist' frames the window beautifully, while valerian provides a striking contrast in the foreground

JANUARY

Midwinter, if true to form, should bring its share of icy winds, frost and snow. It is tempting not to venture out into the garden at all, but those who do are rewarded by a magical dusting of hoar frost on every twig, leaf and stem. The structure of the garden is laid bare and the evergreen mounds made by privet, holly, box and rue are reassuringly solid. At ground level, winter aconites and the first snowdrops are pushing their way through, seemingly oblivious of the ice-hard soil and cold, wet blanket of snow. There are few things more cheering than the opening of these early flowers, bright and beautiful in rare moments of sunshine.

At this time of year a gardener's thoughts turn to boundaries, which are now exposed with all their faults – sparse hedges, wobbly fences and gappy walls. While the problems should not be tackled this month, it is a good time for reviewing the situation and making plans to order new hedging plants or to redesign the fencing altogether. It is also a good time to ponder the pros and cons of evergreen versus deciduous hedging. There is no doubt that privet and yew can look dark and dull in a hot, dusty summer, but in a winter frost the leaves sparkle and shine. Likewise, rose and hawthorn hedges are full of interest in spring, summer and autumn but in winter they disappear into mediocrity. It is a difficult choice. Some writers suggest planting showy climbers, such as clematis, through an evergreen hedge, but to me this seems unnecessarily fussy. View the hedge as a protective arm, slipping itself around the flowers to shield them from wind and cold, and you will find it more easy to accept – and appreciate – for what it is. Apart from planning for the months ahead (and the seed catalogues are loaded with temptation) the gardener can, on those rare sorties outdoors, witness some winter delights. Shrubs in flower in midwinter include winter sweet, witch hazel, Daphne mezereum and the winter viburnums, bringing perfume and colour on the bleakest days.

tasks
FOR THE
month

SNOWDROPS IN THE GREEN
Snowdrops rarely last well indoors, but if you must pick them to enjoy the scent, plunge them into cold water up to their necks and stand in a cool outhouse for twenty four hours before use. Alternatively, clumps of snowdrops that will need to be divided anyway can be dug up while flowering and placed in terracotta cooking pots then the earth covered with moss. Keep them moist, then after flowering, divide and plant them outdoors again.

CHECKLIST

- ☐ Force rhubarb
- ☐ Lift and divide snowdrops and aconites
- ☐ Protect tender perennials
- ☐ Plant deciduous shrubs

FORCING RHUBARB

This is one of the traditional winter jobs for the cottage gardener. Forcing, or 'forwarding' as it used to be called, means selecting one or two rhubarb crowns and protecting them from the cold and light so they grow slender, pale stems, that are earlier and more tender than those produced in early summer. The most attractive device is a terracotta rhubarb forcer, which is open at the bottom with a removable lid at the top. Simply place it over the crowns and lift the lid occasionally to check when the stems are fully grown. A less expensive method is to surround the crowns with straw or to place an upturned bucket or wooden box over them. If you have a plentiful supply of leafmould, make a cylinder of wire mesh around the clumps and cover the crowns with the leafmould.

NOTE

■ *Rhubarb should only be forced when it has been growing successfully for at least three years. Choose different plants to force each year so that the forced plants have chance to recover. (For instructions on planting and cultivating rhubarb, see p.34)* ■

Harvesting rhubarb
The stems should be ready for pulling in one to two months; take only the largest. Place your thumb on the inside of the stem as far down as possible and twist it away from the plant. Discard the leaves which are poisonous.

PROTECTING TENDER PLANTS

This can be one of the worst periods for frost, cold and wet conditions. Old cottage garden plants are generally hardy enough to resist all weathers, but some of the newer plants now grown in cottage gardens are on the borderline of hardiness and will benefit from a little extra protection in winter; this includes autumn-flowering nerines (*Nerine bowdenii*), agapanthus (*Agapanthus*), penstemons (*Penstemon* species) and montbretias (*Crocosmia*). Cover their crowns with a layer of straw or bracken.

LIFTING AND DIVIDING SNOWDROPS AND ACONITES

Both snowdrops and aconites prefer to be moved or propagated when they are in the green', that is, just after they have flowered, but while the foliage is still growing strongly. This is a task for the latter part of this month and next and is particularly useful to rejuvenate clumps that have stopped flowering well. There are many variations on the standard snowdrop species, *Galanthus nivalis*, including those with double flowers and striking markings. If you make only one new year's resolution, promise to order yourself a few interesting snowdrops from the catalogues this month.

Snowdrops (*Galanthus* species)
Use a fork to lift the clumps

PLANTING EVERGREENS AND CONTAINER-GROWN SHRUBS
Evergreens prefer to be planted when the soil is warmer, in mid-autumn or mid-spring. Many nurseries and garden centres now sell their shrubs as container-grown specimens, which means they have been established in containers and have built up a dense root system. Container-grown shrubs can be planted at any time of year.

out of the ground. Divide the bulbs by hand, discarding any that are soft or damaged. Replant the others immediately, 10–15cm (4–6in) apart and 5cm (2in) deep, in moist soil. Choose a site where the plants will receive some shade. The smaller bulbs may take a year or two to reach flowering size.

Aconites (*Eranthis hyemalis*)
Aconites form tuberous clumps. Lift the clumps with a fork and divide the tubers into sections. This can be done by breaking them into pieces or by cutting with a knife. Immediately replant the new sections into a moisture retentive soil, 8cm (3in) apart

Dividing bulbs

and 2.5cm (1in) deep. Like snowdrops, aconites prefer dappled shade, under deciduous shrubs or trees is ideal, particularly if the soil has added leafmould.

PLANTING DECIDUOUS SHRUBS

The main season for planting deciduous trees and shrubs is from mid-autumn to late winter while the plants are dormant — although they are never planted when the ground is frozen, waterlogged or snow-covered. However, if this is a relatively mild month, bare-rooted shrubs can be safely planted.

Preparation
The soil must be workable and fertile; if it is not, dig it over to about a spade's depth and add organic matter such as garden compost or well-rotted manure. Remove the shrubs from their packaging and check the roots are healthy. Trim off any broken roots with a pair of secateurs.

■ Dig a roughly circular hole, deep and wide enough to take the root system. Try the shrub in position to check that the old soil mark on the stem will be level with the top of the hole

■ Add some garden compost, old potting compost or well-rotted manure to the planting hole. Fork the bottom to mix the soil with the added material

■ Hold the shrub by the main stem and place it into the hole. Fill around the roots with the excavated soil, shaking the shrub to ensure that the soil goes down into between the roots. Firm in the soil by gently treading it down. Water thoroughly

plants
OF THE
month

Winter aconite

WINTER ACONITE
(*Eranthis hyemalis*)

The cheerful rosettes of yellow flowers appear at ground level in midwinter, often in the company of snowdrops. Aconites were almost certainly introduced into Britain in the sixteenth century – they appear in Gerard's herbal published in 1597 – and by the time of poet John Clare (the first half of the nineteenth century) they were a regular feature of cottage gardens. In Lincolnshire they go by the name of New Year's Gift, perhaps because of their tendency to open up at the first hint of winter sunshine.

type	Tuberous perennial
flowers	Bright yellow; midwinter to early spring
foliage	A collar or ruff of deeply-divided leaves beneath the flower
height	8–10cm (3–4in)
spread	8cm (3in)
site	In sun while flowering, partial shade for rest of the year so, ideally, under deciduous trees or shrubs
soil	Moist, humus-rich with added leafmould
planting	Plant tubers in late summer or early autumn, 3–5cm (1–2in) deep and 8cm (3in) apart in groups of six or more
care	Apply a mulch of leafmould around the plants in spring to preserve moisture through the year
propagation	Plants will naturally set seed and spread. Alternatively, lift and divide tubers immediately after flowering
hybrids	*E. hyemalis* Tubergenii group are sweetly-scented garden hybrids with larger flowers than the species. They flower slightly later, in early spring.

WITCH HAZEL
(*Hamamelis mollis*)

Based on the ideal that a cottage garden should have something in bloom all year round, no garden can afford to be without a witch hazel. The fragrant, spidery flowers appear before the leaves, which makes them all the more striking. They are fairly tough shrubs, quite resistant to a bit of urban pollution, but the flowers can be spoilt by blasts of icy winds; a hedge or fence will protect them. Witch hazel was named by English settlers in America, who were reminded of the hazel trees from their native Britain by the

Hamamelis virginiana that grew wild in the woods of Virginia. They used the forked twigs for water divining and dowsing as they had used hazel rods at home – hence the supernatural association. *Hamamelis mollis*, the Chinese witch hazel, was a later introduction to gardens.

type	Deciduous shrub or small tree
flowers	Yellow; mid- to late winter
foliage	Mid-green, turning golden in autumn
height	To 3m (10ft)
spread	2.4m (8ft)
site	In sun or partial shade, with some protection from cold winds
soil	Prefers acid soil, but will tolerate neutral soil with added humus
planting	Plant between mid-autumn and early spring, adding leafmould to the planting hole on neutral soils
care	No pruning required. Remove any straggly branches on old plants, after flowering. Mulch with leafmould in spring or autumn
propagation	Layering in early autumn. Seed can be collected in mid-autumn and left to germinate in pots outside or in a coldframe – germination takes up to two years
varieties	*H.* x *intermedia* 'Pallida' is the most popular variety with its dense, soft yellow flowers, but there are many other named garden varieties with flowers ranging from copper to deep crimson
cottage garden value	Witch hazels provide perfume and colour on dreary winter days, and the branches make interesting indoor flower decorations

PRIVET
(*Ligustrum ovalifolium*)

Privet was probably the most popular cottage garden hedging plant and its usefulness is hard to ignore. True, the dull, dusty-leafed, straggly specimens we often see in suburban gardens are hardly an enticement to grow the plant, but a well-trimmed privet makes a quiet, subdued backdrop for riotous planting. Relatively quick-growing, it has the added advantage of being easy to clip into a range of shapes and can been used for making entrance arches to gardens, shady arbours for garden seats and shaped hedges. It was known as 'poor-man's topiary', being quicker to grow and easier to obtain than box or yew, and provided the cottager with a chance to show off his artistic skills: doves, cockerels and globes were typical shapes sculpted out of otherwise plain hedges.

type	Evergreen shrub
flowers	Cream; midsummer; only produced if grown as an unclipped shrub
foliage	Mid-green, oval
height	To 4m (12ft), usually clipped to about 2m (6ft)
spread	2m (6ft)
site	Sun or shade; best used as hedging, but can be grown as a flowering shrub
soil	Any fertile soil
planting	For hedging, choose plants 30–60cm (12–24in) high and set them out in mid-autumn or mid-spring, 30–45cm (12–18in) apart. Before planting, improve the soil by working in some garden compost or well-rotted manure.
care	In mid-spring after planting, cut all shoots by half their length. Repeat this in mid-spring and early autumn of the following year to encourage bushy growth from the base. Continue to cut the shoots back by half in early autumn until the hedge reaches its final height. Established hedges should be trimmed twice a year in late spring and early autumn. The ground beneath a privet hedge can become starved of nutrients, so apply an annual mulch of well-rotted manure or compost
propagation	Take hardwood cuttings in mid-autumn. Insert in a sheltered border and plant out into permanent positions the following autumn
varieties	*L. ovalifolium* 'Aureum', golden privet, was a favourite of Victorian gardens and is still widely available. The leaves are edged with wide bands of golden-yellow. 'Argenteum' has leaves variegated with a gentler yellow. Both are slower-growing than the green form and need sunshine to retain their colour
cottage garden value	Few plants are more resistant to abuse, more tolerant of pollution and give such effective screening

SANTOLINA
(*Santolina chamaecyparissus*)

The silvery foliage of this Mediterranean herb should withstand the coldest winter and will shine out from the borders on even the dark-est days. Santolina (also known as cotton lavender) makes low-growing mounds of aromatic foliage which can be used as an effective edging for paths or beds. It came into vogue during the Elizabethan period for use in knot gardens where, like box, it could be clipped into neat shapes.

type	Evergreen dwarf shrub
flowers	Bright yellow button-like flowers; midsummer, if unclipped
foliage	Silver, finely-divided, woolly, aromatic
height	45–60cm (18–24in)
spread	45–60cm (18–24in)
site	Full sun; as path edging, at the front of borders or in containers
soil	Any well-drained, but a light, sandy soil is best
planting	Set out young plants in early to mid-spring, 40cm (16in) apart for hedging
care	Pinch out the growing tips twice during the first year of growth to encourage dense foliage. When fully grown, use shears occasionally through the summer to retain a compact shape. Old plants that have become woody should be cut back hard into the old wood, in mid-spring, to encourage new shoots from the base (see p.41)
propagation	Take semi-ripe cuttings in late summer and grow on in a coldframe. Pot up the following spring and plant out into permanent positions in autumn
varieties	*S. chamaecyparissus* var. *nana* is a more compact 30cm (12in) high which is ideal for edging. *S. c.* 'Lambrook Silver' is a full-size variety with finely-cut silver foliage
related species	*S. pinnata* subsp. *neapolitana* forms a larger mass of foliage – grey, rather than silver – but with the same, sunny yellow flowers in summer. *S. rosmarinifolia* has deep green foliage
cottage garden value	When so much in the cottage garden is herbaceous, with only fleeting flowers, it is invaluable to have some plants that hold their shape and foliage through the winter. The dried leaves and stalks can be used in pot pourri and are reputed to have an insect repellent quality

Top to bottom: witch hazel, privet and santolina (NB: the flowers of the santolina will not appear until midsummer.)

practical project

CREATING THE COTTAGE GARDEN BOUNDARY

Enclosing the plot of land was vitally important to the cottage gardener. It was what distinguished his garden from a piece of common land or from the surrounding fields. Garden writers, painters and poets have given us lots of clues to what the traditional cottager might have chosen for his boundary. The Northamptonshire poet John Clare speaks of the garden being enclosed by painted pales – the traditional palisade or picket fence. Thomas Hyll, writing in the sixteenth century, suggests hedging the plot with 'either privet alone, or sweetbriar and whitethorn, interlaced together'. In eighteenth-century paintings we see dry stone walls, broken by a wooden gate or stile. Neat privet or 'quickset' (hawthorn) hedges were a feature of tidier Victorian gardens. William Robinson, writing in the late nineteenth century, recommends holly and 'quick' mixed with sweet briar (*Rosa rubiginosa*), dog rose (*Rosa canina*) and bramble, with perhaps an odd bush of sloes (blackthorn). He was very scathing about iron railings as a garden boundary which, he wrote, 'bids fair to ruin the beauty of the English landscape'.

Whatever material was chosen for the boundary, it was rarely above waist or chest height. Presumably the cottage gardener liked to look out on his neighbours and, naturally, passers-by liked to look in. The cottage garden boundary should reflect the local environment – so if stone walls or hedges are commonplace in your neighbourhood, let this be your guiding principle.

FENCES, PALES AND HURDLES

The term 'dead hedge' is used in the countryside to describe a boundary that is not living. Rural fences developed as temporary divisions and were used to fill in the gaps in old field hedges or to give protection to newly-planted hedging shrubs.

Picket fencing

Waist-high picket fencing imposes orderliness on chaotic planting and has the advantage that plants can happily poke their heads through the gaps and seed themselves on the other side. Originally made from roughly-hewn timber, it can now be bought in ready-made lengths, in natural wood or painted. White and green look good in most gardens, but it can be painted to match the house, the front door, or some other feature in the garden. The lengths of picket are attached to stout upright posts which should have been pressure treated with preservative. If the posts are erected securely and the pales are well painted, a picket fence can last for years.

Wattle hurdles

Wattle hurdles are usually made from willow or hazel rods, cut from coppiced trees. The pliable lengths of wood are woven between upright stakes which have pointed bases and are stuck directly into the ground. Originally, craftsmen would have put up the stakes in the position where the hurdle was needed and woven in situ. Nowadays, they are available as 2m (6ft) panels, which can be nailed to upright posts, although local craftsmen can still be found who can make the traditional wattle. This is not intended to be a long-lasting method of fencing, but is decorative and useful for sheltering a young hedge.

FIXING FENCING POSTS

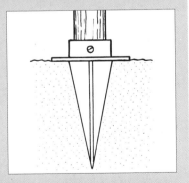

■ Posts last longer if set in a hole filled with hardcore (broken bricks or stones), which ensures that any water drains away quickly from the bottom. The hole is then filled with concrete to hold it in position ■

■ On ground that is firm, but not too stony, metal post holders can be driven into the earth. The post is held firmly in the metal casing and never comes into contact with the ground ■

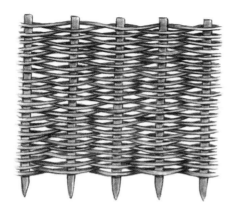

Chestnut paling

This is a very inexpensive, simple type of fencing, made from chestnut (or other) pales, secured to three lengths of wire; it is flexible and is usually bought on a roll. Although not particularly strong, it is useful for marking the boundaries of large areas, and shrubs or small trees can be planted in front of it.

LIVING BOUNDARIES

In a true cottage garden, the boundary has to work just as hard as the rest of the plants, that is, it must be useful as well as decorative. Hedges of all types serve the purpose well, offering shelter to plants, protecting them from the worst extremities of frost, wind, rain and sun. However, in a small plot, the commonly planted privet, which takes lots of nutrients and moisture from the soil, may not be the best use of the precious space. The cottage garden can also be separated from its neighbours by espalier fruit trees (see p.119) which have blossom in spring and a good crop of apples or pears later in the year.

Hedging plants

Yew (*Taxus baccata*). Yew makes one of the best hedges, but patience is needed as the plants are very slow-growing. It is fully evergreen and hardy, tolerating wind and drought. The foliage is dense and can easily be clipped into topiary or shaped hedges. For hedging choose plants 45cm (18in) high and plant them in mid-autumn or mid-spring, 45cm (18in) apart. Clip once a year, in summer. All parts of the plant are poisonous.

Privet (*Ligustrum ovalifolium*) see page 14. A quick-growing evergreen with glossy leaves, which can be easily trimmed into neat hedges and topiary shapes. Choose 45cm (18in) high plants and set them out 40cm (16in) apart. All parts of the plant are poisonous.

Hawthorn (*Crataegus monogyna*). Hawthorn grows at a medium pace and is a good multi-purpose hedging shrub. It makes a thorny, impenetrable barrier and can be clipped closely or allowed to form a more natural-looking boundary. The spring flowers are scented and attractive to bees and insects; they are followed by colourful hips or 'haws' which were used to make a vitamin C-rich jelly. Choose 45cm (18in) high plants and set them 40cm (16in) apart, between autumn and early spring. Trim in the summer.

Blackthorn (*Prunus spinosa*). Once a common hedgerow shrub, blackthorn is now quite scarce. The bluey-black fruit, known as sloes, are very acidic and not good to eat. However, they can be used to make a potent drink – sloe gin. They had many medicinal uses for the old cottagers. Blackthorn makes a thick hedge which provides an excellent habitat for nesting birds. Choose plants that are no taller than 45cm (18in), and set them out, 40cm (16in) apart, between autumn and early spring.

Roses (*Rosa* spp.). Sweet briar (*Rosa rubiginosa*) makes a dense hedge, reaching about 2.2m (8ft) high, with single pink flowers and huge orange-red hips. *Rosa rugosa* is also excellent for hedging, particularly the varieties 'Rubra' and 'Roseraie de l'Hay', which have scented flowers and showy hips. Plant the bushes from autumn to early spring, setting them 40cm (16in) apart. In winter, cut them back to within 45cm (18in) of the ground to produce dense growth.

POISONOUS HEDGES
Yew is another widely planted hedge, but being poisonous to livestock (and humans), it must be used with care if the garden adjoins farmland. As a hedge was intended to keep animals out of the garden, perhaps unscrupulous cottagers planted it to keep their neighbours' stock at bay.

INFORMAL BOUNDARIES
To make a more informal boundary which does not need regular clipping, combine small native trees and shrubs such as field maple (Acer campestre), elder (Sambucus nigra), hazel (Corylus avellana), cherry (Prunus avium), holly (Ilex aquifolium), bullace (Prunus domestica) and crab apple (Malus sylvestris). The result will be a much taller, less cultivated boundary but one which might suit a large garden or one with a wild area.

FEBRUARY

This is one of the months where forward planning reaps rich rewards for the cottage gardener. It is tempting to think that nothing grows in this dark, damp time, but a cottage garden planted for winter as well as summer will surprise with its bounty. Pulmonarias (once only available as the native lungwort) have been developed into an interesting and attractive group of plants with variegated foliage and a range of flower colours. Periwinkle (Vinca minor and V. major) is always excellent evergreen ground cover, but also produces flowers out of season, in shades of mauve and purple. Windflowers (Anemone blanda) are coming into bloom, creating patches of pink, blue and purple. Snowdrops reach their peak early in the month and crocuses will be poking their colourful chalices above the frozen ground.

Nor are shrubs disappointing: native hazels begin their annual cycle with delicate catkins and tiny suggestions of leaves, and a more exotic shrub which also shines at this time of year is Garrya elliptica – an evergreen with beautiful long, silvery catkins. The flowering quince (Chaenomeles speciosa), a widely grown cottage garden shrub, produces its blossom in winter, particularly if given the warmth and protection of a wall.

If cottage gardening is about making the most of the garden in every season, then this is not a month to put our feet up. It is easy to miss the 'deadlines' for seed sowing: sweet peas, perennials and vegetables should be sown indoors or in a coldframe this month. Out in the garden, established perennials can be moved or divided if the ground is not frozen. Depending on local conditions, new perennials can also be bought and planted. Gooseberry bushes need to be pruned to open them up for healthy growth and easy picking. Finally, this is the last chance for planting bare-rooted fruit trees, roses or deciduous hedges while the plants remain dormant.

tasks
FOR THE
month

CHECKLIST

- Prune gooseberry bushes and shrub roses
- Lift and divide overgrown perennials
- Sow perennial seed indoors

PRUNING

The traditional cottage garden always includes a few gooseberry bushes, and now is the time for pruning them. The aim is to produce bushes which are goblet-shaped and open in the centre, making it easy to pick the fruit. If the branches are allowed to cross in the middle, harvesting is difficult and uncomfortably thorny.

Many of the old-fashioned cottage garden roses, such as the Rugosa and Gallica roses, come under the heading of shrubs and do not need the severe pruning of hybrid tea bushes. These shrub roses have a more relaxed, natural appearance and the only pruning they

need at this time of year is the removal of dead wood and a light 'tidying up' of the branches.

Gooseberry bushes
- Cut out any crossing or inward-growing branches completely. Remove any dead wood.

- Shorten the leading shoots by about one quarter of their length, always cutting to an outward-facing bud. Any side shoots (laterals) should be cut back to about 5cm (2in).

Shrub roses
- Remove dead or very old stems as near to the base of the plant as possible.

- Cut back any particularly

long shoots which are spoiling the shape of the plant.

- 'Tip' all the stems by cutting off a few inches. This will encourage the formation of flower-bearing side shoots. 'Tipping' can be done very easily with hedging shears, although many gardeners still prefer to cut each stem individually.

DIVIDING PERENNIALS

Any perennial plants that have formed large clumps can be divided this month or next. Division not only provides a stock of new plants for the year ahead, but also prevents large specimens from outgrowing their allotted space.

Some herbaceous perennials, such as golden rod (*Solidago*), cuckoo flower (*Cardamine pratensis*) and aquilegia may be easier to divide in autumn (see p.111), while the foliage is still visible. However, if the winter has been mild, new growth may already have appeared and they will be easy to identify.

PRUNING GOOSEBERRIES

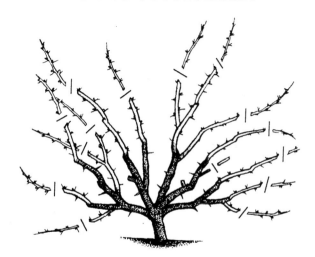

PRUNING SHRUB ROSES

Do not lift plants if the weather is frosty — wait until there is a comparatively mild spell.

■ Ease the plant out of the ground with a garden fork, working around it, levering it gently on all four sides.

■ Divide the plant immediately. If necessary, wash away the soil from around the roots to make them easier to see. If the roots are not too matted, pull apart sections of the plant by hand, complete with roots, and replant immediately.

■ If the plant roots are very old and matted, insert two garden forks, back to back, into the clump and lever the roots apart. This seems a bit brutal, but the sections of the plant will survive.

■ Replant sections immediately and water lightly if the ground is not moist. Remember to leave sufficient distance between the plants, to allow for their eventual spread.

SOWING SEED INDOORS

Seed of perennial plants (either bought in packets or saved and stored from last year) should be sown this month. Ideally, the sown seed needs to be kept at a temperature of 15°C (59°F) so a small heated propagator is useful. If you do not have a propagator, seedlings can be raised in a closed coldframe or cool greenhouse, although they may take longer to germinate.

How to Sow

■ Fill the seed trays or pots with seed compost to 2.5cm (1in) below the rim. Water the compost with the fine rose spray.

■ Sprinkle the seeds over the surface, as thinly as possible. It is best to put a small

amount in the palm of your hand and take 'pinches'.

■ Cover with a fine layer of compost 5mm (¼in) thick. Use a sieve so the compost is distributed evenly and does not disturb the seed.

■ Cover the trays with sheets of perspex (or glass masked with a sheet of white paper; this allows light to filter through to the seeds but stops

the sunlight from being magnified by the glass). Pots should be covered with polythene bags secured with string or plastic garden tie.

■ Place the pots or trays in a propagator, on a greenhouse bench, or in a coldframe with the lid closed.

Aftercare

Ensure that the compost is kept moist by regular misting with a fine water spray. As soon as the seeds have germinated (usually between three and six weeks), remove the covers. Keep the seedlings in a warm place and gradually increase the ventilation by opening the coldframe or greenhouse ventilators on mild days.

Pricking out

When the seedlings have produced at least one pair of true leaves (the ones that appear after the initial seedling leaves), they must be pricked out into new pots to give them more room to grow. Fill the pots with multipurpose potting compost, water and allow to drain. Make holes in the compost using a pencil or dibber. Lift the seedlings carefully including the roots, and place them in the new holes. Firm the compost gently with your fingers.

Hardening off

Once the plants are growing vigorously (usually by late spring), transplant them into individual 10cm (4in) pots of potting compost. Keep watered and gradually introduce them to the outside world by opening the coldframe or the greenhouse doors. The pots can be stood outside during summer, provided they are protected from strong sunlight, kept well watered and checked regularly for damage from slugs and snails. Plant out in the garden in mid-autumn (see p.110).

PLANTS TO DIVIDE

Oriental poppy (Papaver orientale)
Soapwort (Saponaria officinalis)
Betony (Stachys officinalis)
Daisy (Bellis perennis)
Rudbeckia (Rudbeckia spp.)
Michaelmas daisy (Aster spp.)
Phlox (Phlox maculata and P. paniculata)

PERENNIAL AND HERB SEEDS TO SOW

Bellflower (Campanula species)
Gold dust (Alyssum saxatile)
Hyssop (Hyssopus officinalis)
Perennial sweet pea (Lathyrus latifolius)
Toadflax (Linaria purpurea)
Lupin (Lupinus polyphyllus)
Musk mallow (Malva moschata)
Marjoram (Origanum vulgare)
Oriental poppy (Papaver orientale)
Sage (Salvia officinalis)

TIP
The little forks provided with take-away foods, and plant labels with V-shaped ends are ideal for pricking out seedlings

plants
OF THE
month

Mezereon
'Though leafless, well attired
and thick beset with blushing
wreaths, investing every spray'
WILLIAM COWPER,
'THE WINTER WALK AT NOON'

MEZEREON
(Daphne mezereum)

Mezereon, known as Mezell in Hampshire and the Paradise plant in the West Country, was once a common wild shrub of woodland, pastures and shrubland. Cottage gardeners have grown it for generations, most probably because of its early flowers and heady perfume. It is compact and has a long season of interest: the flowers appear on bare stems, to be followed by the leaves and bright red berries. It is also slow-growing, which in small gardens can be a blessing. All parts of the plants are poisonous especially the berries.

type	Deciduous shrub
flowers	Pale, purple-pink; late winter to early spring
berries	Bright red; after flowers
foliage	Dull grey-green; after flowers
height	To 1.5m (5ft)
spread	To 1.4m (4½ft)
site	In sun or light shade
soil	Well-drained
planting	Plant in early autumn or early spring
care	Keep the roots cool by mulching in spring. No pruning required; it dislikes being cut back, but if growth is very straggly, snip off the tips of the branches in early spring
propagation	Take cuttings from non-flowering shoots in late summer or collect and sow seed when ripe (midsummer to early autumn). Seed may take a year or two to germinate, so look out for seedlings growing beneath an existing shrub
varieties	The white-flowered form, 'Alba' has amber yellow berries
related species	The evergreen *D. odora* comes into flower slightly earlier than *D. mezereum* and has a very exotic perfume. It would not have been available to early cottage gardeners, but is just as useful, if not quite as elegant. It has a variegated form, *D. odora* 'Aureomarginata'
cottage garden value	Daphnes were undoubtedly grown for their perfumed flowers, which is as attractive to early butterflies and bumblebees as it is to humans. The bark, used in folk medicine, has pharmacological properties, although all parts of the plant are poisonous

CROCUS 'OLD TOMMY'
(Crocus tomasinianus)

Of the myriad of crocus species and varieties now available to the cottage gardener, few have the charm of *C. tomasinianus* – affectionately known as 'Old Tommy'. The lilac buds open at the first hint of sun to reveal deeper-coloured inner petals, with bright orange stamens. Old Tommy looks best grown in grass beneath a tree, or wherever it can seed and spread and take on a more natural appearance.

type	Corm
flowers	Lilac, purple; late winter to early spring
foliage	Narrow, grassy leaves each with a silver stripe
height	15cm (6in)
spread	15cm (6in)
site	In sun or light shade; naturalized in grass or in groups between ground-cover plants
soil	Well-drained
planting	Plant corms 7.5cm (3in) deep and 10cm (4in) apart, in early autumn
care	No special care needed. Allow flowers and leaves to die down naturally. If growing in grass, mow as late as possible in spring, to allow time for the corms to build up food reserves from leaves
propagation	Self-seeds easily and should increase without difficulty. Seeds can also be collected in early summer. To propagate from the corms, lift clumps as the leaves turn brown, remove the offsets and replant immediately
varieties	*C. tomasinianus* 'Barr's Purple' and *C. t.* 'Whitewell Purple' are deeper coloured than the species. *C. t.* 'Albus' is the white form
related species	*Crocus aureus* was described in Gerard's Herbal as a flower of a 'most perfect shining yellow colour' – a wonderful contrast to the purple forms. Sometimes known as *Crocus luteus* or *C. flava*, it is 10cm (4in) high and can also be naturalized in grass
cottage garden value	Although a relatively late (nineteenth century) introduction to cottage gardens, Old Tommy has the two essential qualities of a cottage garden plant: it is easy to grow and has a tendency to self-seed. It is also a useful plant for early bees

SNOWDROP
(Galanthus nivalis)

Although not a native to Britain, the snowdrop has been with us since medieval times and was a common flower in early cottage gardens. It began its garden career by being dug up from the hedgebanks and woodlands where it had colonized freely. Its close association with the Feast of the Purification, or Candlemas, on February 2nd, ensured that it was widely planted around churches and abbeys, from where, no doubt, the local cottagers purloined a few bulbs to purify and beautify their own plots.

type	Bulb
flowers	White, with green-tipped inner petals; mid- to late winter
foliage	Narrow, grass-like
height	13–20cm (5–8in)
spread	15–20cm (6–8in)
site	Partly shaded, under deciduous trees or hedges where it will receive some sunlight in winter and early spring
soil	Any, but grow best in moist, humus-rich soils
planting	Plant as dry bulbs in early autumn, 5cm (2in) deep and 8–15cm (3–6in) apart, or 'in the green' in early spring
care	May take two or three years to get established, but then needs no special care
propagation	Sets seed and spreads naturally. Alternatively, lift and divide clumps immediately after flowering
varieties	All the widely available varieties make good cottage garden subjects. *G. nivalis* 'Viridapicis' has green markings on the outer as well as the inner petals. The double 'Flore Pleno' is very showy and a great favourite with cottage gardeners. *G.* 'S. Arnott' is taller, about 20cm (8in) high, and has a good scent
cottage garden value	The snowdrop's fragrance is delicate rather than powerful and really only gives itself up when warmed by unseasonal sunshine or by bringing the blooms in to the house. The bulb was supposed to have made a good wound dressing and this may have been the reason that monks first imported it from Italy to form part of their comprehensive physic gardens

LUNGWORT
(Pulmonaria officinalis)

Although technically spring flowerers, in sheltered gardens lungworts often brave the weather to bloom from midwinter onwards. The real delight is the colour of their flowers which changes from pink on opening, to violet-blue as they age. The common lungwort would have found a place in many a shady corner of the cottage garden, providing interesting ground cover with its silver-spotted leaves, marked, it was believed, by the tears of the Virgin Mary. In many areas it is called Sage of Jerusalem or the Jerusalem cowslip, but its reputed ability to cure diseases of the lung account for its most commonly-used name.

type	Herbaceous perennial
flowers	Pink fading to blue and violet; midwinter to mid-spring
foliage	Green with white spots, heart-shaped
height	30cm (12in)
spread	60cm (24in)
site	In partial or full shade
soil	Any moist soil
planting	Plant between mid-autumn and early spring, 45cm (18in) apart
care	Mulch in spring and autumn to retain moisture
propagation	Divide roots when soil is moist in mid-autumn. Replant immediately
varieties	*P. officinalis* 'Sissinghurst White' has spotted leaves and white flowers
related species	*P. rubra* is one of the earliest to flower and has plain green leaves. *P. rubra* 'Redstart' has rosy-red flowers which will bloom for several months. *P. saccharata* is grown for its strong silver markings. *P. saccharata* 'Argentea' has leaves of almost pure silver
cottage garden value	The leaves were used as a pot herb and to make an infusion which was said to cure lung troubles. Pulmonaria's association with lungs dates back to the sixteenth century when physicians believed that a plant's appearance was a clue to its medicinal properties – the spotted leaves were thought to resemble the inside of a lung: the relationship has no foundation in fact. Nevertheless, the plant provides excellent ground cover and welcome early flowers

Top to bottom: crocus, snowdrop and lungwort

practical
project

MAKING PATHS AND
CHOOSING EDGING

TRADITIONAL COTTAGE
GARDEN DESIGNS

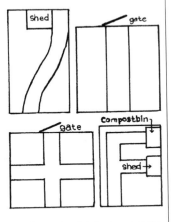

A curved path helps to reduce the length of a long narrow garden. A path from gate to door is the classic 'two halves' layout. A cross design enables access to all parts of the garden. An E-shape breaks up a long garden

For the original cottage gardener, the best path was the shortest route between two points. Design did not come into the equation – a path was simply a way of getting to the vegetables, flowers, herbs or compost with the minimum of fuss. Simplicity is still the key concept to keep in mind when planning cottage garden paths. A path should lead somewhere – to a seat or to a shed, for instance – and not merely meander for the sake of it. Make use of natural routes, starting the path at the back or front door of the house and allowing it to stretch to which ever part of the garden you use most.

Of course a path is part of a garden's design and it can be used to divide a large, square plot into manageable 'chunks'. The lines do not have to be straight, particularly if the plot is rectangular, but keep any curves subtle. This not only retains an uncluttered layout but also makes laying the path much easier.

MATERIALS

Well-trodden earth between privy and compost heap may have been the reality of a sixteenth century cottage garden, but most people would opt for something a bit more secure underfoot. Pea shingle makes a simple, low-cost path that requires no building skills or tools to lay. Chopped bark is a good material for an instant path, although it can be expensive if you have long stretches to cover. More durable paths can be made from broken paving stones, log 'rounds', bricks or pavers. The choice of materials for a path should, in some degree, be dictated by the local building stone and the character of the house: brick paths work well for Victorian terraces, broken paving or shingle for white-walled, thatched cottages.

DIMENSIONS

■ *Mark out the shape of your path with pegs and string, making sure it is the same width all the way along – 60cm (24in) is the minimum width for walking and 1m (3ft) will make access more comfortable* ■

Grass
If you are creating the garden from a former lawn or field, the beds can be dug from the turf leaving strips of grass to form the paths. The drawback with grass paths is that they

tend to get muddy in winter and need close mowing in summer, but they are a cheap alternative if you do not want any hard landscaping in the garden. A compromise is to set stepping stones into the turf – low enough to allow the mower to pass over them – on the parts that get the heaviest wear.

Shingle
Choose a stone colour that suits the local building materials: sand and beige shades for sandstone areas, greys for granite areas.

■ Dig a trench 8cm (3in) deep and level the earth using a garden roller or by firming it down underfoot.

■ Fill the depression with shingle and rake level. If perennial weeds are a problem, a layer of perforated plastic sheeting beneath the shingle will stop tough weeds growing up through the stones.

Attractive plants can be allowed to self-seed in the shingle and weeded out selectively to maintain a natural effect. One of the drawbacks with shingle is that it tends to get kicked into the flower beds, so an edging can be used to separate the stones from the soil . The level of shingle will need to be topped up from time to time.

Bricks
Old bricks are quite in keeping with a cottage garden and if they happen to be ones from an old outhouse or barn, they will match the house perfectly. It is usually recommended that engineering bricks are the most suitable for paths but, although they are undoubtedly hardwearing, they rarely complement this type of garden. Although old house bricks do have a tendency to crumble, the laying technique is simple so it is a straightforward matter to replace individual bricks from time to time. Porous bricks also attract moss and lichen, which is part of their charm of course, but care is needed in winter when they can become slippery when wet. Modern, purpose-made brick pavers are available for garden use and, as their texture and colour improves with age, they come quite close to looking like weathered bricks.

The following method is recommended for laying bricks and pavers, but manufacturers of pavers may have their own suggestions which should be followed:

■ Dig the trench deep enough to allow for the hardcore, sand and the depth of your particular bricks. Level the base using a garden roller or by treading in heavy garden boots.

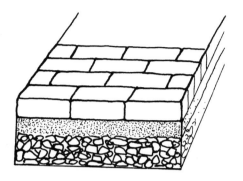

■ Add the layers, levelling each one firmly. After laying the bricks, brush more sand into the joints.

Timber and bark

Coarse chopped bark makes a natural-looking, easy-to-lay path. Like shingle, it needs an edge to prevent the chippings spreading into the flower beds and it may need to be topped up after a year or two. As with gravel, a layer of perforated polythene sheeting will prevent perennial weeds.

Sawn log rounds, if available, make an economical path, but they must be treated with a wood preservative, and like brick, they can become slippery in winter. Surround them with chopped bark for a decorative finish.

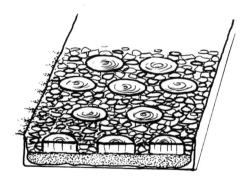

Broken paving

Although the term 'crazy paving' conjures up pictures of lurid coloured mosaics, a broken, natural stone paving path is quite in keeping with a cottage garden. It is a slightly more technical job than the other paths but is an economical use of old paving stones if you happen to have them. Aim for pieces that are 4–5cm (1½–2in) thick. Follow the method for laying bricks. Then after laying the hard-

core and sand, use the larger pieces of paving to form the edges of the path, securing each stone with a few blobs of mortar (1 part cement:6 parts sand). Use the smaller pieces to fill in the gaps. Make sure each stone is bedded in the sand to form a level surface (a spirit level is essential). Brush a dry mortar mix (without water) into the gaps.

CHOOSING EDGING FOR PATHS AND BEDS

Edging has a role to play in the cottage garden, but it should be used with care so as not to destroy the informal look. This is particularly so with tiles and bricks, although when used subtly they can serve an important function in separating gravel from soil.

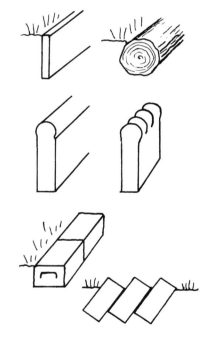

A variety of materials can be used to edge your paths: wood strips or logs, roll- or rope-topped tiles or bricks laid end-to-end or on their side

NATURAL EDGING

Although cottage garden paths are at their best when the plants are allowed to spill over from the beds, a slightly neater appearance can be achieved by planting a row of a single type of plant along each side, such as pinks (*Dianthus*), thrift (*Armeria*) or dwarf lavender.

ATTRACTIVE PATHS WITH PAVING STONES
If only whole paving stones are available, they can be spaced out to create an informal path. The paving can be interplanted to soften the edges and create a more pleasing effect. You don't need to keep to a straight design; this arrangement will work just as well for a curved path.

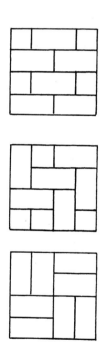

Different patterns for laying bricks (from top to bottom): running bond, herringbone and basketweave – the easiest for beginners

MARCH

'And in the wood, where often you and I,
Upon faint primrose beds were wont to lie'

WILLIAM SHAKESPEARE: A MIDSUMMER NIGHT'S DREAM

No flower belongs more essentially to spring and to the cottage garden than the primrose. Shakespeare might well have taken the inspiration for Hermia's lovelorn verse from the primrose-covered bank leading to the door of Anne Hathaway's cottage. No cottager would have dreamed of not including them in the flower beds, on a bank or under an old fruit tree.

But there are other, equally authentic, cottage flowers to brighten this part of the year. The seventeenth-century herbalist John Gerard, described country gardens as full of narcissi; this was probably the native daffodil, Narcissus pseudonarcissus, which would have been a natural and very attractive subject for cottagers to introduce. Two other narcissi soon found their way into gardens, the poet's narcissus (Narcissus poeticus), which was known to the Ancient Greeks, and Narcissus tazetta, which has a history stretching back over 3,000 years.

Spring advances and retreats with alarming frequency this month: brilliant sunshine, flurries of snow, driving rain and infamous winds, make gardening something of a lottery. Yet it is surprising how little the thrusting of the spring bulbs and the opening of the buds are affected by this inconstancy – leaves continue to unfurl, blossom continues to break and perennials continue to make steady progress towards full growth. This is the season of excited anticipation and occasional despondency when winter seems reluctant to leave. The way to deal with this uncertainty is to continue the time-honoured round of garden work – prune shrubs when their winter flowering is over, plant perennials between the bouts of bad weather and sow seed under cover of a greenhouse or coldframe.

tasks
FOR THE
month

**PERENNIALS TO PLANT
THIS MONTH**

Acanthus mollis
Bellflower (*Campanula* spp.)
Crane's bill (*Geranium* spp.)
Globe flower (*Trollius europaeus*)
Golden rod (*Solidago* x *hybrida*)
**Japanese anemone (*Anemone* x
hybrida)**
Oriental poppy (*Papaver orientale*)
**Phlox (*Phlox maculata* and *P.
paniculata*)**
Red campion (*Lychnis flos-jovis*)
Soapwort (*Saponaria officinalis*)
Yarrow (*Achillea millefolium*)

CHECKLIST

- ☐ Plant hardy perennials
- ☐ Take basal cuttings
- ☐ Mulch borders
- ☐ Prune winter-flowering shrubs
- ☐ Plant evergreen hedging plants

PLANTING HARDY PERENNIALS

Many of the common cottage-border perennials can be planted this month. If you have your own stock, grown from seed or cuttings, this is the time to plant them out, otherwise, garden centres and nurseries will be selling young plants in pots. (Note: Hardy perennials may also be planted in mid-autumn.)

■ Prepare the border ready for planting. Dig over the soil, breaking up any large clumps of earth. Add a bucketful of garden compost to each square metre/yard of soil. Mix it in well with the soil and rake level. If the soil is particularly poor, sprinkle on a few handfuls of granular or powdered general-purpose fertilizer. (Note: If perennials are to be fitted in between other plants in an established border, lightly fork over the soil and sprinkle on the fertilizer.

■ Check the eventual spread and height of each plant and plan the border accordingly, putting in tall plants at the back and low spreading plants at the front. Although conventional perennial borders are planned carefully, with plants usually positioned in groups of three or five of the same species, this is not necessary if a more random, cottagey effect is the aim.

■ Make a hole for each plant with a trowel or spade, according to how large the root system is. Set the plant into the centre of the hole, spreading out the roots. Push the soil back around it and firm in by hand. Water immediately and firm in again, adding more soil around the plant if

necessary. Continue until all the plants are in place.

TAKING BASAL CUTTINGS

Some perennials (including delphiniums, heleniums, lupins and scabious) can be increased from cuttings taken in spring, from new shoots appearing at the base of the plant.

■ Scrape away the soil around the clump and look for the new shoots emerging at the edge .

■ Choose shoots that are about 10cm (4in) long and cut them off at ground level.

■ Put the cuttings into pots of cuttings compost – three cuttings to a 15cm (6in) pot.

■ Place the pots in a coldframe, and water with a mist sprayer. Keep the frame lid closed.

Aftercare
Keep the cuttings moist by spraying with a mister. After a week or two, gradually harden them off by opening the coldframe lid by a few inches, increasing the ventilation. After six weeks, pot the cuttings into individual 9cm (3¹/₂in) pots of potting

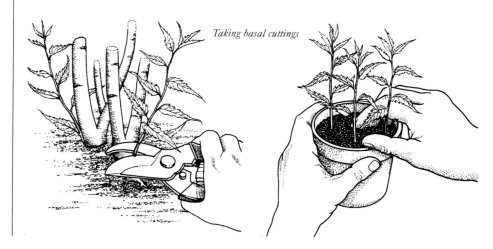

Taking basal cuttings

compost. They can be placed outside during the summer as long as they are shaded from the sun, ready for planting out in the garden in the autumn.

PRUNING WINTER-FLOWERING SHRUBS

Winter jasmine (*Jasminum nudiflorum*) tends to get very tangled and congested if left unpruned. Prune it after flowering has finished, usually this month (see illustration left).

■ Cut back all the shoots that have just flowered to within 5–7cm (2–3in) of the main stem. Cut out any dead or straggly stems to open up the shrub. Winter jasmine is usually grown against wires, trellis or up an arch. If so, tie in the remaining stems to their support.

Winter sweet (*Chimonanthus praecox*). If trained as a wall shrub, winter sweet should be cut back this month; freestanding shrubs only need pruning if growth is congested.

■ On wall shrubs, cut back all the shoots that have just flowered to within 5–7cm (2–3in) of their base. Free-standing shrubs may be thinned out by removing any dead or weak growth.

MULCHING BORDERS

The best time to apply a mulch to the garden is in early spring when the herbaceous plants are just reappearing and it is easier to see the layout of the borders. Because the cottage garden is often densely planted it is vital to give it this once-a-year boost. An organic mulch of garden compost, well-rotted manure or mushroom compost will regenerate the soil, providing nutrients and humus, helping to conserve moisture and to keep down weeds.

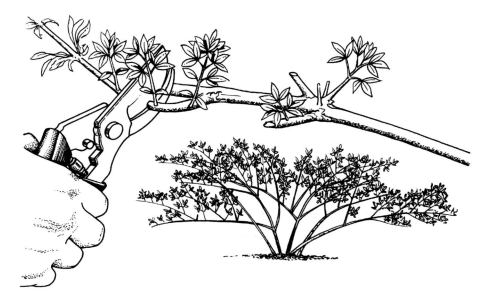

■ Remove any weeds and make sure the ground is moist.

■ Spread a generous layer (at least 5cm/2in thick) of the organic matter over all the bare soil in the garden, particularly around woodland plants like foxgloves, primulas, violets and lily-of-the-valley. Flowering shrubs like *Ribes* will also appreciate an annual mulch and it is particularly important for climbers like *Clematis* to help to keep their roots cool through the summer.

■ On rock gardens and alpine areas apply an alternative mulch of gravel or pebbles which deters weeds and ensures that the rain water drains away quickly from the surface. A gravel mulch is also preferable for plants that thrive on light soils in a hot, dry position such as lavender, thyme and rosemary.

PLANTING EVERGREEN HEDGES

Evergreen, aromatic plants can be used to create decorative low-growing hedging, for edging paths, borders and herb gardens. Young plants of

lavender, rosemary, santolina, southernwood and box should be planted out this month (or next, if the ground is still cold and wet). Choose small, compact, healthy specimens.

■ Dig over the ground thoroughly, removing any stones. Perennial weeds should be dug out or treated as they are impossible to remove once the hedge is planted.

■ Mark out the line of the hedge with short pieces of bamboo cane or a garden line.

■ Set out the plants about 40cm (16in) apart: dwarf varieties of lavender and box should be spaced 23cm (9in) apart.

■ Pinch out the growing tips to encourage bushy growth. Repeat this in late summer.

■ Water the new plants thoroughly and keep watered through their first spring and summer.

Aftercare
Once established, clip over with secateurs or garden shears once or twice during the summer. (See p.77.)

PLANTS FOR HEDGING AND EDGING

FOR LOW HEDGES AND EDGING
Buxus sempervirens **'Suffruticosa'** 23cm (9in) slow growing, compact
Lavandula angustifolia **'Loddon Pink'** 60cm (24in) pale pink flowers
Lavandula angustifolia **'Hidcote'** 45cm (18in) deep purple-blue flowers
Santolina chamaecyparissus var. *nana* 45cm (18in) more compact than other varieties

FOR TALLER HEDGES
Rosmarinus officinalis **'Miss Jessop's Upright'** 1.2m (4ft) upright grower, best hedging variety

plants
OF THE
month
1

'*Daffodils*
That come before the swallow
dares, and take
The winds of March with beauty'

WILLIAM SHAKESPEARE:
A WINTER'S TALE

COTTAGE GARDEN DAFFODILS
(*Narcissus spp.*)

The native Lent lily, Narcissus pseudonarcissus, *must have been the first daffodil to find a place in village gardens, removed, perhaps, from nearby meadows and stream sides. They were said to be so plentiful around London in the sixteenth century that the markets of Cheapside were overflowing with bunches of the bright little flowers. This daffodil is now increasingly rare in the wild but, naturalized in grass, it makes a good garden subject. Cottage gardeners became more adventurous and Mediterranean species such as Jonquils, the Poet's narcissus and Tazettas found favour in gardens. These delicate plants and their intricate, double-flowered forms suit the smaller cottage garden far better than the large, rather clumsy, trumpet daffodils that are so often used for bedding and displays in lawns.*

Jonquil narcissus (*N. jonquilla*)

flowers	Deep yellow, 5cm (2in) wide, with a short central cup, scented; mid-spring
height	30cm (12in)
varieties	*N.* 'Baby Moon' has several soft yellow flowers per stem and is highly scented
requirements	Warm, sheltered position

Hoop-petticoat narcissus (*N. bulbocodium*)

flowers	All yellow, 2.5cm (1in) long trumpets, insignificant petals; late winter to early spring
height	5–15cm (2–6in)
varieties	*N. bulbocodium* var. *citrinus* is pale lemon-yellow.
requirements	Sunny position, moisture-retentive soil

Poet's narcissus (*N. poeticus*)

flowers	5–7cm (2–3in) across, white petals with small, yellow-red central cups, ringed with red, fragrant; mid- to late spring
height	38–45cm (15–18in)
varieties	*N. poeticus* 'Old Pheasant's Eye' (syn. *N. poeticus* var. *recurvus*) has a deep red eye and is late flowering
requirements	Most suitable for wild corners of the garden

Tazetta narcissus (*N. tazetta*)

flowers	2.5cm (1in) across, white or yellow petals with short, yellow central cups, scented, many flowers to a stem; midwinter to early spring
height	30–45cm (12–18in)
varieties	*N.* 'Paper White' is a very early flowering, all-white, scented form
requirements	Not hardy in all areas, can be grown indoors in pots

Double Narcissus

Many of the small-flowered, double narcissus are ideal for cottage gardens. These include 'White Lion', which is 45cm (18in) tall and has creamy-white, overlapping petals, and another pretty form, 'Irene Copeland', which is a creamy-yellow and 35cm (14in) high.

FLOWERING CURRANT
(*Ribes sanguineum*)

The early-flowering *Ribes* does not have a particularly ancient garden pedigree, nor is it a native to Britain, yet it still has all the hallmarks of a classic cottage garden shrub – the deep rose-coloured flowers appear at the end of winter and last for anything up to three months, it is hardy and can almost be totally forgotten about once planted and, despite its lack of perfume, it will be swamped by bees throughout the spring. It was imported from North America in the nineteenth century and, often planted as a hedge, has become a feature of many country gardens.

type	Deciduous shrub
flowers	Deep rose-red; late winter to mid-spring
foliage	Mid-green, gooseberry-like
height	To 3m (10ft)
spread	2m (6ft)
site	In full sun or partial shade
soil	Any
planting	Plant in autumn or early spring. For hedging, set young plants 40cm (16in) apart and pinch out the growing tips to encourage bushy growth
care	Mulch with well-rotted manure or garden compost in mid-spring. Cut out old wood at ground level, after flowering in late spring. For hedges, continue to pinch out growing shoots in first year of growth. In subsequent years trim twice, in late spring and late summer.
propagation	Take hardwood cuttings in late autumn. Grow on and put in permanent positions the following autumn

varieties *R. sanguineum* 'Pulborough Scarlet' was discovered in Sussex in the 1930s and has flowers of a rich claret colour. Several white and paler pink varieties are available, but look rather washed-out in comparison with the red forms

PERIWINKLE
(Vinca minor)

For small gardens, *Vinca minor* is unbeatable for covering difficult areas with poor soils; larger gardens or those with a wild area can take the more rampant *Vinca major*. Although both will tolerate dry, infertile ground, like most plants they are at their best when given a little moisture and nourishment. Gardeners should note its Latin name *vinca* means 'to conquer', as it can easily swamp other less vigorous plants.

type	Spreading evergreen perennial
flowers	Violet-blue, sometimes white; early to late spring; often produced intermittently until autumn
foliage	Dark green, oval
height	60cm (24in)
spread	1m (3ft)
site	In full or partial shade; as ground cover under shrubs, hedges or on banks
soil	Any
planting	Plant in early autumn or early spring
care	No special care needed
propagation	Trailing stems root wherever they come into contact with soil. To transfer the plant to a new site, take 15cm (6in) stem cuttings (with roots attached) in early spring and plant directly into flowering position
varieties	*V. minor* 'Aureo-variegata' has variegated leaves. *V. major* reaches 75cm (30in) high. *V. major* 'Elegantissima' has variegated leaves and paler blue flowers
cottage garden value	Miss Mitford, writing about nineteenth-century Hampshire in 'Our Village', called this *'the very Robin-redbreast of flowers, a winter friend'* and, indeed, it does flower in the bleakest months. The plant had many medicinal uses, including curing toothache and stopping nose bleeds. Culpeper declared that the leaves, when *'eaten by man and wife together, cause love between them'*: it seems to have a similarly dizzying effect on bees

PRIMROSE
(Primula vulgaris)

One of the oldest garden flowers, the primrose was already a popular garden perennial by the sixteenth century. The pale yellow wild form was probably cross-pollinated with a red-purple subspecies bought in from the East in the seventeeth century to produce the many colours we know today. Double flowers were also extremely popular and many gardeners (mistakenly) thought they were produced by regular transplanting. Most primulas look good in a cottage garden setting but the old-fashioned doubles are particularly suitable.

type	Herbaceous perennial
flowers	Pale yellow, pink, red, purple; early to mid-spring
foliage	Rosette of mid-green leaves, with pale undersides
height	15cm (6in)
spread	23cm (9in)
site	Sun or partial shade; beneath deciduous trees or hedges, on grassy banks or by streams
soil	Fertile, moisture-retentive soil
planting	Prepare the ground by breaking up the soil and adding well-rotted manure. Plant seedlings 23cm (9in) apart in autumn or early spring
care	Mulch around plants in spring to retain moisture
propagation	Divide and replant after flowering, in late spring. Collect seed when ripe (usually early summer) and sow in a shaded coldframe. Put into planting positions in early autumn
varieties	The double 'Quaker's bonnet' (*P.v.* 'Lilacina Plena') which has frilly lilac petals and 'Double White' (*P. v.* 'Alba Plena') are long-standing cottage garden classics
primrose curiosities	Jack-in-the-Greens have a ruff of green around the petals which makes each flower look like a posy. They were popular in Tudor times and a few varieties such as *P.* 'Dawn Ansell' – a double white – can be bought from nurseries. Hose-in hose primroses, also known as cup and saucers, have one bloom appearing to be growing out of another although the lower 'flower' is actually a calyx. Some nurseries still stock a small collection including *P.* 'Wanda Hose-in-Hose', which has claret petals

Top to bottom: flowering currant, periwinkle and primrose

practical
project

GROWING COTTAGE
GARDEN VEGETABLES

POTATOES
Potatoes were surprisingly little known in cottage gardens until the latter end of the eighteenth century – except in Ireland where they were a staple food. English cottagers had always shunned the potato and, in remote areas, it was unknown until well into the nineteenth century. Although garden landscapers and advisers tried to encourage it (Loudon suggested about a quarter of the plot should be given over to the crop), there is no evidence that cottagers took it up. Perhaps they were right to be conservative, as it was the Irish reliance on the potato crop that led to such terrible tragedy and famine. Eventually, cottagers took to the potato and few self-respecting country people would be without it today. But for gardens of less than a quarter of an acre, there are other vegetables which will add more colour and variety.

The medieval gardener did not have a lot of time for vegetables – partly through ignorance and problems with availability, but partly through lack of interest. Cottagers put their meagre resources into raising a pig, a cow or a few chickens and if there was any space left, would perhaps grow cabbage, onions and spinach. These vegetables were rarely eaten as such, but were more likely to be boiled to pulp in a pottage. Herbs, of course, were always grown to deal with a variety of ailments and household problems and would have been used to flavour the pot as well.

Interest in vegetables for their own sake did not really get going until Elizabethan times, when gardeners began to emulate Flemish growers who raised their crops in neat rows. By 1557, beets, endive, asparagus, carrots, beans, turnips and parsnips were all widely grown, along with a surprising number of salad crops (see p.36); other early crops included skirret – a perennial parsnip – and wild celery. It made sense to cottage gardeners to grow edible plants in ground that was made fertile from pig and cow dung. Soon cauliflowers, broccoli, pumpkins, and by the nineteenth century, potatoes and tomatoes, were all being grown. Many of the improvements in crops must have come about through the cottagers choosing healthy, high-yield plants from which to collect seed. No doubt they were spurred on to produce better vegetables by the highly competitive world of the village show.

CROP ROTATION

In a cottager's yard, which contained nothing more than an old fruit tree and a few wattle hurdles, the earliest and simplest form of crop rotation was simply a case of moving the pig or chickens around each year, with the

THREE-PLOT ROTATION

	Plot 1	Plot 2	Plot 3
Year 1	Root crops	Brassicas	Legumes
Year 2	Legumes	Root crops	Brassicas
Year 3	Brassicas	Legumes	Root crops

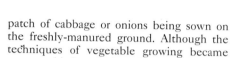

patch of cabbage or onions being sown on the freshly-manured ground. Although the techniques of vegetable growing became more sophisticated, the principle of a three-year crop rotation (see below) has never been improved upon.

■ This system allows a two year break before any piece of land is used for the same crop, which prevents carry-over of pests and diseases.

■ In winter or early spring, manure or garden compost is dug into the plot that is to take the peas, beans, onions that season – that is, the crops which require the richest ground.

■ Root vegetables dislike freshly-manured ground so are always grown on ground that has been used for other crops. The plot which will take root vegetables should be dug deeply to allow roots to develop freely.

■ If there is no space for the three-plot system, brassicas (cabbages, broccoli and so on) and roots should be grown in separate areas and swapped over every year. Salads and runner beans can then be grown wherever there is space, or in pots.

Seed sowing

■ Lightly fork over the ground to a depth of 5–8cm (2–3in). This allows the top surface to dry and become crumbly. Tread down (with boots) to form a firm, even surface.

■ Rake over to remove any stones and provide a fine tilth for the seeds.

■ Mark out the rows using a measuring stick (if available), stakes and line. Use a draw hoe to make the drills.

■ Sow seed thinly, push soil over the drill, then rake level.

SIX COTTAGE GARDEN VEGETABLES

Leeks
SOW: Late winter to early spring
DRILL DEPTH: 1cm ('/₂in)
TRANSPLANT: Early to midsummer
ROW SPACING: 38cm (15in) apart
DISTANCE APART (AFTER THINNING): 15cm (9in)
HARVESTING: Late autumn to late winter. Lift as needed

Spring cabbage
SOW: Mid- to late summer
DRILL DEPTH: 2cm (³/₄in)
TRANSPLANT: Early autumn
ROW SPACING: 45cm (18in) apart
DISTANCE APART (AFTER THINNING): 38cm (15in)
HARVESTING: Mid- to late spring. Cut off heads when firm

Parsnip
SOW: Early spring
DRILL DEPTH: 2.5cm (1in)
ROW SPACING: 30cm (12in) apart
DISTANCE APART (AFTER THINNING): 23cm (9in)
HARVESTING: Late autumn to midwinter as required

Runner beans
SOW: Late spring
DRILL DEPTH: 5cm (2in)
ROW SPACING: 45cm (18in) apart
DISTANCE APART (AFTER THINNING): 30cm (12in)
HARVESTING: Pick regularly while beans are young and tender.

Globe Beetroot
SOW: Early to mid-spring
DRILL DEPTH: 2.5cm (1in)
ROW SPACING: 30cm (12in) apart
DISTANCE APART (AFTER THINNING): 23cm (9in)
HARVEST: Summer to early autumn, as needed

Early Carrots (Stump-rooted)
SOW: Early to mid-spring
DRILL DEPTH: 2cm (³/₄in)
ROW SPACING: 23–30cm (9–12in) apart
DISTANCE APART (PLANTS, AFTER THINNING): 10cm (4in)
HARVEST: Mid- to late summer. Pull by hand or with a fork

SUCCESS WITH VEGETABLES

Remove all perennial weeds before sowing. If necessary cover the plot with old carpet or black polythene for a season to ensure they have all been eradicated

If weather has been particularly dry, water the plot the day before sowing

To help the seeds get off to a good start, sprinkle a little vermiculite or peat substitute into the bottom of the drill and sow the seed directly onto this

Water the plot regularly with hose and spray attachment – particularly during the early stages of growth

Thin out the seedlings as soon as they are large enough to handle, leaving the plants spaced out at their ideal distance

CARROT TIP
Thin carrot seedlings after sunset and water the plot thoroughly afterwards to lessen the chance of attracting carrot fly

PLANTING RUNNER BEANS
Runner beans are conventionally planted in straight rows on crossed canes, but they can also be planted in a circle – for example in a small bed. For four plants the diameter of the circle should be 75cm (30in). The canes or sticks can be secured at the top with twine.

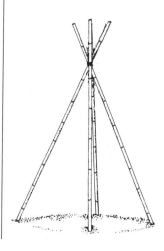

plants
OF THE
month
2

VEGETABLES FOR THE
FLOWER BORDER

Globe artichoke showing the large 'king' head and a smaller head from the lateral branches

GLOBE ARTICHOKE
(Cynara scolymus)

In gardening it is always a delight to find a plant that it is as ornamental as it is deliciously edible. The globe artichoke is a fine plant in its own right and the grey-green leaves and tall stately stems are an asset at the back of the border. However, there is a dilemma for the gardener once the heads begin to appear: whether to cut them for the succulent leaf bases and hearts, or to leave them to develop into dramatic, thistle-like, purple flowers. The Elizabethans thought them far too tasty to leave to flower and the seventeenth-century gardener John Parkinson recommends them served with oil, vinegar *and* a butter sauce. It is doubtful that they were grown in the poorest gardens; like many vegetables they became popular with the upper classes first and the fashion filtered downwards only very slowly. However, for all but the tiniest garden, they fit perfectly into the cottage garden scheme.

type	Short-lived herbaceous perennial (not hardy in all areas)
flowers	Thistle-like, purple, 13cm (5in) across; mid- to late summer
foliage	Silver-grey, deeply cut
height	1.2–1.5m (4–5ft)
spread	1m (3ft)
site	Open, full sun; borders or vegetable plot
soil	Well-drained, fertile soil
planting	In the winter before planting, dig in plenty of well-rotted manure or garden compost. Plant out in mid-spring, setting the plants 1m (3ft) apart
care	Mulch around the plants in late spring with garden compost or well-rotted manure. To encourage larger heads, snip off the flower buds in the first year. In the second year allow 4–6 stems to develop. In late autumn, cut the stems down to almost ground level. In all but the mildest areas, cover the plant with a layer of straw or bracken to protect from frost. Plants over three years old should be discarded after the suckers have been removed (see propagation). They will go on flowering for approximately six years, but the best eating heads are from two- or three- year olds
harvesting	Heads should be ripe in early to late summer. Cut with secateurs, while the scales are still green and tightly wrapped. Take the 'king' head first, then the smaller heads from the lateral branches
propagation	Detach rooted suckers in mid-spring and replant immediately
varieties	'Green Globe' is hardy in most areas, other than those with particularly fierce winters in which case, 'Purple Globe' is a better choice

RHUBARB
(Rheum rhaponticum)

Technically, rhubarb is a vegetable, even though because we tend to serve it sweetened as a dessert, we think of it as a fruit. It has an old cottage garden pedigree and was, until the 1800s, not considered either fruit or vegetable: it had many medicinal uses and the discovery that it made very acceptable pies was possibly an accident. It is a vigorous plant and not ideal for the smallest gardens, but one or two can be grown in a larger border. The leaves are large and coarse, but the stems are colourful and of course delicious when cooked. Rhubarb naturally matures from mid-spring onwards, but can be forced to produce an earlier crop. Terracotta rhubarb forcers are very decorative, but cottagers would have adapted any utensil they had in the household – probably a bottomless bucket or old wooden crate.

type	Herbaceous perennial
foliage	Wavy, dark green. Note: the leaves contain a mild poison (oxalic acid) and should not be eaten
height	60–90cm (24–36in)
spread	1m (3ft)
site	Open, full sun; borders or vegetable plot
soil	Any, well-prepared soil (see planting)
planting	Prepare the ground in the winter before planting by digging the required number of planting holes 60cm (24in) deep by 60cm (24in) wide and 1m (3ft) apart. Work in plenty of well-rotted manure and refill the holes, marking their position with a stake. In early spring, plant the crowns in the holes so that the top bud is 5cm (2in) below the soil surface. Firm in well and water
care	Mulch around the plants with well-rotted manure and water in dry spells. Feed with a liquid fertilizer in spring and summer. Remove any flower spikes as soon as they appear

harvesting	In the first year, do not harvest any stems. In the second and third years, pull a few fully grown stems. In following years, harvest as many stems as needed, but always leave three or four on each plant. Harvesting begins in spring and can go on until early summer
forcing	For earlier stems, cover one or two plants with a rhubarb forcer in midwinter. This encourages the stems to shoot upwards towards the light and makes them pale and slender with very few leaves
propagation	Rhubarb plants should be lifted and divided approximately every seven years. Dig up a clump in late winter and divide with a spade. Replant the roots, making sure there is a growing tip on each new plant
varieties	'Timperley Early' – for forcing; 'Hawkes Champagne' – an early nineteenth-century variety with red stems, also suitable for forcing

FRENCH BEANS
(*Phaseolus vulgaris*)

Climbing beans with attractive pods, such as 'Purple Podded', can be trained to grow up a wigwam of hazel rods or canes where they will create height and interest in a flower border. They also give a good crop which matures earlier than runner beans. If you have neither the room nor the inclination for climbers, dwarf beans like 'Purple Queen' and 'Royal Burgundy' are beautifully coloured and need no staking. Purple beans turn green when cooked.

type	Tender annual
foliage	Mid-green, oval
height	Climbers to 3m (9ft); Dwarf 30cm (12in)
spread	Climbers 1m (3ft); Dwarf 45cm (18in)
site	Open, full sun; borders or vegetable plot
soil	Light, well-drained
planting	Prepare the ground in the winter before planting by digging deeply. If soil is heavy, incorporate plenty of leafmould. Sow seed outdoors *in situ* in late spring or in pots in a coldframe in early spring (to be planted out after the danger of frost has passed). Seeds are sown in pairs, 5cm (2in) deep and 23cm (9in) apart. As the first leaves

	appear, remove the weaker of the two seedlings
care	Keep well watered. Support climbing beans with a wigwam of hazel rods or canes. They can also be supported by a trellis or wire mesh
harvesting	Pick pods when they are young and tender – they usually start to appear eight weeks after sowing. The more they are picked, the more they produce; do not allow them to get too long and stringy
propagation	Grow from fresh seed each year
varieties	Climbing: 'Purple Podded', 'Coco-bicolor' (purple-red markings on pods); Dwarf: 'Purple King' – dark purple stems and pods. Leaves are also tinged purple; 'Royalty' – deep purple pods

KALE
(*Brassica oleracea* vars.)

Kale is closely related to the wild cabbage and probably more like the cabbages that early cottage gardeners grew. The leaves, which do not form heads, are a valuable winter vegetable being extremely hardy – it is even said that frost improves the flavour. They are also very decorative in a variety of curled, flat, ribbed and cut forms. Colours range from bright green, through smoky blues to crimson reds. Kale is not difficult to grow and is equally at home in a flower border as in a vegetable bed.

type	Annual
foliage	Curled or plain, green, pink, red
height	30cm (12in)
spread	60cm (24in)
site	Sunny, open position in vegetable or flower beds
soil	Well-drained, fertile
planting	Manure ground before planting. Set out young plants in midsummer, 60cm (24in) apart
care	Keep watered and weed-free
harvest	Cut leaves from midwinter onwards as required. When the plants start to flower, pull them up and put them on the compost heap
propagation	Sow seed in mid-spring, 2cm ($\frac{1}{2}$in) deep, outside in beds or pots. Thin out to 5cm (2in) apart and leave to form sturdy plants. Transplant into final positions in midsummer (see planting above)
varieties	'Cottagers' – purple-tinged leaves, 'Dwarf Green Curled' –tightly curled green leaves

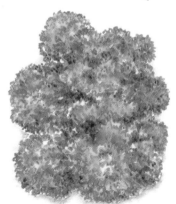

Top to bottom: rhubarb, French beans and kale

practical project 2

GROWING SALAD CROPS

In 1400 a short verse entitled *The Feate of Gardening* liste d almost a hundred plants which we can assume were commonly grown in gardens; it included garlic, lettuce, onion, mustard, radish and salad burnet. What is surprising is that, at a time when all but the most basic vegetables were shunned in the kitchen, it seems salads were already an established meal. By the Elizabethan period, the list had expanded to include cress, succory (chicory), cucumbers, purslane, rocket and sorrel – quite a sophisticated choice even by today's standards. Only the tomato, arguably the most popular modern salad ingredient, is missing – it was a latecomer to cottage gardens, becoming widely grown late in the Victorian era.

GROWING SALAD VEGETABLES

Salads can be grown as part of the main crop rotation in the legume plot (see p.32) or, where space is limited, as an *intercrop*. Fast-growing plants like radishes and spring onions can be grown in rows between slower-growing vegetables, such as parsnips. Miniature lettuces such as 'Little Gem' or 'Tom Thumb' will fit between rows of runner beans or cane tomatoes. If space is very short, salad crops can be raised in a growing bag. The grow-bag may not have been available to cottagers in the past, but it is certainly an invention which, being compact, inexpensive and utilitarian, is very much in the spirit of cottage gardening.

COTTAGE GARDEN SALAD VEGETABLES

Succory *(Cichorium intybus)*
Succory, now better known as chicory, was an early cottage garden plant, grown originally for its root, which can be roasted and ground to produce a coffee substitute or boiled as a vegetable. Today, it is most commonly grown to produce a forced head of crisp leaves in winter when there are few fresh salads available. This lifting, forcing and blanching is quite a complicated process and less energetic gardeners can grow the variety 'Sugar Loaf' the leaves of which can be picked in summer. Chicory is also a pretty plant in the flower border, with startling blue flowers from midsummer to early autumn.

TYPE: Perennial
HEIGHT: 60–90cm (24–36in)
SOW: Early summer
DRILL DEPTH: 5mm (¼in)
ROW SPACING: 45cm (18in) apart
DISTANCE APART (PLANTS, AFTER THINNING): 23cm (9in)
CARE: Water and hoe through the summer. Pick fresh leaves of 'Sugar Loaf' for salads. In autumn, lift the roots of forcing varieties and cut off the foliage, 2.5cm (1in) above the roots. Trim the roots from the base to 20cm (8in) and store in a frost-free shed. Take 4 or 5 roots and set them 5cm (2in) apart in a 23cm (9in) pot of soil. Water and cover with another pot. Place in a warm place (a kitchen or heated greenhouse).
HARVESTING: One month later, cut off the

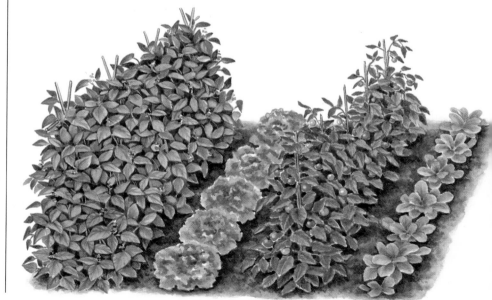

Intercropping lettuce and radishes with runner beans and cane tomatoes

'chicons' which should be about 15cm (6in) high. The combination of warmth and darkness should have encouraged white shoots which have a slightly bitter taste. They can be used as raw leaves in salads or steamed as a vegetable. Although chicory is a perennial, when forced it is treated as an annual and the roots are thrown away (or put on the compost heap)

VARIETIES: 'Witloof' – reliable variety for producing chicons; 'Sugar loaf' – green leaves for summer picking

Sorrel *(Rumex acetosa)*

Sorrel was first discovered growing wild by field labourers, who chewed the leaves to quench their thirst (the leaves have a cooling, acidic taste). In appearance, it is rather like a dock, an upright, coarse-looking plant with plume flowers. French Sorrel *(Rumex scutatus)* is a less untidy plant, with rounder leaves and more slender stems. It was the French, in fact, who exploited the plant's full potential, transforming the leaves into classic soups and piquant sauces. It was used, much as we use lemons today, to counteract the richness of certain meats and to make a well-known 'green sauce' to accompany fish. In salads, the young leaves have the best flavour but should be used sparingly – as a flavouring, not as a substitute for lettuce.

TYPE: Herbaceous perennial
HEIGHT: 60cm (24in)
SOW: Spring
DRILL DEPTH: 5mm (¼in)
ROW SPACING: 60cm (24in) apart
DISTANCE APART (PLANTS, AFTER THINNING): 30cm (12in)
CARE: In autumn, lift and divide established plants and replant immediately
harvesting Take leaves as needed – the larger ones for soups, the smaller ones for salads

Salad burnet *(Sanguisorba minor)*

A native plant of British downlands, salad burnet was an important component of herb and kitchen gardens from Roman times onwards. It had a host of uses – as an aromatic herb, as a medicinal plant for wounds, and as a salad ingredient. The leaves have a nutty, cucumber-like flavour when crushed and can be mixed with other salad leaves, chopped into the dressing or used to decorate summer drinks. Its country name, poor man's pepper, gives an indication of its culinary value, but it also makes an attractive border plant, with globe-shaped, shaggy, red to yellow flowers. It can be grown in rows, but for most households, two or three plants will provide enough leaves.

TYPE: Herbaceous perennial
HEIGHT: 30–45cm (12–18in)
SOW: Early to mid-spring
DRILL DEPTH: 1cm (½in)
ROW SPACING: 30cm (12in) apart
DISTANCE APART (PLANTS AFTER THINNING): 30cm (12in)
CARE: Water well until plants are established and hoe to keep weeds at bay. Cut off the flowering stems as they appear to encourage more young foliage. Established plants may be divided in autumn and replanted immediately
HARVESTING: Pick the young tender leaves. If the plant is to be allowed to flower, take the young leaves before flowering

Radish *(Raphanus sativus)*

The Elizabethans used to eat radishes on their own as an appetizer, flavoured only with salt and accompanied by bread. They were said to stimulate the appetite and as such were considered to be a suitable *hors d'oeuvre*. Summer radishes are quick-growing and easy to cultivate. The key to having a succession of young, crisp roots is to sow little and often, lifting them before they have a chance to get old and woody. Because radishes mature so quickly they are ideal for sowing between rows of peas or parsnips which will be in the ground much longer. Winter varieties (see below) can be eaten raw or cooked.

TYPE: Biennial (grown as an annual for the roots)
SOW: At 3 week intervals, from mid-spring to early autumn
DRILL DEPTH: 6mm (¼in)
ROW SPACING: 15cm (6in) apart
DISTANCE APART: 2.5cm (1in). If sown this distance apart no thinning will be necessary
CARE: Water frequently
HARVESTING: Pull roots 3–4 weeks after sowing
VARIETIES: 'French Breakfast' – mild; 'Scarlet Globe'; 'Long White Icicle' – white
WINTER VARIETIES: Radishes such as 'China Rose' and 'Black Spanish Long' which produce much larger roots are designed for winter harvesting. They can be eaten raw but are also suitable for cooking, rather like turnips. Sow the seeds in summer, in rows 30cm (12in) apart. Thin the seedlings out to 15cm (6in) and water well until the autumn. The roots may be pulled up as required from early autumn onwards. Like other root crops, winter radishes prefer a well-dug soil which was manured for a previous crop.

Top to bottom: succory, sorrel, salad burnet and radish

APRIL

'When daisies pied and violets blue
And lady-smocks all silver white
And cuckoo-buds of yellow hue
Do paint the meadows with delight'

WILLIAM SHAKESPEARE: LOVE'S LABOUR'S LOST

Spring brings forth not only a rush of flowering and blossoming, but
also an outpouring of verse from the pens of poets and playwrights.
Shakespeare was unable to contain his enthusiasm for the new season,
neither was Coleridge whose passion was not for the usual cheerful
flowers, but for the delicately pale lily-of-the-valley. Some flowers, he
says 'rush upon the eye with garish bloom....Not such art though,
sweet Lily of the Vale!'
Yet it is not the individual flowers that make the spring tapestry so
fresh and enticing, but the burst of new growth from trees, shrubs and
flowers together. Hedgerow leaves unfurl, neat shrubs make wayward
shoots and perennial foliage pushes its way upwards to fill the once
empty borders. Spring bulbs are at their peak and the vegetable garden
has not yet become a tyrant. But there are still essential jobs to be
done. Winter-flowering shrubs can be clipped to size and low evergreen
edging should be coaxed into shape to set the stage for summer flowers
that will decorate this ordered backdrop. Spring showers and bursts of
sun are to be expected and the gardener must work around them; it is
a good idea to stake border plants that are starting to shoot upwards,
so that they can resist heavy downpours without collapsing.
If the cottage garden includes a lawn, the mowing season will begin
this month. It is a mistake to think that the principle of relaxed
planting can be transferred to lawn maintenance. A scraggy lawn will
detract from the flower-filled borders; mowing little and often will keep
the grass neat and create the best foil for cottage plants.

tasks

FOR THE

month

HARDY ANNUALS TO GROW FROM SEED

California poppy *(Eschscholzia californica)*
Larkspur *(Delphinium consolida)*
Love-in-a-mist *(Nigella damascena)*
Mignonette *(Reseda odorata)*
Night-scented stock *(Matthiola bicornis)*
Poached-egg plant *(Limnanthes douglasii)*
Poppy *(Papaver rhoeas* and *P. somniferum)*
Sunflower *(Helianthus annuus)*
Ten-week stock *(Matthiola hybrids)*

CHECKLIST

- Sow seed of annual flowers
- Divide primulas
- Lift and divide crocuses
- Trim and prune evergreen hedges

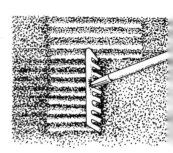

SOWING ANNUAL FLOWERS

It is true that annual seed can be sprinkled on bare patches in the flower beds, but by preparing the soil beforehand and sowing the seed more carefully, the chances of success are far higher. It is safe to sow the hardy annuals this month although any half-hardy varieties should wait until late spring. The usual way to sow the seed is in rows or drills which can then be thinned out later. If you prefer to sow in patches rather than rows, this is quite acceptable, although it makes it more difficult to identify the competing weeds. You can either use seed saved from last summer's plants or buy packet seed. Bought seed will be more uniform and you will know exactly what size, colour and form the flower will be, but home-collected seed does introduce a lot more variation into the garden.

Preparing the ground
Annuals grow well on quite poor soil, but the surface must not be baked hard.

- Clear the ground of weeds and large stones and fork some potting compost into the top layer of soil to make it more friable. The exhausted compost from last year's grow-bags or pots is good for this job as it does not need to be full of nutrients. Rake over to give a level surface.

- Water the ground thoroughly before sowing.

- Mark out drills 1cm ($\frac{1}{2}$in) deep, using a draw hoe or stick. Alternatively, simply make depressions in the soil with your fingers ready to take the seeds.

- Place the seed in the palm of your hand and take a single seed (or a small pinch if they are very fine and impossible to pick up individually) and sow in the individual holes or along the drill.

- Thinly cover the seeds by drawing a rake over the sown areas.

- Water again with a watering can fitted with a fine spray rose.

Aftercare
Remove any weeds as soon as they appear and water the bed in dry spells.

DIVIDING PRIMULAS

Most members of the primula family, including primroses *(Primula vulgaris)*, cowslips *(P. veris)*, polyanthus *(Primula hybrids)* and drumstick primulas *(Primula denticulata)* can be divided after they have finished flowering — usually mid- to late spring. Lift the clumps with a fork and pull apart with your hands. Replant the sections immediately in their new planting positions and water well.

LIFT AND DIVIDE CROCUS

After a few years in an established position, crocus corms start to produce offsets or mini-corms underneath the ground. It is simple to produce new plants from these offsets. As soon as the crocus leaves have died back, lift the clumps and put the corms into a shallow wooden box to dry off for a few days. When the leaves are dry, pull them off and separate the offsets from the old bulb. Grade the offsets into sizes: the larger ones will flower sooner than the tiny ones. The parent corm can be replanted — or discarded if it is no longer firm and plump.

*Pruning cotton lavender
(santolina)*

STORING CROCUS CORMS

If the crocus beds are needed for annual flowers, all the corms can be lifted and dried and stored until the autumn. Remove any dead roots or leaves and put them into trays or wooden boxes in a cool, airy place such as an outdoor shed. It is important that the shed has good ventilation and that the corms do not get damp or they will rot. Replant in autumn (see p.102)

Replanting

They can be replanted in their original positions or in a new site: choose a well-drained position in full sun (this can be under a deciduous shrub or tree, as the leaves will not appear until after the crocuses have flowered). Plant the larger corms in groups, 5cm (2in) deep and 10cm (4in) apart. If you have room, plant the smaller ones, 5cm (2in) deep and 5cm (2in) apart, in a separate bed where they can grow on for an extra year until they are ready for flowering. The following year, they can be lifted and put out into the garden.

CLIPPING EVERGREEN HEDGES

Holly, privet, and yew when grown as shaped hedges, tend to produce straggly new shoots at this time of year. These should be removed by lightly clipping over the hedge with a pair of shears, cutting the new shoots flush with the old hedge.

PRUNING EVERGREEN SHRUBS AND HEDGING

Low-growing evergreen hedges, used as path edging, such as santolina, artemisia, lavender and rosemary, can be cut back this month to keep a good shape.

Cotton Lavender (*Santolina*) has a tendency to lose its compact shape after a few years' growth, but pruning will help to prevent it from getting too straggly. Using secateurs, prune each main stem to where a cluster of new shoots is appearing near the base. Ensure that all the stems are cut back to roughly the same height to retain a good outline.
If the plant is only slightly straggly, simply go over the plant lightly with a pair of hedging shears to remove a few inches of growth.
Artemisia or Wormwood (*Artemisia absinthium*) can be cut back hard each spring. Use secateurs and cut the

wood to about 15cm (6in) above ground level, making the cut just above a leaf joint. Southernwood (*Artemisia abrotanum*) needs only light pruning — follow the instructions for lavender.
Lavender (*Lavandula*) does not need to be as hard pruned as Santolina or wormwood — in fact cutting back into the old wood can cause the plant to dieback. Using a pair of hedging shears, cut off all the old flower spikes and a small amount (about 2cm/1in) of leaf growth. Aim to keep the plant's rounded outline.
Rosemary (*Rosmarinus*). For old plants that have become leggy, cut back all the shoots by half. Younger plants can be lightly clipped with hedging shears.
Rue (*Ruta*). To keep rue as a compact bush, trim back to (but not into) the old wood, with shears or secateurs. It is advisable to wear gardening gloves as rue can cause allergic skin reactions in some people (see also p.124).

Pruning lavender

plants
OF THE
month
1

The seed pods of honesty caught the imagination of country people, hence the wealth of interesting names given to the plant: Judas pence, two pennies-in-a-purse and moonflower. Gerard called it the white satin flower; Parkinson, the pennyflower. Its name in French (herbe aux lunettes) means spectacle plant

HONESTY
(Lunaria annua, syn. *Lunaria biennis)*

This is an old cottage garden favourite which frequently escapes into lanes and roadsides around country villages, although it rarely gets established there. Cottagers traditionally grew it for the decorative, papery seed pods which are used in indoor flower arrangements, but the purple flowers in late spring are equally striking. The seed pods have three layers or 'skins', the outer two being cloudy, but the inner one being perfectly transparent; it is this transparency that led to the common name of honesty. Honesty is technically a biennial, setting seed and germinating in late summer to produce flowers for the following spring. However, it self-sows so readily that it easily becomes a permanent fixture of the garden.

type	Biennial
flowers	Purple-mauve; mid- to late spring
foliage	Mid-green, coarsely toothed
fruit	Disc-shaped, translucent silver seed pods
height	60–75cm (24–30in)
spread	30cm (12in)
site	Partly-shaded; in borders or against fences and hedges
soil	Any garden soil, preferably light
planting	Put out new plants grown from seed in early autumn
care	No special care needed. Unwanted self-sown seedlings can be dug up in autumn and discarded or transplanted to a new position
propagation	Sow packet seed outdoors in late spring or early summer. Alternatively, collect pods in mid- to late summer and sow immediately. Thin out the seedlings to 15cm (6in) and put into flowering position in early autumn. Once established in the garden, self-sown seedlings should supply plenty of stock
varieties	The leaves of *L. annua variegata* are edged in cream and the flowers are an intense crimson. There is also a white-flowered form, *L. annua alba*
related species	The perennial honesty, *L. rediviva,* looks similar, but is taller and has paler, more fragrant flowers
cottage garden value	In Tudor times the roots were grated and used in salads or boiled to be eaten as an accompaniment to meat. Mainly, though, for its unusual seed pods

CUCKOO FLOWER
(Cardamine pratensis)

This plant has two equally well-known common names – lady's smock and cuckoo flower. The latter name is obvious – it is in bloom when the first cuckoo sings – but the former relates to its resemblance to the milkmaids' white smocks hung out on the washing lines of Shakespeare's England. It is a native flower, favouring damp, streamside meadows where, from a distance, the waves of lilac-white might just have resembled newly-washed garments. Cottage gardeners have grown it for centuries, particularly the double form 'Flore Pleno' whose flowers last longer than the species. It makes a good border plant, as long as it can be given a moist soil, and when established will spready easily by self-seeding. It is also suited to growing around the margins of a pond or in a damp, wild area.

type	Herbaceous perennial
flowers	White, flushed with lilac; mid-spring to early summer
foliage	Forms a rosette at the base of the plant
height	30–45cm (12–18in)
spread	30cm (12in)
site	Partial shade
soil	Any, moist
planting	Plant in autumn or late winter
care	No special care needed. Mulch plants with leafmould or garden compost in spring to retain moisture
propagation	Lift and divide roots of established clumps straight after flowering (or in late winter). Replant immediately
varieties	*C. pratensis* 'Flore Pleno' is a blowzy, lilac, double, which makes more impact than the single-flowered varieties. *C. pratensis* 'Edith' is a neater double form
cottage garden value	Attractive to bees and hoverflies, and a food plant for young and adult Orange-tip butterflies

PASQUE FLOWER
(Pulsatilla vulgaris, syn. *Anemone vulgaris)*

The Pasque flower, takes its name from the Christian Pasque festival, its flowering coinciding with Easter. It is a native of the chalk downs, turf meadows and slopes of northern Europe and was, in the sixteenth century at least, a common wild flower. As more and more meadows came under the plough, it became something of a rarity in the wild and in Britain it is now confined to a few locations in East Anglia and the Cotswolds. Its demise may well have been prevented by the cottage gardener who removed it to the safety of his border. There are several legends associated with the flower, the most prevalent being that it represents the blood of Danes shed on English soil; in Hertfordshire, Cambridgeshire, Suffolk and Norfolk, where many ninth- and tenth-century battles were fought, it goes by the name of Dane's Flower.

type	Herbaceous perennial
flowers	Pale to deep purple with yellow stamens; mid-spring to early summer
foliage	Mid-green, fern-like
height	23–30cm (9–12in)
spread	30cm (12in)
site	In full sun but sheltered (if possible) from heavy winds or rain which can spoil the flowers; in borders or rockeries
soil	Well-drained, with added garden compost
planting	Plant out in early autumn, adding plenty of humus (leafmould or compost) to the soil
care	No special care needed
propagation	Divide the rhizomes after flowering and replant. Collect seed in midsummer and sow immediately in a coldframe. Pot up the seedlings when new leaves begin to show (the following spring) and plant out into the garden in early autumn
varieties	*P. vulgaris* var. *rubra* has deep wine-coloured flowers and there is also a creamy white form, *P. vulgaris alba*
related species	The closely related spring Pasque flower (*Pulsatilla vernalis*) is a mountain species, not native to Britain but widely grown in gardens. It is more compact (15 x 15cm/6 x 6in) and produces white flowers, flushed with violet, from mid- to late spring
cottage garden value	The only traditional use recorded for the Pasque flower is to produce a bright green dye to decorate Easter eggs. Members of the court of Edward I are known to have dyed 400 eggs for Easter, using *P. vulgaris* (among other flowers) as a dye. All parts of the plant are poisonous

GOLD DUST
(*Alyssum saxatile*,
syn. *Aurinia saxatilis*)

The sunny, golden alyssum is a familiar feature of spring gardens, to be seen spilling over banks and growing from old stone walls. The 'Cottage Gardener's Dictionary' of 1863 advises that *'to have them in perfection they should be used as rock or hillock plants'* and they do indeed look best on walls or rocky banks where they can be allowed to spread freely. The plant is a native of Crete; it found its way to Britain in the eighteenth century and in some places has become naturalized.

type	Evergreen perennial
flowers	Bright yellow; mid-spring to early summer
foliage	Grey-green leaves in a basal rosette
height	23–30cm (9–12in)
spread	45cm (18in)
site	In full sun; walls, banks, terraces, rockeries
soil	Any, well-drained soil
planting	Plant out in early autumn or early spring
care	To improve drainage and prevent rotting in winter, mulch the surface of the soil around the plants with horticultural grit
propagation	Take softwood cuttings in early summer and grow on in sandy soil in a coldframe to plant out the following spring. Sow seed in early spring in a coldframe and pot on to plant out in the garden in autumn
varieties	*A. saxatile* var. *citrina* is a softer lemony yellow and *A. saxatile* 'Gold Ball' is a more compact 15cm (6in) high. *A. saxatile* Dudley Nevill Variegated' has buff flowers against cream and green foliage
related species	*A. maritimum* (now *Lobularia maritimum*) is the plant cottage gardeners know as Sweet Alison. It is a summer annual, creating carpets of white against a backdrop of silver grey foliage. Pink forms include *L. maritimum* 'Wonderland'
cottage garden value	*A. saxatile* does not seem to have any traditional uses in the home and we can assume cottagers grew it purely for the cheerful waves of colour

Top to bottom: cuckoo flower, pasque flower and gold dust

practical project

USING CLIMBING PLANTS 1: ARCHES, ARBOURS AND PORCHES

CLIMBERS FOR THE ARBOUR
The whole point of an arbour is to provide the gardener with a sheltered spot where he can enjoy the last rays of the summer sun. The plants around the arbour are selected partly for their shade-giving properties but mainly for their ability to perfume the evening air. Thomas Hyll recommended the summer-flowering jasmine (Jasminim officinalis), Parkinson suggests honeysuckle and John Clare records sweet briar (Rosa eglanteria) and old man's beard (Clematis vitalba)

In a small cottage garden, climbers are one of the few ways of achieving height: tall trees are too hungry and cast too much shade; herbaceous plants die down in winter, so it is left to the archway or pergola to add some structure and to break the monotony of a one-level garden. Many cottages had brick-built or rough wooden porches where the family could take a seat from the house and place it outdoors at the end of the day. Another common feature was the arched gateway – either a continuation of the hedge planting or a separate feature. Roses around the door are the trademark of a cottage and these can be trained to grow over the porch. Free-standing arches and pergolas have become a feature of modern gardens and help to accentuate the transition from one part of the garden to another – for example, to mark the entrance to the vegetable plot. Arches, arbours and pergolas should not be seen as a design feature in themselves but as a way of supporting plants and providing shade. If this principle is borne in mind, the cottage garden will not be spoilt by over-complicated structures.

ARCHES

Archways are reasonably simple to make; they are also easily available in kit form and as ready-made features. The choice of materials includes rustic timber poles, traditional wooden uprights, wrought iron and its modern, lighter equivalents. The main considerations should be that it is strong enough to take the weight of climbing plants when they become mature and that it is large enough for people to pass easily underneath it; bear in mind that the plants will 'fill out' into the opening. The usual size is 2.2m (7ft) tall and at least 1.2m (4ft) wide.

Rustic arch
Rustic arches are home-made or bought arches, made from rough-hewn lengths of chestnut, larch or other easily available wooden poles. Shorter pieces of timber can be nailed, ladder-fashion, to the sides and top to give the plants something to climb up. Alternatively, narrow wooden trellis panels can be nailed to the uprights and horizontal bars. Remember to treat the timber with garden preservative before use.

Traditional timber arch
Like rustic arches, these can be made up from a kit, or bought ready-made. With the

ready-made versions there is a choice of rounded top and apex arches, as well as the conventional flat-topped version. The wood – usually a sturdy redwood or cedar – has already been treated with preservative and cut to length.

Metal arch
Although old-fashioned wrought ironwork is still seen in gardens, the most commonly available metal arches are made of steel tubing, covered with a protective black plastic coating. These look attractive and are strong and long-lasting and available in a wide range of widths. For the cottage garden the simple versions with rounded arches are the best choice.

Entrance arches
Entrance arches – with or without a gate – were a traditional feature of the cottage garden. In some a picket fence gave way to an arch of rustic timber smothered with roses; in others, iron railings dictated a metal arch, perhaps covered with variegated ivy. A living entrance arch was another common feature, where the boundary hedge of yew, beech, or privet was extended to make an arch over the gateway.

PERGOLAS

A pergola is really just a longer version of the arch, making an extended area of shade or a small tunnel of plants. If the pergola is too long it can begin to look like a self-consciously architectural feature. To counteract this tendency, the cottage gardener should go for the rustic pole version and cover it with vines, twining jasmine or roses.

THE ARBOUR

The arbour is a covered wooden seat constructed in a corner of the garden, usually situated to get the late afternoon and evening sun – a retreat at the end of a working day. Sometimes the seat is surrounded by a simple arch which is then clothed in plants, but the sides and roof of an arbour can be made of solid timber or slatted wooden boards. The roof may be flat or vaulted. Writing in 1564, Thomas Hyll recommended juniper wood for building arbours which would not need repairing for ten years, or willow which would only last three years.

PLANTS FOR ARBOURS, ARCHES AND PORCHES

Clematis *(Clematis montana* 'Tetrarose', *C.* 'Jackmannii Superba', *C.* 'Perle D'Azur' *C. vitalba)*
White jasmine *(Jasminum officinalis)*
Perennial pea *(Lathyrus latifolius* 'White Pearl'

ROSES FOR ARCHES, PERGOLAS AND PORCHES

Roses are the most popular choice and the ramblers are best suited to the job because of their flexible stems. However, most ramblers only flower once in the year so some gardeners use the repeat-flowering climbers, which can be made to twine if they are trained early while their stems are still pliable.

rose	flower	notes
RAMBLERS		
'Albéric Barbier'	fragrant, creamy yellow	strong grower to 8m (25ft)
'Albertine'	fragrant, pink	strong grower to 6m (20ft)
'Seagull'	small, fragrant, white	not as invasive as 'Kiftsgate' or 'Rambling Rector' to 5m (15ft)
CLIMBERS		
'Gloire de Dijon'	heavily scented, buff yellow	bourbon rose; ideal for pergolas and arches; to 5m (15ft)
'New Dawn'	blush-pink, perfumed	to 3m (10ft)
'Climbing Iceberg'	pure white	to 3m (10ft)

ROSE ARCH

■ *After planting, mulch around the base of the plant and twine the stems around upright post*
■ *Don't let the leading stem get to top too quickly. Pinch out the vigorous shoots in summer to encourage shooting lower down*
■ *In late summer prune once-flowering ramblers Cut back each stem to the post*
■ *Deadhead repeat-flowerers throughout the summer to encourage a long flowering period. Prune in autumn or late winter* ■

plants
OF THE
month
2

Lily-of-the-valley and forget-me-not

LILY-OF-THE-VALLEY
(Convallaria majalis)

Sweet scent and waxy, pendent flowers make lily-of-the-valley a cottage garden favourite. Inexperienced gardeners often find it difficult to grow or find the plants are disappointing. The reason is that, although it is tolerant of many situations, it grows best in a shaded position in rich, moisture-retentive soil with plenty of added humus. The roots need to be kept cool and the dappled shade of a small tree or the protection of a mossy wall is ideal. When grown in sun-baked soil in an open border it will struggle to produce any strong growth.

type	Spreading rhizomatous perennial
flowers	White, scented; mid- to late spring
foliage	Mid-green, elliptical
height	23cm (9in)
spread	60cm (24in)
site	In partial shade; ideally under not too dense shrubs or small trees
soil	Prefers a moisture-retentive soil with added leafmould or compost to prevent the roots from drying out
planting	Plant crowns in early or mid-autumn, 15cm (6in) apart, pointed end up, just below the surface of the soil. Add a layer of mulch; water in well
care	Mulch with a layer of leafmould or garden compost each year, in autumn or spring
propagation	Convallaria spreads naturally by underground rhizomes. To create new plants, lift and divide crowns in autumn or late winter. Replant immediately (see planting above)
varieties	For foliage, the green and-gold-striped leaves of *C. majalis variegata* are popular, and for flowers the pink *C. majalis* var, *rosea*
related species	Solomon's Seal (*Polygonatum* × *hybridum*) is larger (60cm/24in high) and later flowering (early summer). In Elizabethan times, the rhizomes were crushed and applied to the skin. It was said, they would remove 'any bruise gotten by woman's wilfulness in stumbling upon their hasty husband's fists'.
cottage garden value	The flowers of lily-of-the-valley (dried or distilled) were used in many herbal potions to treat everything from gout to memory loss. The plant does have pharmacological properties and should not be taken internally. The berries, produced in late spring or early summer are poisonous

FORGET-ME-NOT
(Myosotis species*)*

The wild forget-me-nots are so commonplace in cottage gardens, often hiding their shining blue flowers under the cover of bolder plants that it is hard to believe they were introduced deliberately. Certainly, they were not thought worthy of any comment by garden writers until the nineteenth century hybrids of the cultivated forms began to be used as spring bedding plants. The field forget-me-not (*M. arvensis*) is a rather insignificant plant and it is the water forget-me-not (*M. scorpoides*) that probably holds the key to the legend of the plant's name. A German knight was said to be gathering the blue riverside flower for his lady, when the current carried him away in the stream, and he cried out in despair *'Forget-me-not!'*.

type	Biennial
flowers	Blue; mid- to late spring
foliage	Mld-green, oblong
height	15–30cm (6–12in)
spread	15cm (6in)
site	In partial shade; edging, borders
soil	Moisture-retentive soil containing garden compost or leafmould
planting	Plant out from early to mid-autumn, 15cm (6in) apart
care	No special care needed. After flowering, pull up plants and shake seed around the flower beds where you want the new plants to appear
propagation	Self-seeds easily and propagation is rarely necessary. Sow packet seed in pots outdoors or in a coldframe in late spring to grow on and be planted out in early autumn
varieties	The varieties offered by seed merchants tend to vary each year, but pink, white, blue and pale blue forms are usually available
related species	The compact alpine forget-me-not *M. alpestris* is a bushy perennial, suitable for cottage rock gardens. The flowers are fragrant and have distinctive yellow eyes
cottage garden value	Forget-me-nots may have found their way into cottage gardens by accident, but as cheerful, easy-care, self-seeders they were encouraged to stay. They remain symbols of friendship and abiding love and no doubt many a bunch has been picked as a lover's token

CROWN IMPERIAL
(*Fritillaria imperialis*)

Introduced from Persia in the sixteenth century, the crown imperial was first planted in the London gardens of the wealthy. By imitation, it soon turned up in the gardens of more humble, country people and so began its cottage garden life. Its attraction is the magnificent stately stem, topped by a ring of bell-shaped flowers and a tuft of green foliage. One of its peculiarities is that it produces nectar as a 'teardrop', clearly visible at the base of each bell. The advice used to be plant crown imperials in very early spring when they had less chance of rotting in the wet, but provided the bulbs are set on their sides (to prevent the hollow bulbs filling up with water) they can be safely planted in autumn.

type	Bulb
flowers	Yellow, deep orange, red; mid-spring
foliage	Glossy green, narrow
height	To 1m (3ft)
spread	30cm (12in)
site	In full sun or partial shade; borders
soil	Well-drained, fertile
planting	Plant bulbs in early autumn, 20cm (8in) deep and 23–30cm (9–12in) apart. Place the bulbs on a layer of sand, on their sides and cover with an extra layer of sand
care	Crown imperials prefer to be left undisturbed. Stems can be cut down when they have died back in the summer
propagation	Offsets can be removed from the bulbs during the dormant period (late autumn to late winter), but avoid disturbing the clumps until four years after planting
varieties	*F. imperialis* 'Maxima Lutea' is a tall, lemon-yellow variety; *F. imperialis* 'Rubra' is deep red; *F. imperialis* 'Crown upon Crown' is an unusual form with two circles of flowers, one above the other; *F. imperialis* 'Aureomarginata' has gold-variegated leaves and red flowers
related species	*F. meleagris* is the delicate chequered snake's head fritillary, also spring flowering and perfectly at home in the cottage garden. The dark, plum-coloured species, *F. persica* with bells arranged all down the stem, makes an interesting plant for the back of the border

WALLFLOWER
(*Cheiranthus cheiri*, syn. *Erysimum cheiri*)

The wallflower was introduced into gardens before Elizabethan times. Parkinson, writing in the seventeenth century grew six varieties, three doubles and three singles including a double red. In folklore, the plant represents a lover's faithfulness in adversity and was often worn by wandering minstrels in their caps as a symbol of lost or unrequited love. Apart from having a wonderful scent, the burnt orange and golden flowers seem to have been made to grow against a backdrop of brickwork and weathered stone and are often found growing on old stone walls.

type	Shrubby perennial (grown as a biennial)
flowers	Yellow, deep orange, red and brown, scented; late spring to early summer
foliage	Mid- to dark green, narrow
height	30–50cm (12–20in)
spread	25cm (10in)
site	In full sun; borders, underneath windows, beside walls
soil	Any well-drained soil
planting	Plant out in mid-autumn, 25cm (10in) apart
care	No special care needed. Remove plants after flowering and replace with new plants in the autumn. Wallflowers will flower for several years, but get progressively leggy and produce less flowers
propagation	Sow seeds outdoors in a shady spot in early summer and grow on until transplanting in mid-autumn. Double varieties are usually increased by cuttings in midsummer
varieties	Several old varieties are still widely available: 'Bloody Warrior', the dark, blood-red double that some say could be Parkinson's double red (45cm/18in); 'Harpur Crewe' a compact double yellow (45cm/18in) possibly Elizabethan, but rediscovered by Victorian enthusiast, the Reverend Harpur Crewe in Hampshire; 'Bowles' Mauve', an old favourite with fragrant mauve flowers and grey-green leaves (75cm/30in)
cottage garden value	The wallflower, with its heady perfume is a prime candidate for planting beneath the cottage window, or by a garden seat

Crown imperial and wallflower

practical project

USING CLIMBING PLANTS 2: WALLS

Cottagers with limited space will always make use of the walls of the house, out-houses or garden to grow plants vertically. Paintings of eighteenth- and nineteenth-century cottage gardens show houses smothered with plants, often including a grape vine, a rose or a trained fruit tree. In the twentieth century the choice of plants widened to included winter-interest shrubs like the winter-flowering jasmine, forsythia and winter sweet, and the berry-bearing cotoneaster. The reflected warmth of the wall helps to ripen buds and produce a good crop of flowers or fruit.

Using the space to grow something edible makes good sense in a small garden, particularly when the plants are decorative as well. However, many people still choose the old-fashioned climbing roses which clothe the wall with colour and fragrance. Wall training suits slightly stiffer-stemmed plants which cannot be coaxed to twine around a pillar or arch. When choosing wall plants, take into account the aspect (north, south, east or west) and choose the plant accordingly. Fruit and many roses need a warm wall, while cold or shady walls can be planted with less demanding climbers.

PLANTING NEXT TO A WALL

Shrubs or climbers, planted next to a wall can suffer from lack of water and nutrients. The earth in front of walls is often dry because the rain is blocked by the angle of the wall and it may also be infertile. Before planting it is vitally important to dig in plenty of well-rotted manure or good garden compost to improve the condition of the soil and to help it to retain moisture.

■ Dig the hole 45cm (18in) away from the wall. Make it roughly circular and deep enough to take the roots of the plant.

■ Position the plant so that the stem is nearest the wall and fan out the roots in the opposite direction – this will enable them to make use of damper soil away from the wall.

■ Replace the soil, firm well and water thoroughly.

WALL TRAINING

Most wall plants (except those that self-cling like ivy and Virginia creeper) will need a framework of wires to which they can be attached. Use large (10cm/4in) vine eyes and set them so that wires will lie 8cm (3in) away from the wall. Fix the wires horizontally, 30–45cm (12–18in) apart.

Tying-in plants
Use soft twine or string (not plastic ties which can dig into the stem of the plants). Loop the tie around wire twice and then tie in the stem so that it is not directly against wire. Tie in the stems no less than 15cm (6 in) apart.

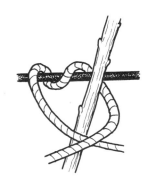

GROWING GRAPE VINES

Grapes were widely cultivated by traditional cottagers and invariably grown against the sunny side of the house. At one time over twenty varieties of hardy outdoor grapes were cultivated in the south of Britain for wine and eating. Among the oldest varieties are the black 'Miller' and the white 'Muscadine'.

The simplest way to grow grape vines against a wall is as single upright cordons. Depending on the length of the wall, buy enough plants to set at 1.2m (4ft) intervals along it. Set up the vine eyes and wires, as described above, and when planting, put a strong cane behind each plant, securing it to the wires. Choose the strongest shoot to grow on as the cordon. Cut off the others to just above the first bud. Tie-in the main shoot to the cane.

First- and second-year care
■ Pinch out the flowers as they appear during spring and summer.

■ In late summer pinch back the side shoots (laterals) to leave about five or six leaves on each.

- In late autumn cut back the leading stem by about one third

Third (cropping) year

- Allow three bunches of grapes to form on each plant (pinch out other flowers as before).

- In late summer cut back the side shoots to five or six leaves.

- In late autumn cut the leading stem by up to one third and cut back the laterals to two buds.

Subsequent years

Gradually increase the number of bunches of grapes that are allowed to develop each year. Continue to prune in autumn only, cutting the leading stem by up to one third and the laterals back to two buds. Apply a mulch of well-rotted compost or manure around the plants each winter.

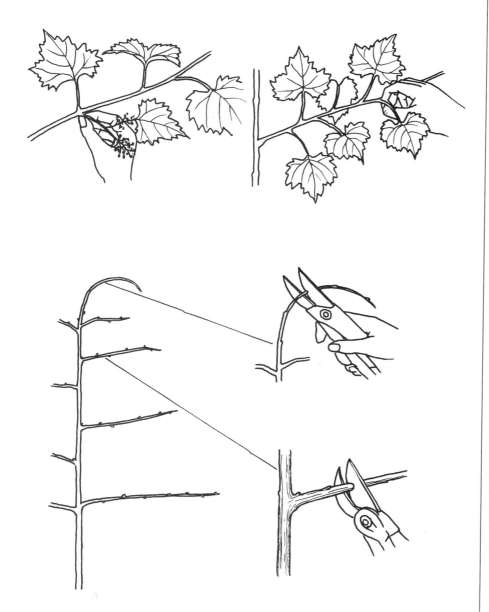

WALL PLANTS FOR WINTER INTEREST

Cotoneaster (*Cotoneaster horizontalis*) – red berries, winter, shady wall

Firethorn (*Pyracantha rogersiana*) – red berries, winter, shady wall

Forsythia (*Forsythia suspensa*) – yellow flowers, early spring, shady wall

Japanese quince (*Chaenomeles speciosa*) – pink, red or crimson flowers, winter and early spring, any aspect

Winter jasmine (*Jasminum nudiflorum*) – yellow flowers, winter, shady wall

Winter sweet (*Chimonanthus praecox*) – yellow flowers, winter, sunny wall

ROSES FOR WALLS

The best varieties are those that flower lower down the stem and do not grow too tall. The following are best on a sunny wall, except 'Zépherine Drouhin', which will flower on a shady wall:

'**Golden Showers**' – yellow flowers on thornless stems, repeat-flowering, height to 2.4m (8ft)

'**Pink Perpétue**' – pink cluster-flowered rose with an autumn repeat, height to 2.4m (8ft)

'**New Dawn**' – pale pink, scented blooms, height to 3m (10ft)

'**Zéphirine Drouhin**' – deep pink, scented bourbon rose, thornless stems, height to 4m (12ft)

OUTDOOR GRAPE VARIETIES

'**Brant**' – sweet black fruit, leaves turn red-gold in autumn

'**Black Hamburg**' – black berries with a blue 'bloom' (may need the protection of a greenhouse in cold areas)

'**Seyval Blanc**' – green fruit for eating and wine making

MAY

In many ways this is the quintessential cottage garden month, when shrubs and flowers grow unbelievably fast and even the laziest gardener can achieve results with little effort – lilac bushes in traditional pinks, purples and white, blush-pink weigela, a few early roses, foxgloves, columbine and carpets of geraniums fill the borders with ease. Garden centres and market stalls are stacked high with snapdragons, stocks and pansies to fill up any spaces left by the fading spring biennials. In most areas, the danger of frost is receding and even if the weeds have thrived in a few spots, the borders are vigorous enough to resist them. In short, this is a month to be cheerful about the garden's summer prospects.

Work does not stop, however. Bulbs need to be divided, evergreens planted, beds mulched and seedlings thinned out. Fruit and vegetables will benefit from watering in any dry spells and should be protected from bird damage with netting. The weather should be warm enough – certainly by the end of the month – to risk putting out tender plants in containers. Pelargoniums are not, strictly speaking, cottage garden plants but few gardeners would want their pots and window boxes without them.

One or two cottage garden shrubs deserve a special mention this month. The old cottage favourite laburnum, with its long tassels of golden-yellow, is often overlooked in favour of newer introductions, but it never fails to give a good show. Hawthorn or May blossom is filling the air with its distinctive scent and climbers such as Clematis montana and the more glamorous wisteria are making their mark. Fruit trees are laden with blossom and the promise of a good crop to come. If a cottage garden could be frozen in time, many gardeners would choose this month to stop the clock.

tasks

FOR THE

month

DIVIDING PASQUE FLOWERS

Pasque flowers (*Pulsatilla vulgaris*) may be divided after they have finished flowering, to create new plants. Lift the clumps carefully and pull root sections apart. Replant immediately.

PLANTING HALF-HARDY BEDDING

When the risk of frost is over (this month in most areas, but in particularly cold regions, it might be wiser to wait until next), it is safe to plant out half-hardy flowers. Tobacco plants (*Nicotiana*), pelargoniums, African and French marigolds (*Tagetes erecta* and *T. patula*) and lobelia (*Lobelia erinus*) add greatly to the colour, form and scent of summer cottage borders. They can be bought as bedding plants from garden centres and markets and are a very economical way to increase the variety of plants in your garden. Simply divide the strips by hand and use a trowel to plant them in spaces in the flower beds, or use them to fill window boxes and pots. Water thoroughly after planting. Remember to allow enough space for the plants to reach their full size. Pansies (*Viola* x *wittrockiana*) and snapdragons (*Antirrhinum*) are usually sold and planted at this time – as bedding plants – even though they are actually hardy.

THINNING OUT SEEDLINGS

Continue to weed and water annuals sown last month. As soon as the seedlings have at least one pair of true leaves (those that appear after the first seedling leaves), thin them out to the recommended spacing – consult the seed packet or see the relevant Plant Profile in this book. As a general guide, they should be about 15–23cm (6–9in) apart.

- Using one hand, press down on either side of the seedling to be removed, use the other to do the thinning. This prevents pulling up neighbouring seedlings.

TIDYING SPRING BORDERS

To keep the cottage borders looking their best, snip off the flowerheads of bearded irises as they fade. Pull up any late spring biennials that have finished flowering and lift bulbs (if the space is needed for other plants, see June) when the foliage has turned brown.

PLANTING EVERGREEN HEDGES

The structural framework of the garden – evergreen hedges such as privet, yew, holly, *Lonicera nitida* and laurestinus (*Viburnum tinus*) can be set out this month. (For choice of hedging species see p.17) Use healthy, two-year-old plants.

■ Mark out the length of the hedge using short lengths of bamboo cane and string. For a curved hedge, set the canes in a curve and tie the string to the first cane. Then follow the canes with the string, making a single loop around each cane.

■ Dig a trench in front of the canes 45cm (18in) wide and 60cm (24in) deep. Remove any stones or weeds. Add a layer of well-rotted manure or garden compost and mix it with some of the loose soil at the bottom of the trench.

■ Set the plants in the trench 45cm (18in) apart and fill around the roots, firming down well.

■ Water thoroughly and keep the hedge bottom free of weeds until the plants are established.

Aftercare

The new shoots of evergreen hedges should be pinched out after planting and in mid- to late spring each year. This encourages the plants to stay bushy, particularly around the lower part of the stem. Once the hedge has reached its full height and thickness, it can be lightly trimmed each spring (see p. 41) and again in autumn.

PRUNING FLOWERING CURRANT

The flowering currant (*Ribes*) is one of the most popular

PRUNING FLOWERING CURRANT

cottage garden shrubs, but it can get very large and woody if left unpruned. Cut it back hard after flowering has finished.

■ Using secateurs, or long-handled loppers if the branches are too high, cut the old wood back to where fresh buds are developing. If necessary, the old wood can be cut back to 45cm (18in) above ground level, although this is not required every year. *Note*: It may be easier to use a pruning saw on thicker branches.

■ Shorten any new shoots as required to keep the plant looking balanced.

plants
OF THE
month
1

Lilac

LILAC
(Syringa vulgaris)

The familiar shade of mauve-blue we now call 'lilac' took its name from this shrub, first recorded in England at Henry VIII's palace at Nonsuch, where the privy garden was planted with six sweet-smelling lilacs. More humble gardens adopted the tree and soon breeders were developing white, pink, crimson and blue forms. It is an easy-care cottage garden shrub, either grown on its own, or as an informal screen.

type	Deciduous shrub or small tree
flowers	Lilac, white, rose-pink, purple; late spring to early summer
foliage	Mid-green, oval
height	3m (10ft)
spread	2m (6ft)
site	In sun or partial shade
soil	Any fertile soil. Add well-rotted manure or garden compost to poor soils
planting	Plant in mid- to late autumn. For hedges or screens, set plants 2m (6ft) apart
care	Prune out weak or crossing branches in late autumn or winter. To rejuvenate old bushes, cut all stems down to 60–90cm (24–36in) above ground level, in winter
propagation	Take semi-ripe cuttings in mid- to late summer
varieties	Many named varieties are available, including the double, lilac-coloured *S. vulgaris* 'Katherine Havemeyer' which is strongly scented and a nineteenth-century French white form, *S. vulgaris* 'Madame Lemoine'
related species	For smaller gardens the spreading *Syringa microphylla* (1.2m/4ft) is a good substitute if it can be allowed to grow over a low wall. It has fragrant, lilac-coloured flowers in shorter panicles

COLUMBINE
(Aquilegia vulgaris)

The native columbine with its deep violet-blue flowers has been known to gardeners for generations. In the wild, its natural habitat is open woodland, grassy banks or marshland, but it adapts well to the garden. Its best asset is its tendency to hybridize freely, so that if the species is planted alongside other varieties, the resulting variations in colour and flower form are endless. It also self-seeds happily, so is an ideal candidate for the care-free cottage garden. The name columbine, is derived from the Latin *columba* – a dove or pigeon (the swept back petals are thought to resemble the bird's wings). In Cornwall it is known as doves-at-the-fountain and in many areas as Granny's bonnet.

type	Herbaceous perennial
flowers	Violet-blue, pale blue, white, pink; late spring to early summer
foliage	Leaves resemble a large maidenhair fern
height	To 60cm (24in)
spread	30cm (12in)
site	Sun or partial shade
soil	Any, well-drained
planting	Plant in autumn or spring, 30cm (12in) apart. Add leafmould to improve drainage on heavy soils
care	Apply an annual mulch of leafmould or compost in spring
propagation	Self-seeds easily. Alternatively, collect seed when ripe (late summer) and sow in seed compost or light, sandy soil in a coldframe. Plant out the following autumn. Seed does not usually come true to type. To propagate a particular variety or form, lift and divide an established plant from mid-autumn to early spring.
varieties	*A. vulgaris* 'Nora Barlow' is one of the few aquilegia varieties to come true from seed. It has double, spiky pompon flowers in two-tone crimson and pale green. It has been around since the nineteenth century and was grown by Miss Barlow, the granddaughter of Charles Darwin. *A. vulgaris* 'Munstead White' (also known as 'Nivea') was one Gertrude Jekyll's favourites, being single, pure white and very elegant. She recommended planting them with white foxgloves and *Campanula persicifolia*
related species	The range of *Aquilegia* species was extended in the nineteenth century by introductions from North America. *A. caerulea* from the Rocky Mountains is the parent of many long-spurred hybrids (such as *A.* 'Mrs Scott-Elliot Hybrids) and is now the state flower of Colorado. The species is smaller than most of the hybrids (about 18in/45cm) and has pretty blue flowers with white centres. Smaller still is *A. viridiflora*

from western China (15in/38cm),
which has a good perfume and
subtle chocolate and cream colouring

cottage garden value	The flowers are attractive to bees. Although mentioned in early herbals *Aquilegia* is poisonous.

HEARTSEASE
(*Viola tricolor*)

Forever associated in the mind with love and affairs of the heart, *Viola tricolor* is the flower whose juice was squeezed into Titania's eyes in *A Midsummer Night's Dream*, making her fall in love with the ass-headed Bottom. It is one of the wild pansies and a favourite old cottage garden plant, going by many local names, including love-in-idleness, kiss-and-look-up and the best known, heartsease. Not until the early 1800s did the breeding of the garden pansies begin and it easy to see how the trinity of purple, yellow and cream, so delicately combined in the wild flower, should inspire generations of breeders to develop bigger and bolder 'faced' pansies. The word pansy itself is taken from the French *pensée* – as Shakespeare puts it, '*pansies, that's for thoughts*'.

type	Spreading herbaceous perennial
flowers	Violet-blue or purple, with yellow and cream; 2.5cm (1in) across; late spring to early autumn
foliage	Mid-green, oval, toothed
height	5–15cm (2–6in)
spread	15–30cm (6–12in)
site	In full sun or light shade; at front of border or rock gardens
soil	Well-drained, neutral soil
planting	Plant out in early to mid-autumn or in early to mid-spring. Set the plants 30cm (12in) apart
care	No special care needed
propagation	Collect seed in mid- to late summer, sow outoors in a shady spot and keep moist. Strong seedlings can be put into planting positions in mid-autumn. Alternatively, seedlings can be overwintered in a coldframe and planted out in spring
related species	*V. cornuta* was introduced into Britain from the Pyrenees in 1775 and was used to breed a whole race of violas. The original species has simple, pastel blue flowers and self-seeds profusely. A pure white variety *V. cornuta* 'Alba' is available
cottage garden value	Cottagers grew heartsease for no other reason than that it is a charming plant. Gerard commented

on the '*beautie and bravery*' of the colours, which '*are so excellently and orderly placed, that they bring great delectation to the beholders*'

DAISY
(*Bellis perennis*)

The common daisy, found in all but the most immaculate lawns, is the parent of the cottage garden double daisy. Daisies were known to the Anglo-Saxons (the name 'day's eye' relates to the fact that it is the first flower to open in the morning). From Elizabethan times onwards, it was the double forms that caught the gardener's imagination, being hardy, colourful and easy to care for. They were grown as edging plants, in rows running alongside a path or border.

type	Herbaceous perennial
flowers	White, pink, crimson; spring to early autumn
foliage	Mid-green, oval
height	15cm (6in)
spread	15–23cm (6–9in)
site	In sun or partial shade; path and border edging
soil	Fertile, moist soil
planting	Plant in mid- to late autumn, 15cm (6in) apart
care	Lift and divide plants regularly to prevent them becoming woody. Alternatively grow as biennials
propagation	Lift plants in early spring or autumn. Pull apart and replant sections, 15cm (6in) apart
varieties	Large-flowered varieties (over 5cm/2in across) include *B. perennis* 'Montrosa', which is available in a range of colours. The miniature varieties grow to only 10cm (4in) tall and have tiny button flowers (1.5cm/1in across). They include *B. perennis* 'Dresden China', a reliable, old-fashioned double pink and *B. perennis* 'Rob Roy' a Victorian red
related species	*B. prolifera* is the 'hen-and-chickens' daisy, an old cottage garden plant, which has tiny replica flowers coming from the central bloom, said to resemble a mother hen and her chicks
cottage garden value	Double garden daisies were unashamedly decorative but the wild plant was used as a wound herb and as a salad ingredient in the fifteenth century

Columbine and heartsease

practical project

COTTAGE GARDEN CONTAINERS

BASKET FAVOURITES

Dwarf nasturtium (*Tropaeolum majus* 'Alaska')
Heartsease (*Viola tricolor*)
Lobelia erinus 'Cascade'
Spanish daisy (*Erigeron karvinskianus*)
Trailing ivy-leaved geranium (*Pelargonium* 'Elégante')
Viola 'Jackanapes'
White alyssum (*Lobularia maritima*)

TIP
Use small plants (rooted 'plugs' and plantlets are ideal) and leave plenty of room for their roots and top growth to develop and fill the basket through the summer

Way back in 1557, Thomas Tusser was recommending a host of flowers to grow in windows and pots, including pinks, daffodils, lilies, marigolds, larkspur, love-in-a-mist, pansies, sweet rocket and wallflowers. The would-be cottage gardener who has only a patio, steps or windowbox could do worse than to follow Tusser's suggestions – none of these plants look out of place in a contemporary cottage garden planting scheme.

The traditional cottager would have utilized whatever containers were available – cattle and horse troughs, old tin buckets, wicker fruit baskets and wooden cider barrels. Swagged pots, leaded urns and Versailles tubs were the domain of the grand house and would seem out of place in the cottage garden. But, there is no need to interpret cottage garden principles too literally – windowboxes and hanging baskets are easier to obtain than cattle troughs and more affordable. To achieve a relaxed effect, it is important to create an impression of profusion by grouping the boxes and baskets together, rather than dotting them about the facade of the house at random. Planting should be soft and generous and the containers themselves should give the appearance of being overflowing with flowers.

COTTAGE HANGING BASKETS

Wire baskets are the simplest choice and produce a more sympathetic effect than plastic or even terracotta – because the plants are inserted through the gaps in the mesh, they soon spread to hide the basket altogether. The basket will need to be lined with moss or a ready-made liner to hold the compost. Fresh moss looks the most natural but conservationists have voiced their concern over the depletion of resources and an alternative such as the cotton-based moss substitutes or a coir fibre liner can be used. Fix the baskets using a cast iron bracket and hook for a traditional effect.

Planting a hanging basket
■ Line the base of the basket with moss or moss substitute. Add a layer of multi-purpose potting compost to fill one third of the basket.
■ Start adding the trailing plants, pushing the roots through the moss from the outside into the compost. Work around the basket, adding more moss and more compost until the top of the wire framework is reached.

■ Add any upright (or more trailing) plants to the top of the basket, firming in well. Water thoroughly and leave to drain before hanging in position.

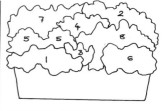

PLANTED WINDOWBOX

KEY

1 *Campanula carpatica* (white or blue)

2 **Cherry pie** (*Heliotropium* x *hybridum*)

3 *Helichrysum microphyllum*

4 *Helichrysum petiolare* 'Aureum'

5 **Mignonette** (*Reseda odorata*)

6 *Nicotiana* 'Domino' and full-sized vars.

7 **Snapdragon** (*Antirrhinum*) dwarf and full-sized

8 **Wallflowers** (*Cheiranthus/ Erysimum cheiri*) dwarf

COTTAGE GARDEN WINDOWS

Windowboxes for cottage gardens should be wooden and can be stained or painted to match or contrast with the paintwork of the house or window frames.

Make sure the wood has been treated with a non-toxic preservative. Drill drainage holes in the base at 15cm (6in) intervals and fix to the wall with brackets for extra security. If the box is to sit on the sill, make sure the sill is strong enough to take its weight. For added stability, use small wooden wedges to tip the box backwards slightly and prevent it slipping off.

TIP
Cover the drainage holes with broken pots (crocks) and add a shallow layer of stone chippings or gravel to help drainage. Use a multi-purpose potting compost.

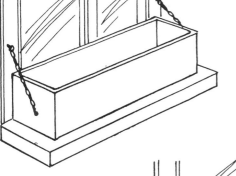

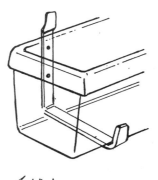

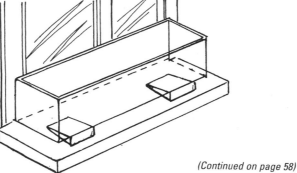

(Continued on page 58)

practical project

COTTAGE GARDEN
CONTAINERS
(continued)

PLANTING AN OLD SINK OR TROUGH

Old horse or cattle troughs were probably the first containers that enterprising cottagers used for their plants; wooden and stone troughs and butler sinks have become a permanent feature of cottage gardens over the centuries, not necessarily for growing rare alpine plants but as a way of recreating the garden in miniature, with small forms of cottage favourites such as aquilegias, campanulas, pinks and phlox. Troughs also make good deep containers for climbing roses and jasmine sited near the door, for scented geraniums, for herbs and for butterfly plants, like sedum and buddleia. Just because they have become known as 'alpine' troughs does not mean that alpines are the only plants that will look the part.

Stone troughs are expensive and increasingly rare, but reconstituted stone versions are cheaper and weather well after a season or two. New timber troughs made in the old 'manger' or cradle style are well suited to cottage garden plants. Old sinks – if available – don't need to be disguised or given a coat of stone-cladding as they often are in smarter town gardens. With judicious planting, the foliage and flowers will soon spill over and soften the brilliant white sides.

Siting the trough
■ Find a permanent site *before* planting up. Choose a site against a wall, under a window or free-standing in a courtyard or patio. Ensure that the eaves of the house or a window sill do not cause rain water to run off directly in rivulets into the trough as this could wash away the compost and damage foliage.
■ Position the trough where it will get sunlight for at least half the day as most of the recommended plants prefer an open, sunny position.
■ Make sure there are no overhanging trees or shrubs that could shed their leaves into the trough or cast too much shade.
■ Once the trough is in position, and before planting, raise it off the ground with bricks or stone blocks.

Planting the trough
■ Cover the plug hole (if any) with a piece of wire mesh and a layer of broken crocks.
■ Add a 15cm (6in) layer of gravel or stone chippings (limestone chippings are suitable for all the plants listed here).
■ Fill the trough with multi-purpose compost and add plants, firming in well.

A BARREL OF PLANTS

Oak casks and barrels, once used for storing ale, cider and mead, soon found a secondary use in the cottage garden. Half-barrels in a range of sizes are widely available from garden centres and, compared to glazed pots of the same size, are very reasonably priced. The natural wood colour blends with most house styles or they can be stained or painted to give a more individual look

Preparing a tub for planting
Give the staves a coat of non-toxic wood preservative. The metal bands should be rubbed down with wire wool to remove rust and then painted with a matt black metal paint. Barrels can also be painted to complement the walls of the cottage – pink or cream for example – or to pick out the colour of the garden gate or front door – dark blue or green. Scrub out the inside with hot water and drill about six drainage holes in the base. Raise the tub on bricks or stone blocks and select a permanent position before planting (see Siting the trough).

UNUSUAL CONTAINERS

■ *Old log baskets painted with waterproof (wood or yacht) varnish. Line with a sheet of black polythene and punch some holes in the bottom for drainage. Do not trim the excess liner at the top until filled with compost – leave 5cm (2in) unfilled below rim. Trim off excess liner or tuck inwards – the plants will soon overgrow the edges and disguise it*
■ *Old chimney pots. (See illustration for how to fill, or rest a pot or hanging basket in the top to reduce compost needed)* ■

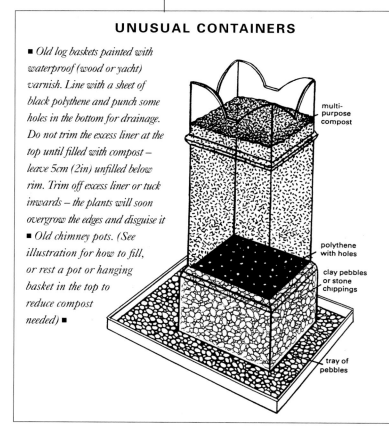

multi-purpose compost

polythene with holes

clay pebbles or stone chippings

tray of pebbles

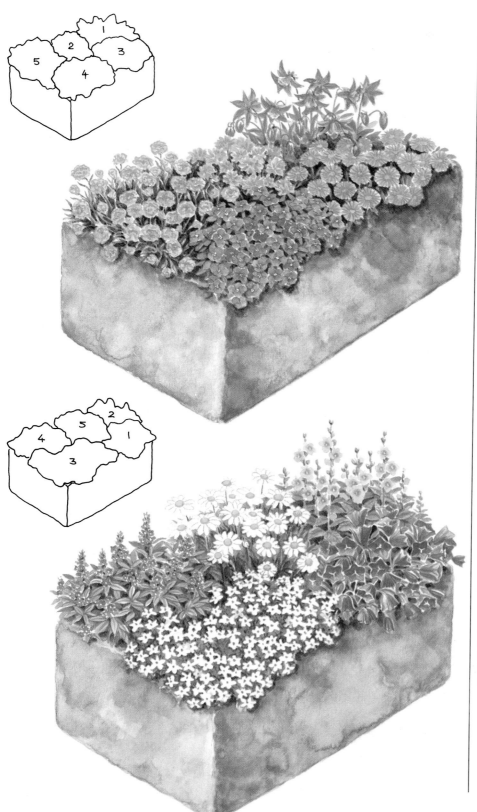

PLANTING PLANS FOR THE COTTAGE GARDEN TROUGH

KEY 1

1 *Aquilegia bertolonii* – dainty blue flowers. ht. 20cm (8in)
2 *Armeria caepitosa* – dwarf thrift, pink flowers. ht. 10cm (4in)
3 *Bellis perennis* **'Dresden China'** – double daisy, pink flowers. ht. 10cm (4in)
4 *Aubrieta deltoidea* **'Aureovariegata'** – purple flowers, variegated leaves. ht. 13cm (5in)
5 *Dianthus* **'Pike's Pink'** – fringed pink flowers, scented. ht. 15cm (6in)

KEY 2

1 *Campanula carpatica* **'Blue Moonlight'** – pale lavender flowers. ht. 10cm (4in)
2 *Diascia vigilis* – delicate pink flowers. ht. 30cm (12in)
3 *Phlox subulata* **'May Snow'** – spreading plant, white flowers. ht. 10cm (4in)
4 *Veronica prostrata* – bright blue flowers. ht. 15cm (6in)
5 *Leucanthemum hosmariense* – daisy-like white flowers. ht. 25cm (10in)

PLANTS FOR A COTTAGE GARDEN BARREL

SINGLE SHRUB
Hydrangea maculata (Mophead or Lacecap)
SUMMER PERENNIALS
Lady's mantle (*Alchemilla mollis*), foxgloves, larkspurs, lilies, astrantias, hardy geraniums

plants

OF THE

month

2

Meadow cranesbill

HARDY GERANIUM
(Cranesbill)

The wild geraniums, familiar from roadsides and hedgerows would have been a natural inclusion in cottage gardens. The common name, cranesbill, clearly describes the long, arching stalks which hold the beak shaped seed pods. The leaves of the plants were also reputed to stop the flow of blood from a wound, which is probably how the bloody cranesbill (Geranium sanguineum) gets its name. These easy-care, perennial plants, with their finely cut foliage and delicate pink or blue flowers have a myriad of uses in the cottage garden. Fanatics will collect the many species and named varieties and claim that a garden can never have too many geraniums. Indeed, there is literally a geranium for every garden situation, be it hot and sunny, dry and shady or damp.

CULTIVATION
of geraniums

planting	Autumn or spring
compost	No special requirements, add some garden compost to planting hole if soil is very poor
care	Cut back stems to ground level after flowering, to keep plant compact and to encourage a new flush of flowers
propagation	Divide in autum or spring and replant immediately. Most self-seed easily. Seeds of species (not hybrids) can be collected in early autumn, sown and grown on in a coldframe for planting out following autumn

MEADOW CRANESBILL
(Geranium pratense)

A native plant of most of northern Europe, the meadow cranesbill extended as far north as Iceland, where it was used to extract a blue-grey dye. The colour seems to have associations – mythical or real – with the warrior heroes of the Icelandic Sagas and it may even have been used to dye their fighting garments. The large clumps of violet-blue flowers can be grown on dry, chalky soils, against stone walls or in rough grass where they will often give two flushes of flowers – in early and late sum-mer. Locally it goes by the name of blue basins.

type	Herbaceous perennial
flowers	Violet-blue; early summer to early autumn
foliage	Mid-green, deeply divided
height	60–90cm (24–36in)
spread	60cm (24in)
site	In full sun or light shade (in full shade it will become leggy); in borders, beside stone walls, path edging or rough grass
soil	Well-drained
care	May need the support of twiggy sticks if grown in isolation
varieties	The double forms are popular in cottage gardens, particularly *G pratense* 'Plenum Violaceum' (lavender-blue) and *G. pratense* 'Plenum Album' (white). *G. pratense* 'Mrs Kendall Clarke' is a pale grey-blue variety

BLOODY CRANESBILL
(Geranium sanguineum)

A much more compact and lower-growing plant than the meadow cranesbill, *C. sanguineum* is a native of rocky slopes, limestone outcrops and coastal sand dunes. It likes light, well-drained soils and produces magenta-pink flowers from midsummer onwards.

type	Herbaceous perennial
flowers	Bright magenta or deep pink; mid-summer to early autumn
foliage	Mid-green, deeply divided
height	23–30cm (9–12in)
spread	45–60cm (18–24in)
site	Full sun; path edging or informal rock garden
soil	Well-drained, sand or chalk
varieties	*G. sanguineum* 'Album' is a white form – one of the best compact white geraniums

FRENCH CRANESBILL
(Geranium endressii)

A slender plant, bearing its silky-pink flowers from early summer onwards, this is a native of the Pyrenees in south-western France and has become naturalized in many parts of Europe as a garden escapee. It makes a pretty cottage garden subject.

type	Herbaceous perennial
flowers	Pale to mid-pink; early to midsummer

foliage	Mid-green, deeply lobed
height	30–45cm (12–18in)
spread	45cm (18in)
site	Sun or light shade; borders
soil	Any fairly moist soil
varieties	Since the 1930s the cottage garden favourites have been *G. endressii* 'Wargrave Pink' (pale pink) and *G. endressii* 'A.T.Johnson' (silvery-pink). Both make good ground cover in a lightly shaded position

DUSKY CRANESBILL
(*Geranium phaeum*)

This plant also goes by the name of 'mourning widow' – no doubt, as a result of its dark, sometimes sombre colour. In fact, the flowers can be quite variable, ranging from almost black, through deep purple, to an almost cheerful wine colour and some believe that this reflects the widow coming out of mourning. It is not quite as tall as the meadow cranesbill but forms a denser clump.

type	Herbaceous perennial
flowers	Dark purple; late spring to midsummer
foliage	Mid-green, partly divided
height	60cm (24in)
spread	60cm (24in)
site	Partial or full shade; borders, streamside or damp hollows
soil	Moist
varieties	*G. phaeum* 'Album' is the widely available white form

Geranium macrorrhizum

This species originates from southern Europe, but has been known in English gardens since the seventeenth century. It has two extra star qualities – it will thrive in poor soils and shade and, as an added bonus to the flowers, the leaves turn a brilliant red in autumn. The leaves are also strongly aromatic when crushed and in the past were used to extract Oil of Geranium for the perfume industry.

type	Herbaceous perennial
flowers	Pale pink or magenta; late spring to late summer
foliage	Five-lobed, aromatic, mid-green; brilliant red in autumn
height	30–45cm (12–18in)
spread	45–60cm (18–24in)
site	Partial or full shade; under trees, borders, hedge banks
soil	Any; tolerates dry or moist soil

varieties	*G. macrorrhizum* 'Bevan's Variety' is an intense pink; *G. macrorrhizum* 'Ingwersens' Variety' has shell-pink flowers

Geranium x *magnificum*

This is a nineteenth-century hybrid, widely grown in Scottish cottage gardens, particularly in the east. It is extremely hardy and tolerant of exposed positions and although it does best in sunshine, will grow quite well in shade. It makes a large, handsome plant and deserves to be more widely grown.

type	Herbaceous perennial
flowers	Purple-blue, 5cm (2.5in) across; early summer
foliage	Mid-green, part divided
height	75cm (30in)
spread	60cm (24in)
site	Sun or shade; borders, woodland edges
soil	Well-drained

Geranium x *magnificum*

Dusky cranesbill

French cranesbill

Geranium macrorrhizum

Bloody cranesbill

JUNE

Summer in the cottage garden comes with an exuberance of flowers.
The borders of larkspurs, delphiniums, verbascum, monk's hood,
campanulas and alliums are towering upwards, and honeysuckles and
jasmine take up their summer duty, filling the evening air with sweet
perfume. Perfume is the key to a successful bee- and butterfly-filled
garden and is achieved with the help of pinks and stocks and white
Madonna lilies.

But the month belongs to the rose. Vita Sackville-West, a great
advocate of flower-filled borders, confessed that in early summer her
pen took charge and she could write about little else but the wonder of
roses. Cottage garden roses have come a long way from the sweet briar
or eglantine, grown around every porch and garden seat. Our quest
for the perfect rose now extends to the four corners of the globe and yet
cottage garden roses still retain two characteristics: hardiness and a
good perfume. Among Sackville-West's favourites were the white
climbing rose Rosa odorata and the equally vigorous Rosa moschata,
both having wonderful scents. She recommended growing them up an
old tree, rather than waste good wall space which, in a cottage garden,
could be used to grow fruit or more tender climbers. For a small
garden, the more compact 'New Dawn' or 'Pink Perpétue' would be
better choices.

Colour schemes in the cottage borders can get exceedingly hot at this
time of year; blazing red poppies, dark purple pansies and deep blue
campanulas can look magnificent if the shades are carefully matched,
but they may need to be cooled with splashes of silver, greens or white.
To some people colour co-ordination is nothing short of serious artistic
endeavour, while others are content to have healthy plants in an artless
jumble. Who is to say whether cottage gardeners of old, planned their
gardens or let nature take its course?

tasks

FOR THE

month

CHECKLIST

- Lift spring-flowering bulbs
- Stake tall-growing perennials
- Trim evergreen hedges
- Collect seed of spring-flowering biennials
- Cut down crown imperials

LIFT AND DIVIDE SPRING-FLOWERING BULBS

All the familiar spring-flowering bulbs (tulips, daffodils, hyacinths, grape hyacinths and bluebells) can be lifted safely this month, now that the foliage has yellowed and died down. Lifting and dividing is particularly important for clumps that did not flower well in the spring — the bulbs may be overcrowded underground — but it may also be necessary in small gardens where the space is needed for summer plants.

■ Lift the clumps with a fork and separate the bulbs. These may be replanted immediately, spacing them out to give room to form another clump. Alternatively, store them by laying them in open boxes in a dry, airy place such as a shed with good ventilation.

■ When the bulbs are thoroughly dry, clean off any excess soil, dead roots or leaves and store them, either in the same open boxes or in plastic mesh bags (supermarket fruit or onion bags are ideal). In autumn, replant at the recommended planting depths (see p.103).

DIVIDING SPRING-FLOWERING BULBS

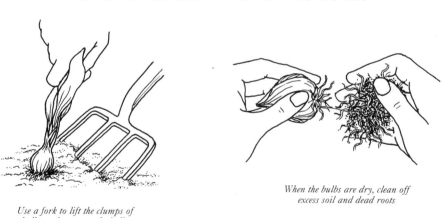

Use a fork to lift the clumps of bulbs and separate the bulbs

When the bulbs are dry, clean off excess soil and dead roots

Store the bulbs in open boxes or plastic mesh bags

SUPPORTING TALL-GROWING PLANTS

Perennial plants like delphiniums and rudbeckias need to be staked as they grow. Single-stem plants like lilies and gladioli can be supported with a bamboo cane tied to the stem, but clump-forming plants are best held by a ring-support. It is important to estimate the final height of the plant and to choose a support that will reach just below the flowers. That way, the support will become invisible as the plant grows above it.

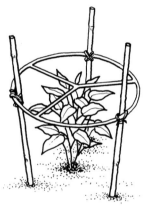

TRIMMING HEDGES

This is a good month to clip the growth on evergreen hedges especially the fast-growing privet (*Ligustrum*), *Lonicera nitida* and conifer hedges. The slower-growing yew (*Taxus*) and box (*Buxus*) can also be trimmed if they have made straggly growth. The aim is to produce a hedge that is slightly wider at the bottom than the top, to give stability and to allow the maximum amount of light to reach the base and to encourage bushy growth lower down. The top of the hedge can then either be sliced off flat or gently curved. Tall, dense hedges should be

TRIMMING TIPS

■ *When using shears, keep the blades flat against the sides of the hedge. To cut the top, turn the shears over* ■

■ *When using an electic hedge-trimmer, always keep safety in mind. Use an electric circuit breaker plug and keep the flex over your shoulder and away from the blades. Tilt the blades slightly in towards the hedge and make smooth, sweeping, upward strokes. It is advisable to wear eye guards to protect against flying twigs* ■

cut with a pair of hedging shears or a power hedgecutter. Small, low hedges, such as box used as edging, should be cut with shears or secateurs.

COLLECTING BIENNIAL SEED

Now that the spring flowers are over, the seed will be ready to harvest. Honesty, wallflowers, sweet William and forget-me-not may need to be removed from the beds to make room for summer annuals. A simple way to 'harvest' the seed is to pull up the plants, shaking the seed back on to the soil as you do so, allowing a random distribution of seedlings. However, if new plants are needed for other parts of the garden, snip off the flower heads and put them into a paper bag. If the seed does not fall off into the bottom of the bag immediately, tie up the bag with a piece of string and hang in a warm, dry place. When the seed separates easily from the plant material it is fully ripe and ready to sow. For best results sow the seed this month or next.

CUTTING DOWN CROWN IMPERIALS

Cut down the foliage and stems of crown imperials (*Fritillaria imperialis*) as they die back. This helps to keep the borders looking tidy and cared for.

SWEET WILLIAM
From the same family as the pinks, sweet William (Dianthus barbatus) is said to have been introduced into England by the Carthusian monks travelling from eastern Europe in the twelfth century. It was certainly established by Henry VIII's day, when bushels of the flowers were ordered for the new Hampton Court palace garden in 1553, at 3d a bushel. It is an easy to grow cottage garden biennial, grown from seed in late spring for flowering the following summer. It likes a sunny spot and will tolerate most garden soils. Colours vary according to the variety, but are usually white, pink or red with distinctive markings. Like the pinks, it has a spicy scent and once introduced into the garden will seed itself freely.

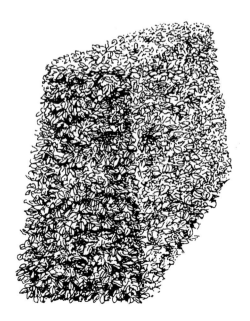

plants
OF THE
month
1

Peach-flowered bellflower

COTTAGE GARDEN CAMPANULAS
(Bellflower)

Campanula medium
Biennial, flowering from late spring to early summer. In the sixteenth century C. medium was known as the Coventry bell and the name Canterbury bell was reserved for another member of the family – C. trachelum, now known as the nettle-leafed bellflower. Despite the confusion, it is the 90cm (36in) high C. medium that became the cottage gardener's favourite with lilac, dark violet-blue or white flowers. The flowers are supposed to resemble the bells carried by the medieval Canterbury pilgrims.

Peach-flowered Bellfower
(Campanula persicifolia)
Evergreen perennial, flowering from early to late summer. This is probably the most graceful of the bellflowers. The single, blue, mauve or white flowers are borne on slender 90cm (36in) stems. The leaves are narrow and unobtrusive, leaving the papery flowers to be shown at their best. C. persicifolia self-seeds easily.

Chimney Bellflower
(Campanula pyramidalis)
Biennial, flowering in midsummer. The chimney – or steeple – bellflower has been grown in gardens since the sixteenth century and later became a favourite pot plant. It was used on windowsills and to decorate the empty fire grate in summer, where the 1.2m (4ft) spires of blue or white flowers, must have created a bold display.

Campanula carpatica
Perennial, flowering from mid- to late summer. This native of the Carpathian mountains is a favourite for growing informally over rocks or old stone walls, or for softening the edges of flagstone pathways. The plant forms compact clumps – 15–23cm (6–9in) high with cup-shaped, china-blue flowers – an ideal subject for the small cottage garden.

Giant Bellfower
(Campanula latifolia)
Perennial, flowering in midsummer. The tallest of the native bellflowers (1.2m/4ft) it makes a good subject at the back of the border.

POPPY
(Papaver spp.)

A whole range of poppy species – both annual and perennial – are available. Some, like the opium poppy, Papaver somniferum, are among the oldest flowers in cultivation; others, like the Iceland poppy, P.nudicale, are relatively new, yet all have the characteristics of a good cottage garden plant, colourful, informal and seeding themselves freely.

FIELD POPPY
(Papaver rhoeas)

This is the red poppy of cornfields and road verges, which no doubt turned up in early cottage gardens. The species is rather small but became the parent of many larger and more varied strains, in particular the famous Shirley poppies, raised by the Reverend Wilks of Shirley, Warwickshire in the 1880s. He is said to have bred selectively from a red and white sport he found growing near his home.

type	Annual
flowers	Red with a black centre, 7cm (3in) across; early to late summer
foliage	Deeply lobed, pale green
height	60cm (24in)
spread	30cm (12in)
site	In full sun; borders
soil	Well-drained; tolerates poor soils, particularly disturbed ground
planting	Sow seed in flowering positions
care	No special care needed
propagation	Self-seeds freely and the seeds may lie dormant in the ground for many years. Sow seeds in flowering position in mid-spring, just covering them with soil. Thin out seedlings as they appear
varieties	*P. rhoeas* 'Shirley Single' is available in mixed shades of pink, salmon, rose and crimson
cottage garden value	Farmers traditionally consider the poppy to be a weed, as it grows prolifically on soil that has been recently cultivated. Old names for it are redweed or headache. However, it was soon hybridized to produce respectable garden plants

OPIUM POPPY
(Papaver somniferum)

This species grows wild in Mediterranean countries and was probably introduced into

Britain by the Romans. According to classical mythology it was created by Somnus the god of sleep – a reference, no doubt, to its narcotic properties. Regardless of its medicinal uses, it is a handsome garden plant and double forms known as 'fringed, curled and feathered poppies' were popular in the sixteenth century. Today, many garden varieties are available, including double forms resembling peonies.

type	Annual
flowers	White, pink or red, 10cm (4in) across; early to late summer
foliage	lobed, pale grey-green
height	75cm (30in)
spread	30cm (12in)
site	In full sun; borders
soil	Well-drained; tolerates poor soils
planting	Sow seed in flowering positions
care	No special care needed. Staking not usually required as *P. somniferum*, despite being tall, has sturdy stems
propagation	Sow seeds in flowering position in mid-spring, just covering them with soil. Thin seedlings as they appear
varieties	Most popular are the peony-flowered strains, particularly *P. somniferum* 'Pink Chiffon' a frothy, pink double
cottage garden value	The ripe seeds were used to decorate cakes and breads and pressed to produce a salad oil, which, according to Gerard *'is pleasant and delightful to be eaten'*. But he also issued a dire warning against extracting the juice of the plant: *'It mitigateth all kinds of paines, but it leaveth behinde it a mischiefe worse than the disease it self...Opium, too plentifully eaten doth also bring death...'* All parts are poisonous except the seeds

ICELAND POPPY
(*Papaver nudicaule*)

The Iceland poppies are actually from Siberia and were introduced into England in the eighteenth century. Their popularity must in part be due to the fact that they are quite distinctive from the other poppies. They have translucent, tissue paper flowers which appear on slender, leafless stems making them ideal as cut flowers. The natural colour is white or yellow and has thus been used to develop strains that tend towards the yellow/orange end of the spectrum rather than pink.

type	Half-hardy annual
flowers	Yellow, white, orange; 2.5cm (1in) across; mid- to late summer
foliage	Soft green leaves in a basal rosette
height	45–60cm (18–24in)
spread	30cm (12in)
site	In full sun; borders
soil	Well-drained soil
planting	Sow seed in flowering positions
care	No special care needed. For long-lasting cut flowers, choose buds that are just showing some colour
propagation	Sow seed outdoors in late spring
varieties	*P. nudicaule* 'Kelmscott Strain' contains a range of apricot, orange, yellow and scarlet shades
cottage garden value	Excellent for cutting and bringing indoors. Adds splashes of bright colours to 'hot' borders

ORIENTAL POPPY
(*Papaver orientale*)

This poppy originates in Armenia where it was discovered by a French botanist in the early 1700s. Seeds arrived in London sometime before 1714 where it was grown by the nursery of London and Wise (famous for the Brompton Stocks). It is a hardy, clump-forming perennial, which makes a more substantial and permanent feature of the cottage garden than the randomly seeding annuals.

type	Herbaceous perennial
flowers	Scarlet with black blotches at the base of the petals, 10cm (4in) across; late spring to early summer; sometimes produces a small second flush in autumn, in mild areas only
foliage	Deeply cut, coarse, dark green
height	90cm (36in)
spread	60cm (24in)
site	In full sun; borders
soil	Good, well-drained soil
planting	Set out young plants in mid-spring or mid-autumn, 60cm (24in) apart
care	Staking may be necessary as plant stems grow. After flowering cut down the stems to encourage a second flush of flowers in autumn
propagation	Divide and replant the roots in early to mid-spring. Alternatively, take root cuttings in winter and grow on in a coldframe. Seed can be sown in a coldframe in mid-spring, but named varieties will not come true from seed
varieties	*P. orientale* 'Mrs Perry' is soft salmon pink with dark markings; *P. orientale* 'Perry's White', introduced in 1913, was the first white oriental poppy
cottage garden value	A handsome and easy-care border plant and a good alternative to the annual poppies

Top to bottom: field, opium and oriental poppies

practical project 1

BRINGING THE GARDEN INDOORS

POT POURRI BORDER FOR A SMALL GARDEN

KEY

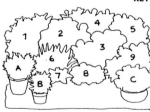

1 Philadelphus (*Philadelphus 'Manteau d'Hermine'*)
2 & 3 Old-fashioned shrub roses: *Rosa* 'Alfred de Dalmas' and 'Gloire de France
4 Lemon verbena (*Aloysia triphylla*)
5 Southernwood (*Artemisia abrotanum*)
6 Lavender (*Lavandula angustifolia 'Hidcote'*)
7 Violets (*Viola odorata*)
8 Pinks (*Dianthus* 'Sops-in-Wine')
9 Marjoram (*Origanum marjorana*)

In pots:
A Bay
B Peppermint
C Scented geranium

Cottage gardeners have always tended their plants with an eye to which ones would be useful or decorative inside the house. The Elizabethan 'strewing' herbs were our equivalent of *pot pourri*, but instead of putting fragrant plants in little bowls, the branches and leaves were dried and strewn on the floors to perfume and disinfect the rooms. Any plant that had a good scent was pressed into household service – sprigs of rosemary in the living quarters, garlands of violets above the bed, lavender on the washroom floor and bowls of snapdragon, roses and sweet Williams on the kitchen table.

MAKING POT POURRI

The ingredients of a successful pot pourri are a matter of personal preference and most people have their favourite flowers and scents. Rose petals are a basic requirement and most recipes include different mixtures of roses, herbs and other scented flowers and leaves. Part of the fun is collecting whatever flowers are available and trying out different mixtures. All the plant material must be thoroughly dried before use.

■ Pick the flowers and foliage on a dry day, after the morning dew has disappeared. Aim to pick petals and leaves that are in peak condition and discard any that have insect damage or are diseased.

■ Lay the petals or leaves on an old-fashioned metal or wooden flour sieve (a large garden sieve is even better). Alternatively use trays lined with sheets of absorbent kitchen paper.

■ Place the sieve in a warm, dry airy place – out of strong sunlight. An airing cupboard is ideal, or the warming oven of an Aga or Rayburn-type cooker.

WARNING

■ *It is not a good idea to put the leaves into a conventional oven as they are liable to dry too quickly and shrivel and there is also a danger of the wood/paper catching fire* ■

■ Toss or turn the petals frequently during drying to ensure all the pieces are dried thoroughly.

■ Store the dried material in cardboard boxes (shoe boxes are ideal) lined with tissue paper, or in darkened glass jars. The material can be used as soon as it is dried or can be stored for months as long as it is kept dry.

■ Add some powdered orris root to help 'fix' the perfumes and essential oils. It slows down evaporation and keeps the scent of the flowers and leaves for longer.

POT POURRI RECIPES

Traditional

1 cupful of rose petals (*Rosa canina, Rosa gallica* or any fragrant garden rose)
$^1/_2$ cupful of clove-scented pink petals
$^1/_4$ cupful of marjoram and rosemary leaves
1 teaspoon of ground or powdered cloves

Orange Spice

1 cup of rose petals
$^1/_2$ cup of mock orange blossom petals (*Philadelphus* hybrids)
Peel of one orange, dried and ground to a powder
A few bay leaves
1 teaspoon ground cinnamon and nutmeg

Lemon Zest

1 cup of lemon-scented geranium leaves (*Pelargonium crispum* 'Variegatum')
$^1/_2$ cup of southernwood leaves (*Artemisia abrotanum*)
$^1/_4$ cup of lemon-scented thyme (*Thymus* x *citriodorus*)
Peel of 1 lemon dried and powdered
1 teaspoon of mixed spice

■ Mix all the ingredients thoroughly. Put into china bowls or pot pourri containers. Traditional china boxes or balls are functional as well as decorative. They are sealed except for several air holes which allow the perfume to escape, but keep the contents dry, dust-free, and avoid spillages.

FLOWERS FOR INDOOR ARRANGEMENTS

Some gardeners like to have special flower beds for 'cutting' in a well-stocked cottage garden, but there is really no need. In spring and summer particularly, the borders will be overflowing with suitable plant material. Ironically, the art of cottage garden floristry is its artlessness'; it should need no wire, no florists' foam, no precise lengths or geometrical formula. The best cottage flowers are simply picked at their peak, combined with some sprigs of complementary foliage, and placed in plain pottery jugs, glass tumblers or china bowls; highly decorated containers only detract from the flowers. Cottage flowers are best picked fresh and replaced frequently.

Scented or colourful plants can be chosen according to the season: primroses and cowslips in spring, *Nigella*, stocks and roses in summer, and late in the year, flower heads of hydrangeas and statice, and the seed pods of honesty can be cut, tied in bunches and hung to

SUMMER
Pink roses ('Louise Odier' or 'Constance Spry')
Sprigs of mock orange blossom (*Philadelphus* 'Virginal' or 'Manteau d'Hermine'*)*

Alternative arrangement (not illustrated)
Alchemilla mollis
Gypsophila paniculata
Love-in-a-mist (*Nigella damascena*)
Aquilegia spp.
Scabious *(Scabious atropurpurea* and *Scabiosa caucasica)*

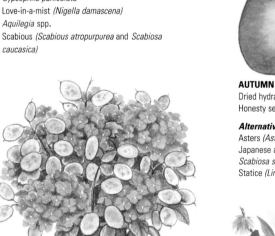

WINTER
Winter sweet (*Chimonanthus praecox*)
Periwinkle (*Vinca major*)

Alternative arrangement (not illustrated)
Daphne (*Daphne mezereum*)
Jasmine (*Jasminum nudiflorum*)
Forsythia (*Forsythia x intermedia*)

SEASONAL INDOOR ARRANGEMENTS

SPRING
Flowering currant *(Ribes sanguineum)*
Bluebells *(Scilla nonscripta)*

Alternative arrangement (not illustrated)
Daffodils *(Narcissus* spp.*)*
Tulips **(***Tulipa* spp.**)**
Sweet rocket *(Hesperis matronalis)*
Primroses *(Primula* spp.*)*
Lilac *(Syringa)*

AUTUMN
Dried hydrangea *(Hydrangea macrophylla)*
Honesty seed pods *(Lunaria annua)*

Alternative arrangement (not illustrated)
Asters *(Aster x frikartii)*
Japanese anemones *(Anemone x japonica)*
Scabiosa stellata
Statice *(Limonium sinuatum)*

plants
OF THE
month
2

MADONNA LILY
(*Lilium candidum*)

One of the oldest cultivated flowers in existence and a centrepiece of the cottage garden, the Madonna lily was known throughout the Roman world and, since it was a proven cure for corns, it was grown near roadside camps to treat foot weary soldiers. It was once so common in Elizabethan gardens that it hardly merited a mention in garden texts or poetry and was treated more or less as a native. Cottagers may even have grown it in rows like a vegetable, as the medical properties of the bulb interested them more than the flowers. Its popularity waned in the Victorian period, until the introduction of a rival, *Lilium auratum*, began a new wave of interest in lilies. The Madonna lily still has the best fragrance, a honey-sweet perfume that has eluded the perfume manufacturers for centuries.

type	Bulb
flowers	White with golden anthers; early to midsummer
foliage	Pale green; after the stems die down in autumn, a rosette of basal leaves is formed which lasts through the winter
height	1.2–1.4m (4–5ft)
spread	23cm (9in)
site	In full sun and, if possible, in the company of lower plants that can provide some shade around the roots. Also, in pots and tubs
soil	Ordinary garden soil, preferably slightly alkaline
planting	Plant bulbs in late summer or early autumn. *L. candidum* is basal rooting and therefore needs to be shallow-planted. Set the bulbs 5cm (2in) deep 23cm (9in) apart
care	Water frequently in dry weather. Mulch in spring with well-rotted compost or manure. Leave undisturbed if possible; if transplanting is necessary do this is early autumn
propagation	*L. candidum* will increase naturally if left undisturbed. If necessary, lift and divide the bulbs in late summer or early autumn when the foliage has died down. Ripe seed can be collected in late summer and sown in seed compost, in a coldframe
related species	The regal lily, *L. regale* is one of the easiest species to grow in borders or pots. It has fragrant white trumpet flowers and increases easily. Unlike the Madonna lily, it is stem

rooting, which means it should be planted more deeply, at 15–23cm (6–9in).

cottage garden value	Originally cultivated for the medicinal properties of the bulb – reputed to cure everything from hair loss to corns – it is now grown purely for the pleasure of its scent and flowers.

HONEYSUCKLE (WOODBINE)
(*Lonicera periclymenum*)

Most gardeners would agree that of all the honeysuckles, wild honeysuckle still has the best scent, if its flowers are less showy and its growth more untidy than the cultivated forms. Every cottage garden would have had a native woodbine twining over the porch or arbour, by a seat or window where its perfume could be savoured on a summer evening. The stems twine naturally upwards, but need the support of a tree, hedge, wooden arch or trellis.

type	Deciduous climber
flowers	Creamy-yellow, tinged with purple; early summer to early autumn
berries	Red berries in late autumn
leaves	Mid-green, oval
height	Up to 6m (20ft) but generally adjusts to the height of the support
site	Ideally with the roots in shade and the top in sun. Against the wall of the house, over an arch or through a tree
soil	Any well-drained soil
planting	Plant in autumn or spring. To ensure the base remains cool in summer, plant among leafy perennials such as periwinkle (*Vinca major*), geraniums or astrantias which will shade the roots
care	Mulch around the base with well-rotted manure or garden compost in late spring. No regular pruning required, but large plants can be given a light top pruning after flowering. Any old wood can be thinned out from the base
propagation	Take hardwood cuttings or layer the stems in autumn. Seed can also be collected from the berries in early autumn and sown in a coldframe
varieties	The two best known varieties are Belgian honeysuckle (*L. periclymenum* 'Belgica') which begins flowering in late spring, and Dutch honeysuckle (*L. periclymenum.* 'Serotina') which goes on flowering into mid-autumn. Both plants have deeper coloured

Madonna lily. The connection with the Virgin Mary dates to the first century when it was said that her tomb was found empty except for roses and lilies. The white flowers became a symbol of purity, the petals being the symbol of her body, the golden anthers her soul glowing with heavenly light

flowers than the wild form. 'Belgica' is the more compact of the two

cottage garden value Grown mainly for its perfume, the honeysuckle is also supposed to ward off evil powers and protect cattle and their produce.

STOCKS
(Matthiola spp.)

This group of annual and biennial flowers is invaluable for the cottage garden for summer colour and scent. It includes the famous Brompton stock, bred in London in the eighteenth century, and the night-scented stock, the best choice for evening perfume. From the nineteenth century comes the ten-week stock, reputedly bred by the weavers of Saxony who, according to Jane Loudon, 'take as much pleasure in growing and saving the seed of their stocks, as the Lancashire weavers do in England in growing their pinks and carnations'. By mutual consent, the weavers of each village bred only one colour or one variety and so kept them absolutely distinct.

Matthiola incana

Of southern European origin, this is the parent of all the garden hybrids commonly grown today. It was has been known in gardens since Elizabethan times and shows no sign of decreasing in popularity. The advice for growing stocks was quite precise: sow the seed in mid-spring at a full moon, transplant the seedlings for three consecutive months (always at full moon) and then set them out into their final positions at Michaelmas, for flowering the following year. These days gardeners are usually content to follow a somewhat simpler programme of cultivation.

BROMPTON STOCKS

This strain dates back to the 1720s when only the finest doubles were raised by the nursery of London and Wise in Brompton, London, and supplied to the gardens of Blenheim Palace in Oxfordshire.

type	Biennial
flowers	Red, pink, white, yellow, scented; mid- to late summer
foliage	Felty, narrow, grey-green
height	45cm (18in)
spread	30cm (12in)

site	In full sun; will tolerate shade, but in deep shade they will become leggy
soil	Fertile soil
planting	Set out plants in autumn, 30cm (12in) apart, adding garden compost or well-rotted manure if the soil is poor
care	No special care needed
propagation	Sow fresh seed each year in early summer and grow on to plant out in autumn

TEN-WEEK STOCK

These are the easy to grow annual stocks which give an almost instant summer display, ideal for filling gaps in summer borders. A huge range of dwarf and giant strains are available.

type	Annual
flowers	Pink, crimson, white, yellow, scented; mid- to late summer
foliage	Linear, grey-green
height	23–60cm (9–24in), depending on strain
spread	30cm (12in)
site	Full sun; open borders
soil	Fertile soil
planting	Grow from seed sown directly in flowering positions
care	Water during dry spells
propagation	Sow seed in flowering positions in mid-spring. Cover the seeds lightly and water in. Thin out the seedlings as they appear

NIGHT-SCENTED STOCK
(Matthiola bicornis)

This probably has the best fragrance of all the stocks, but only from dusk onwards. During the day the flower petals close up and the plant does not look particularly attractive. To get the best of both worlds, mix the seed of *M. bicornis* with Virginia stock (*M. maritima*) which is also an annual.

type	Annual
flowers	Lilac, single, night scented; mid- to late summer
foliage	Narrow, grey-green
height	40cm (16in)
spread	23cm (9in)
site	Full sun; open borders, beneath windows and seats
soil	Fertile
planting	Sow seed in flowering positions
care	Water in dry spells
propagation	Sow seed outdoors in mid-spring and cover lightly with soil. Thin out seedlings as they appear

Honeysuckle and Brompton stocks

practical project 2

GROWING COTTAGE GARDEN PINKS

PINK OR CARNATION?
It is generally accepted that pinks are smaller and daintier with a slender stem, compared to carnations which are taller and more sculptured as the illustration below shows

'But what shall I say to the Queene of delight and of flowers, Carnations and Gilloflowers, whose bravery, variety and sweet smell joined together, tyeth every one's affection'

To John Parkinson, writing in the early seventeenth century, carnations and pinks or gillyflowers were already such a widespread phenomenon that he almost despaired of writing anything new about them. They were – and are – the perfect cottage garden flower, 'brave' (hardy), compact and sweetly scented.

The difference between carnations and pinks has never been clear cut. All the *Dianthus* species have, at one time or another, been labelled as carnations and pinks. The term gillyflower is derived from the French *giroflier* – a clove tree – and was used for any clove-scented *Dianthus*. However, of the two original species, *D. caryophyllus*, which has tall stems, can be said to have been the parent of the carnations and *D. plumarius*, which is smaller and carries single flowers, the parent of pinks.

Dianthus caryophyllus is a native of southern Europe, where it is found growing on rocky limestone outcrops. The story is that it entered Britain on the stones brought by the followers of William the Conqueror and was found growing on the walls of several Norman buildings including Rochester Castle and Fountains Abbey. It still grows wild in Normandy today.

Although border and perpetual carnations are popular for cut flowers, the cottage gardener would usually plump for the less labour-intensive pinks, particularly the old-fashioned varieties. They have the honour of being a garden plant with an almost uninter-

rupted popularity, from Chaucer's time when the petals were used to flavour wine and produce syrups and conserves, to the eighteenth century when they were one of the eight selected and approved 'florists' flowers (see p.106). They lost none of their charm in the Victorian era when gardeners in industrial areas bred more and more elaborate forms for show. Despite competition from modern pinks, which have a longer flowering period, the old-fashioned varieties, which flower only in early summer, are enjoying something of a revival.

GROWING CONDITIONS

■ Pinks like full sun and a well-drained soil. They prefer a limey soil, but extra lime is only necessary if the soil is below pH 6.5. Dress the soil with lime in autumn if this is needed.

■ Pinks are tolerant of exposed, windy positions, salt spray and pollution. Their only dislike is of moisture around the roots. If the soil is heavy, consider growing them in raised beds or a rockery where the soil can be replaced with a mixture of compost and horticultural grit.

OLD-FASHIONED PINKS

Dianthus plumarius from southern Europe is the parent of the old-fashioned pinks, so loved by cottage gardeners. It produces compact hummocks of rich pink flowers with ragged petals and the characteristic clove scent. Fortunately, many of the varieties produced in past centuries have survived, if not

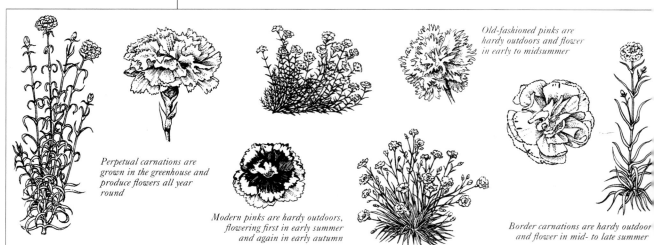

Old-fashioned pinks are hardy outdoors and flower in early to midsummer

Perpetual carnations are grown in the greenhouse and produce flowers all year round

Modern pinks are hardy outdoors, flowering first in early summer and again in early autumn

Border carnations are hardy outdoor and flower in mid- to late summer

continuously, then at least from a nineteenth-century revival:

D. **'Green Eye'**, also known as 'Charles Musgrave', after whom it was named in the seventeenth century, has fringed white petals with a green centre.

D. **'Mrs Sinkins'** is a nineteenth-century variety with double creamy-white flowers.

D. **'Paddington'** was raised in London in 1920 and has pink fringed double flowers.

D. **'Painted Lady'**, a sixteenth-century discovery, has small fringed white petals flashed with purple.

D. **'Sam Barlow'** is a Victorian favourite with double white flowers.

D. **'Sops-in-Wine'**. This fourteenth-century form still survives in cottage gardens and is available from nurseries. It has fringed white flowers with black centres. The name relates to the time when the flowers were steeped in wine, and pinks could be found growing in tavern gardens.

D. **'White Ladies'** is the Victorian show pink with fringed white flowers.

● LACED PINKS

These intricately patterned flowers were the product of selective breeding by Victorian industrial workers in the north of England and Scotland. In particular, the weavers around Paisley in Scotland raised the breeding of laced pinks to an art form, producing striped and flashed flowers in every conceivable colour, said to parallel the designs of the famous Paisley patterned textiles. In the nineteenth century there were around 190 laced varieties; today they are collected by a few enthusiasts and only a handful survive, among them the weavers' *D.* 'Paisley Gem', raised in 1798, a very fragrant white with purple lacing.

● MODERN PINKS

Modern pinks were produced by crossing *D. plumarius* with a perpetual-flowering carnation, retaining the form and habit of a pink, but achieving a longer flowering period. The main breeder was Montagu Allwood, and modern pinks are listed as *Dianthus × allwoodii*. Most retain the perfume and charm of the old-fashioned pinks and they should not be dismissed from the cottage garden just because of their recent pedigree. Among the hundreds of modern pinks *D.* 'Doris' is a popular pale pink double and *D.* 'Haytor White' is a reliable white.

CULTIVATING OLD-FASHIONED AND MODERN PINKS: CALENDAR

EARLY SPRING

Set out new plants, 30cm (12in) apart, taking care not to bury the stem (1). Water in well

MID-SPRING

'Stop' modern pinks to encourage side shoots (1st year only). Break top off main shoot, just above a joint, about 7 joints from base of plant (2)

LATE SPRING

Support plants (if necessary) using branched twigs (3). Use twigs that will stand 15cm (6in) above the plant so stems can grow through them

EARLY SUMMER

Cut flowers for indoor arrangements if required. Cut stems near their base in the morning and stand in deep, clean water until needed

MIDSUMMER

Take cuttings after flowers have finished. Select a strong shoot and cut it off close to the main stem. Remove lower leaves. Trim to just below the last joint beneath the remaining leaves (4). Insert in sandy compost and water in. Place pots in a coldframe

LATE SUMMER

Remove old flower stems completely. Apply a high potash fertilizer

EARLY AUTUMN

Plant out rooted cuttings in flowering positions

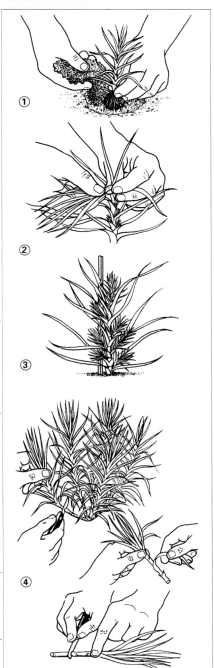

JULY

At the height of summer, the cottage garden should be at its absolute peak, with a wealth of flowering plants all jostling for attention. During the day, lilies, stocks, pinks and roses are rivals for the best perfume; at dusk, the climbing honeysuckles, evening primrose and summer jasmines have their hour of glory. The borders are overflowing with campanulas, columbines, alliums and poppies. In shady beds, foxgloves and lady's mantle ensure that no corner of the garden is left unclothed.

This is the time for relaxation, for taking out a chair and enjoying the sounds, colours and scents of the summer garden. In fact, probably the only attention the plants will need this month is an occasional evening watering, to keep them at their best. However, for the dedicated gardener who cannot bear to sit in or stroll through his patch without a pair of secateurs, there are flowers to be deadheaded, seeds to be saved and sown, and shrubs to be trimmed. Seeds of biennials like foxgloves, hollyhocks and wallflowers can be sown now to produce plants for next spring and summer. It is also a good time to put in autumn-flowering bulbs. Sweet pea enthusiasts will be busy removing side shoots and tying in their plants to produce the larger blooms for cutting. Those of us who grow them for pleasure rather than show content ourselves with picking a bunch for the table each day, secure in the knowledge that cutting the blooms actually encourages more flowers.

Unexpected, heavy summer showers can play havoc with the most carefully tended border. If plants are flattened by the rain, it might be necessary to add a stake here and there, or clip back any flowers that are past their best. But this month can just as happily be spent in a haze of inactivity, soaking in the pleasures of a garden buzzing with wildlife and scented with flowers.

tasks

FOR THE

month

PLANTING AUTUMN-FLOWERING BULBS

Nerines, colchicums and the autumn-flowering crocuses (*Crocus sativus* and *Crocus autumnalis*) should be planted this month or next. They are ideal for growing in rockeries, raised beds, as path edging, or at the front of a border. These bulbs prefer a light, well-drained soil and plenty of sunshine so choose the position accordingly. If the soil is heavy, add sharp sand or grit to improve drainage. Plant the bulbs 10cm (4in) deep and 15cm (6in) apart and cover with soil.

SOWING BIENNIAL SEEDS

Most of the biennial flowers can be sown this month for flowering next spring and summer. Honesty, wallflowers and sweet William seed collected last month can be sown now, along with foxgloves, evening primroses, sweet rocket and hollyhocks. (These can all be grown from packet seed if the garden flowers are not available or have not yet set seed.) Seed can be sown outdoors in pots or in a nursery bed if there is room available. Choose a lightly-shaded position where the seedlings will get some protection from the hot summer sun. Fill the pots with seed compost and/or rake the bed to a fine tilth.

Sowing the seed

■ Sow the seed as thinly as possible, covering it with a light layer – about 1cm ($^1/_2$in) – of sieved compost or soil. Fine seed, like that of foxgloves, can be mixed with silver sand to make it easier to sow.
■ Water the seeds with a watering can fitted with a fine spray rose. Use labels to mark the different flowers.
■ When the seedlings are about 8cm (3in) high, thin them out by transplanting them to new pots or beds.

Aftercare

■ Keep the plants well watered and pinch out the growing tips in late summer to encourage bushy growth.
■ In mid-autumn, transplant the biennials into their final flowering positions. This gives them a chance to establish themselves before the worst of the winter weather.

EXTRA PLANTS
In a particularly bad winter, some young biennial plants will die off because their root systems are not sturdy enough to resist a period of wet and cold. Therefore it is a good idea to have a few extra plants in pots on standby, in case there are gaps in the borders that need to be filled.

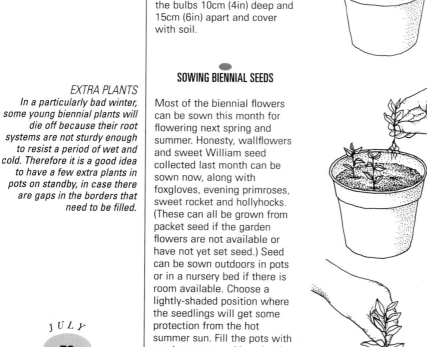

PRUNING CLEMATIS AND HONEYSUCKLE

The two most popular climbing shrubs *Clematis montana* and the common honeysuckle *Lonicera periclymenum* do not need regular pruning and will go on flowering year after year with very little attention. However, eventually they may grow beyond their supports or threaten to swamp other plants and will need to be cut back. The best time for this is after they have flowered; for honeysuckle you may need to wait until the end of the month.

Cutting back
■ Carefully detach the plant from its support; if it has become very entwined, you may need to cut the top growth down first and allow it to die back before tackling the lower part.
■ Cut the main stem down to a young shoot lower down the stem. Remove all the lateral (side) growth to leave a low, bare framework of stems.

MONTHLY REMINDERS

■ *Deadhead roses – cut back the fading flowers to a new bud or shoot*

■ *Cut sweet peas regularly – snip off flowers for indoor use and remove any fading flowers to stop them setting seed*

■ *Water and feed containers and hanging baskets – water daily and use a liquid feed weekly*

■ *Clip privet and box hedges – use hand shears to remove any straggly growth and retain a compact shape*

DIVIDING IRISES

Overcrowded clumps of flag irises (*Iris germanica*, *Iris pallida* and garden hybrids) may be divided now that flowering is finished.

Making new plants
■ Simply lift the old clump out of the ground and break or cut off the new rhizomes from the old woody centre.
■ Cut back the leaves to about 23cm (9in) to prevent wind-rock when replanted.
■ Replant the new rhizomes immediately, firming them into the soil well, but leaving the top of the rhizome exposed to the air.
■ Water regularly, especially in dry weather, until established.

CUTTING DOWN PERENNIAL PLANTS

Cottage garden borders can start to look rather bedraggled by midsummer, as some perennial plants finish flowering, leaving their stems to die back naturally. Geraniums, delphiniums, perennial poppies and globe flowers may be past their best and trimming off the flowering stems with a pair of secateurs will retain the compact shape of the plant. Geraniums and delphiniums in particular respond well to this treatment and may reward you with a late flush of flowers in early autumn. Cut the stems back to just beneath the foliage.

TRIMMING ARTEMISIAS AND SANTOLINAS
These silvery-leaved plants are often grown as low foliage hedges to edge a path or to contain a herb border, and are not required to flower. Lightly clip them over this month with a pair of hedging shears, to remove any flowers and to retain a compact shape. This treatment applies to wormwood (Artemisia absinthium), southernwood (Artemisia abrotanum) and cotton lavender (Santolina chamaecyparissus).

plants
OF THE
month
1

Hollyhock and sweet rocket

HOLLYHOCK
(Alcea rosea)

No other flower lends the garden such an air of antiquity as the hollyhock. It grows to its full height in the space of a few months, yet looks as though it might have been in place for centuries. It was certainly recorded in gardens of the fifteenth century and became so commonplace by the seventeenth century that the Reverend Samuel Gilbert – a rather supercilious clergyman – described it as one of the flowers 'adored by countrywomen' and therefore, by default, *not* in the best of taste. The countrywomen evidently did not take offence and continued to grow hollyhocks in profusion, until a rust disease struck the plant in the late nineteenth century, wiping out many of the old varieties. It will function as a perennial, but tends to get taller and taller, easily reaching 3m (10ft) and producing fewer and fewer flowers lower down the stem. The best plants are produced as biennials, which will stay a compact 2m (6ft). Sowing new plants every one or two years also minimizes the chances of rust problems.

type	Short-lived perennial, usually grown as a biennial
flowers	Pink, crimson, white, cream, yellow; mid- to late summer
foliage	Pale green, rough
height	To 3m (9ft)
spread	45–60cm (18–24in)
site	In a sheltered position, in sun or light shade – the back of a border, or against a sunny wall is ideal
soil	Heavy, rich soil preferred, but will tolerate others
planting	Plant out pot-grown plants in mid- to late spring. If grown as a biennial, sow seeds in pots from late spring to midsummer. Overwinter the young plants in a coldframe and put into their permanent positions the following spring
care	Water frequently in dry weather. If plants are going to be retained from year to year, cut down the stems to 15cm (6in) after flowering and apply an annual mulch of well-rotted manure or garden compost in spring. Stake tall plants as necessary
propagation	Collect ripe seed in early autumn and store in a cool dark place until spring. Sow outdoors from late spring to midsummer
varieties	Double forms like 'Chater's Double' have an old-fashioned, blowzy appearance that suits the cottage garden well. The dwarf variety, 'Majorette', 60cm (24in) tall, is semi-double and comes in a range of pinks and lavendar shades, and could be grown in containers. Single flowers in yellows, pinks, apricots and whites are available
related species	The first *Alcea* to be grown in gardens was probably the native marsh mallow *A. officinalis* which is also a tall plant with simple, pale-lilac pink flowers. The sticky substance used to make sweet marshmallows was extracted from the roots and the plant was used to prepare ointments for all kinds of ailments
cottage garden value	Hollyhocks and marsh mallows are both attractive to bees and were an essential cottage garden subject

SWEET ROCKET
(Hesperis matronalis)

Locally known as dame's violet or sweet rocket, this summer roadside flower has a sweet fragrance and an informal appearance – a perfect candidate for the cottage garden. A native of field boundaries and verges, it had found its way into gardens by the seventeenth century, and probably much earlier. It self-seeds with abandon and its perfume is strongest in the evening – two more reasons for including it in the summer border.

type	Short-lived perennial, usually grown as a biennial
flowers	White, mauve or purple; early to late summer
foliage	Mid-green, serrated
height	60–90cm (24–36in)
spread	45cm (18in)
site	Sun or partial shade
soil	Prefers moist soil, but tolerates others
planting	Plant out young plants in autumn
care	No special care needed
propagation	Self-seeds easily. Alternatively, sow seeds outdoors in trays from late spring to midsummer and grow on in a sheltered spot until planting out in the autumn. Roots can be divided in autumn or spring
varieties	Single varieties can look rather sparse unless planted in dense clumps. Double forms are popular with cottage gardeners, but they do

need a rich soil and regular dividing – *H. matronalis* 'Lilacina Flore Pleno' is a reliable double.*H. matronalis* var. *albiflora* is white

cottage garden value	All varieties have a strong perfume which attracts butterflies. It is the food plant of orange tip and green-veined white butterfly larvae

FOXGLOVE
(Digitalis purpurea)

The wild foxglove, with its intense purple flower spikes is difficult to improve on, but selective breeding and casual crossing in cottage gardens has led to the development of taller, larger-flowered varieties in a range of colours from white, through pink, to the darkest maroon. Its natural habitat is the moist woodland edge, often among ferns or low-growing shrubs, and it is very suitable for a wild garden. It is hard to imagine a cottage garden without foxgloves and the white and cream forms look magnificent in pastel borders. In folklore, the fox, wearing foxgloves, could silently creep up to unsuspecting chickens, and away from cottagers or farmers; the juice of the plant was believed to ward off fairies and to bring back children who had been snatched by them. The fact that it was poisonous increased the superstition surrounding it. It is used commercially to extract the drug digitalin, for use in the treatment of heart conditions. All parts are poisonous.

type	Biennial; occasionally perennial
flowers	Purple, pink, white, cream, with darker spots inside; early to late summer
foliage	Oval leaves in a basal rosette
height	1–1.5m (3–5ft)
spread	45cm (18in)
site	In partial shade, in borders or tubs
soil	Any moisture-retentive soil
planting	Put out young plants in autumn or spring, 60cm (24in) apart
care	Mulch around the plants with leafmould, bark or garden compost in spring. To prolong the life of plants, cut down spikes after flowering (leaving selected plants to set seed). Discard plants after two or three years
propagation	Collect seed in early autumn and sow outside from late spring to midsummer. If sown in pots, plant out into borders in autumn for flowering the following year
varieties	The white foxglove, *D. purpurea alba* is highly prized by cottage gardeners and is widely available.

cottage garden value	Cottagers grew them for their stately spires of colour, but they are also excellent bee and butterfly plants; in Somerset the flowers are known as 'bee-catchers'.

LARKSPUR
(Delphinium consolida, syn. *Consolida ambigua)*

The annual larkspur has been recorded in gardens since the sixteenth century and was cultivated in many colours and double forms before the better known perennial delphinium was introduced; Shakespeare knew it as the 'lark's heel', one of its country names. It was held to possess properties for strengthening eyesight and the distilled flowers were used to make an eye wash. However, the seeds and other parts of the plants are poisonous like other members of the *Delphinium* family.

type	Annual
flowers	Blue, purple, white, pink; early to late summer
foliage	Finely-cut, mid-green leaves
height	1.2m (4ft)
spread	30–38cm (12–15in)
site	In full sun
soil	Any, or light soil
planting	Set out young plants in mid-spring, 30cm (12in) apart
care	No special care needed
propagation	Collect the seed in late summer or early autumn and either sow immediately or store until spring. Autumn sowings can be protected under cloches through the winter and will produce earlier flowers
varieties	The tall 'Giant Imperial' strain is widely grown in borders; the 'Hyacinth-flowered' group is more compact (about 60–90cm/24–36in) and is a favourite for cut flowers. Both are available in a mixed colour range of violet, lavender, pink and white
cottage garden value	Larkspurs were traditionally grown in rows and used to fill in the gaps between perennials. Despite the fact that the plant is poisonous, many medicinal properties have been claimed for it, including (ironically) a cure for poisoning. However, Gerard in his *Herbal* was very disparaging about its medicinal uses, saying that such claims were 'not worth the reading'

Foxglove and larkspur

practical project 1

A GARDEN FOR BEES

Beekeeping was an essential cottage garden skill, providing the household with a ready supply of honey. Honey was a highly valued food stuff and, as sugar was not widely available until the late Victorian era, it served the cottagers' needs for sweetening. There is no proof that cottagers in previous centuries actually planned their gardens with bees in mind, but the number of traditional cottage garden plants which also happen to be good for bees is so extensive, that it seems likely.

At first, the successful bee plants were probably introductions from the countryside – wild thyme and mignonette, field scabious, knapweeds and deadnettles, but as the range of plants available to gardeners increased, so did those that were attractive to bees – lavender, borage, red valerian are all of Mediterranean origin and excellent for bees. So too are the nineteenth-century introductions like the spring-flowering *Ribes* (flowering currant) and *Limnanthes douglasii* (poached egg plant). Bees range far and wide in search of nectar and pollen, but for the beekeeper the joy of watching them working a patch of flowers near the hive may have encouraged the planting of nectar-rich plants. A well-stocked cottage garden will offer plenty of choice to the foraging bee and provide enough for a healthy population of honey bees, bumble bees and solitary bees.

THE ECOLOGY OF THE BEE GARDEN

The bees we are most likely to see are the easily identifiable bumble and honey bees. Both groups live in social colonies: honey bees are usually in hives, although wild colonies nest in old tree trunks: the bumble bees are in nests underground, often taking over an old mouse or vole hole. The bumble bee colony will find a new home every year, but honey bees need a permanent home where the queen can remain undisturbed for many years, hence their willingness to take up residence in man-made hives. There are also many species of solitary bee, such as the mason bee, which likes to nest in wall crevices, and the leaf-cutter bee, so-called because of the female's habit of cutting pieces out of rose leaves to line her nest.

HOMES FOR BEES

Even if you don't wish to become a full time beekeeper, there are ways you can attract a range of different bees to the garden.

The honey bee
A colony of honey bees is only likely to be attracted to a well-constructed hive or to an

THE SOLITARY BEE
Solitary bees usually prefer the security of a small hole or crevice in brickwork, stone walls or fallen trees. The same habitat can be created by taking a large, old log or tree stump and drilling holes in the wood.

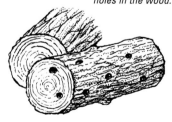

old hollow tree, whose inner walls will give the necessary support to the building of the honeycombs. The only difference between a man-made hive and a naturally occurring one is that the man-made hive has a series of inner 'drawers', allowing the beekeeper to extract a honeycomb while the bees continue working in the other compartments.

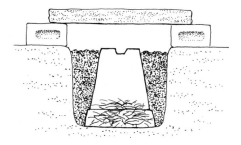

The bumble bee

Most bumble bees nest underground and will use a man-made nest. Dig a hole big enough for a 30cm (12in) clay flowerpot. Add some dry grass or leaves to the hole and place the flowerpot upturned in it. Fill the earth back around the pot, leaving the drainage hole uncovered. Support a tile on a couple of bricks or stones to keep the rain out.

PLANTING FOR BEES

Bees are perfect for the cottage garden ecology. They can provide honey of course, but in searching for the nectar and pollen they need to feed themselves and other members of their colonies, their bodies are dusted with pollen which they carry on to other flowers thus aiding fertilization; without their efforts, many flowers would simply not reproduce. To the bee, it is the flower's scent and colour that provides the attraction – the lighter perfumes seem to suit them best. As for colour, bees are capable of seeing ultra-violet light and therefore are most attracted to those colours that show up the strongest in this light – blues, purples and reds, particularly. Plants like foxgloves have clearly visible markings on the flowers, guiding the bees into the nectar tunnel, but others, like the yellow evening primrose, have markings which we can only see under ultra-violet light. Having been guided into the flower, the bee's relatively long tongue enables it to reach nectar at the base of tubular flowers like campanulas, bluebells and honeysuckle. Sometimes the sheer weight of the bee governs its success rate with flowers like snapdragons which remain stubbornly shut until a bumble bee lands and forces the 'mouth' apart.

MEAD
The drink produced from naturally-fermented honey was made and drunk by all levels of society, from the poorest cottager to the yeoman farmer, the monk and the squire. There were as many recipes as there were households, but most included water, honey, lemon rind (when available) and an assortment of spices such as caraway, cloves, nutmeg or ginger. Herb flavourings were added according to local taste; thyme, sage and strawberry leaves were popular. Mead was matured in stoppered casks for a year or more and emerged strong in alcohol and very sweet.

(continued on page 82)

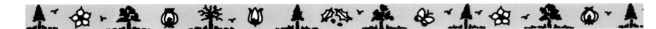

SEASONAL BEE BORDERS

Contented bees need a succession of nectar- and pollen-bearing plants from early spring to late autumn. Even in winter, a few flowers like snowdrop, crocus and lungwort will provide for those that stir early from hibernation. A border of bee plants need not be large and different areas of the garden can provide for the various seasons.

SPRING BED

plant	type	height × spread	description	flowering
Bluebell *(Scilla non-scripta)*	Bulb	30cm (12in)	Nodding blue flowers; strap shape leaves	Mid-spring to early summer
Crocus *(Crocus chrysanthus* and *Crocus tommasinianus)*	Bulb	8cm (3in)	Purple or yellow-goblet shaped flowers	Late winter to mid-spring
Deadnettle *(Lamium maculatum)*	Perennial	30cm (12in) × 60cm (24in)	Pink or purple flowers; silver-striped foliage	Late spring
Flowering currant *(Ribes sanguineum)*	Shrub	3m (9ft) × 2m (6ft)	Deep rose-coloured flowers; mid-green leaves similar to a redcurrant	Early to late spring
Forget-me-not *(Myosotis sylvatica)*	Biennial	15cm (6in) × 15cm (6in)	Brilliant blue flowers with a good fragrance. Use as path edging or bedding	Late spring to midsummer
Lungwort *(Pulmonaria officinalis)*	Perennial	30cm (12in) × 30cm (12in)	Spreading, groundcover plant with narrow spotted leaves and pink, blue or purple flowers	Late winter to late spring
Snowdrop *(Galanthus nivalis)*	Bulb	15cm (6in)	White flowers with green markings, slightly scented	Midwinter to early spring

SUMMER BED

plant	type	height × spread	description	flowering
Giant bellflower *(Campanula latifolia)*	Perennial	1.2m (4ft) × 45cm (18in)	Bell-shaped, violet-blue flowers on tall, upright stems	Midsummer
Borage *(Borago officinalis)*	Annual	60cm (24in)	Blue, star-shaped flowers; rough, hairy leaves. Self-seeds freely	Early summer to early autumn
Globe thistle *(Echinops ritro)*	Perennial	1.2m (4ft)	Steel-blue, globe-shaped flowerheads; thistle-like leaves	Mid- to late summer
Honeysuckle *(Lonicera periclymenum)*	Climber	5m (15ft)	Creamy-yellow flowers, flushed with pink. Very fragrant	Mid- to late summer
Lavatera *(Lavatera* 'Barnsley'*)*	Shrub	2m (6ft) × 1.2m (4ft)	Pale pink, trumpet flowers. velvety leaves. 'Barnsley' is more compact than other varieties	Midsummer to mid-autumn
Lavender *(Lavandula angustifolia)*	Evergreen shrub	60–90cm (24–36in) × 60cm (24in)	Blue flower spikes; aromatic, grey-green leaves	Midsummer to early autumn
Thrift *(Armeria maritima)*	Evergreen perennial	23cm (9in) × 30cm (12in)	Compact mounds of grey-green foliage with pink, pompon flowers	Late spring to midsummer
Thyme *(Thymus serpyllum* 'Coccineus'*)*	Evergreen sub-shrub	5cm (2in) × 45cm (18in)	Low-growing, spreading plant for front of the border. Tiny, deep crimson flowerheads and aromatic leaves	Mid- to late summer

AUTUMN BED

plant	type	height × spread	description	flowering
Calamintha *(Calamintha nepetoides)*	Sub-shrub	30cm (12in)	Low-growing plants, closely related to the thymus. Aromatic foliage and lavender-blue flowers	Midsummer to mid-autumn
Colchicum *(Colchicum autumnale)*	Bulb	15cm (6in)	Rose- or lilac-coloured flowers, similar to crocus	Early to late autumn
Golden rod *(Solidago canadensis* and hybrids)	Perennial	1.2m (4ft) × 60cm (24in)	Tall, clump forming plants with yellow flower plumes	Late summer to late autumn
Sedum *(Sedum spectabile)*	Perennial	45cm (18in) × 45cm (18in)	Flat pink flowerheads primarily attract butterflies, but bees also visit	Mid- to late autumn
Teasel *(Dipsacus fullonum)*	Biennial	2m (6ft)	Pink-purple flowers attract bees and butterflies and are followed by spiny seedheads	Midsummer to early autumn

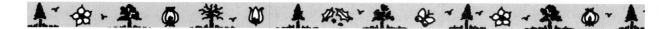

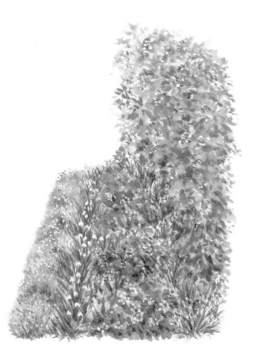

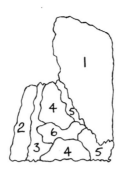

PLANTING PLAN FOR A SPRING BEE BORDER

Height: 2.5m (8ft) Depth: 1.2m (4ft)

KEY
1 Flowering currant
2 Forget-me-not
3 Crocus and snowdrop
4 Dead nettle
5 Bluebell
6 Lungwort

PLANTING PLAN FOR A SUMMER BEE BORDER

Height: 2.5m (8ft) Depth: 1.7m (5ft)

KEY
1 Honeysuckle
2 Lavatera
3 Globe thistle
4 Lavender
5 Borage
6 Thyme
7 Giant bellflower
8 Thrift

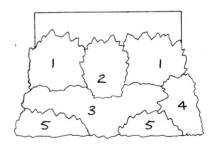

PLANTING PLAN FOR AN AUTUMN BEE BORDER

Height: 1.2m (4ft) Width: 2m (6ft)

KEY
1 Golden rod
2 Teasel
3 Sedum
4 Calamintha
5 Colchicum

plants

OF THE

month

2

FLOWERING PEAS

*'Training the trailing peas in bunches neat,
Perfuming evening with luscious sweet'*
The Shepherd's Calendar *(1821–24)*

*John Clare's poems are full of references
to the common garden flowers that the
average cottager grew, and peas are no
exception. The 'sweet peas' referred to in
gardening books and manuscripts as far
back as the sixteenth century were not
the annual sweet pea we know today but
a smaller-flowered perennial plant, which
we now call the everlasting pea. The
perennial pea is enjoying something of a
revival in popularity as nurserymen and
enthusiasts seek to restore traditional
cottage garden plants. That is not to say
that the modern sweet pea has no place
in the garden; since Edwardian times it
has become probably the best-loved cut
flower for wedding bouquets, formal table
decorations and simple cottage flower
arrangements.*

type	Annual climber
flowers	Pink, mauve, salmon, white; early summer to early autumn
foliage	Oval leaves with tendrils
height	2–3m (6–10ft)
spread	23cm (9in)
site	Open sunny position; beneath windows or in open borders
soil	Fertile, well-drained
planting	Dig the ground well, adding plenty of garden compost or well-rotted manure. Set the plants out in late spring, 30cm (12in) apart and insert canes or twiggy sticks beside them for support
care	Mulch with garden compost or well-rotted manure in late spring. Flowers can be cut to take indoors throughout the season; in fact cutting the flowers increases production and if not cut, they should be deadheaded regularly. Collect seed and discard plants at the end of the growing season
propagation	Sow seeds outdoors in planting position in mid-autumn – cover the

SWEET PEA

(Lathyrus odoratus)

We owe the introduction of the sweet pea to a
Sicilian monk, Father Franciscus Cupani,
who having discovered it in his home country,
sent seeds to Dr. Uvedale, a schoolmaster and
avid plant collector, in Enfield, Middlesex.
The first plants were sparse specimens with
tiny reddish flowers but giving off a powerful
fragrance. They were certainly grown in gardens from 1700 onwards, but only one variety,
'Painted Lady', with its scented, pink and
white bicoloured flowers, was a real success.
The real passion for sweet peas began at the
end of the nineteenth century when breeding
produced the 'Grandifloras', a range of plants
with larger flowers and a huge range of
colours. By the time of the Sweet Pea
Exhibition at Crystal Palace, London in 1900,
264 varieties were on show. These 'old-fashioned' sweet peas were very nearly wiped out
by the popularity of a new frilled-petal variety,
raised by the Spencer family at Althorp,
Northamptonshire in the early 1900s. The
frilled 'Spencer' varieties make up most of the
seed catalogue offerings today; the
'Grandifloras' can still be found, although only
about 20 varieties remain.

*SUCCESS WITH
SWEET PEA SEEDS*
*The outer coating of sweet pea
seed can be very hard and for
the best chance of germination it
is advisable to soak the seeds
for 24 hours before sowing.
Another tip is to rub the outer
coating with sandpaper to make
it more pervious to water.*

*CAUTION: SWEET PEA SEEDS
ARE POISONOUS*

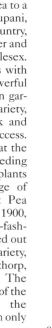

Sweet pea mixture

seedlings with cloches if frost is likely and thin out in mid-spring. Alternatively, sow indoors in late winter in pots or trays and plant out in late spring

varieties Unlike some other plants, sweet pea varieties do come true from seed. A few of the old-fashioned 'Grandiflora' types are still available. 'Painted Lady' is one of the oldest in cultivation, a highly scented pink and white bicolour variety. New varieties of the 'Spencer' frilled types are launched regularly so the names listed in the catalogues vary each year. There is a certain excitement in trying out the new colours which come in every conceivable shade of cream, crimson, mauve, blue, pink

cottage garden value A jug of sweetly-scented peas on the cottage windowsill is probably the best way to appreciate these flowers. In the garden they will add height, perfume and colour to the summer border

EVERLASTING PEA
(*Lathyrus latifolius*)

This is the original 'sweet pea', a climbing perennial pea with rose-purple flowers which was widely used to clothe arches and arbours. It scrambles and climbs vigorously, and although it does not have quite the range of colours of the modern sweet pea, it is a more authentic cottage garden plant. Mysteriously, it seems to have lost its scent over the centuries; botanists of the seventeenth century claim it had a pretty perfume. The perennial pea's greatest asset is its ability to cover unsightly fences or outhouses with flowers that last all summer and well into autumn.

type	Perennial climber
flowers	Purplish-pink or white with pink veins, in clusters; early summer to early autumn
foliage	Dull green, linear to oval
height	2–3m (6–10ft)
spread	45cm (18in)
site	In full sun; over porches, arches, pergolas and arbours; on trellis against walls and fences
soil	Fertile, well-drained
planting	Set plants out in mid-spring, 45cm (18in) apart, at the base of a strong support. Add well-rotted manure to the planting hole
care	Snip off flowerheads as they fade (leaving some to set seed). Cut down all the current year's growth in mid-autumn
propagation	Collect seed when ripe (early autumn) and sow immediately or store until spring. Grow on in a coldframe – autumn sowings can be planted out the following spring; spring sowings can be set out in autumn
varieties	'White Pearl', 'Pink Pearl' and 'Red Pearl', three self-coloured varieties are widely available
related species	*L. grandiflorus* has larger deep pink flowers and reaches only 1.2–2m (4–6ft) high. However, it is just as vigorous as *L. latifolius* and is best grown beside a low wall where it can trail over the brickwork and not swamp other plants
cottage garden value	A purely decorative plant, the everlasting pea comes into its own when allowed to tumble over walls or grow up through old trees. Plant with care, as once established, it is difficult to remove

Everlasting pea

TRAINING SWEET PEAS
Exhibition sweet pea growers raise their plants on cordons using a single cane for each plant, the aim being to produce fewer – but larger – flowers by removing any unnecessary side growths. For the cottage garden, sweet peas look more natural when grown up a wigwam of canes or twiggy sticks. Insert the supports at planting time and tie the tops together for extra strength. Canes or twigs about 2m (6ft) tall should be suitable for most standard sweet peas. Tie in the young growth to the canes until the plants are vigorous enough to twine unaided.

practical
project
2

COMPANION
PLANTING

**PLANTING FOR
BENEFICIAL INSECTS**
*Some of the best plants for
hoverflies (which feed on aphids)
are those with flat, easily
accessible, open flowerheads.
Make sure you include some of
the following in the garden:
angelica, chervil, dill, lovage,
sunflower and yarrow*

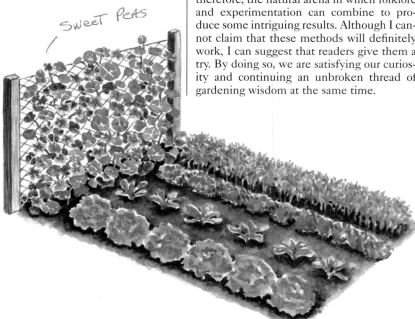

SweeT PeAs

Cottage gardeners of old were dedicated organic and wildlife gardeners – if not by choice, then certainly by circumstance. Chemicals, as we know them today, were simply not available and gardeners used a range of herbal and other methods to combat pests and grow healthy plants.

The idea of companion planting is as old as gardening itself. Simply put, it is the practice of growing plants as companions to one another, so that one may benefit the other. One plant can help another in a number of ways: it may directly effect the soil, by releasing nitrogen for example and making it available to other plants; it may help to create the right microclimate for its neighbour – a good example of this would be growing herbaceous perennials, such as geraniums, around the base of a climbing clematis, which likes shade around its roots – other plants attract beneficial insects, which can wipe out the pests on neighbouring plants and a few actually release chemicals into the soil which inhibit weeds.

It has to be said that the body of knowledge on companion planting built up by experience and handed down over generations is, in the main, unproven by scientific investigation. Yet, gardeners all over the globe will tell you that certain combinations of plants really do 'work'. Cottage gardens, by their very nature, house an eclectic mixture of fruit, shrubs, vegetables, flowers and herbs, all grown in close proximity. They are, therefore, the natural arena in which folklore and experimentation can combine to produce some intriguing results. Although I cannot claim that these methods will definitely work, I can suggest that readers give them a try. By doing so, we are satisfying our curiosity and continuing an unbroken thread of gardening wisdom at the same time.

INHIBITING WEEDS

This is the least proven area of companion planting, but it is suspected that the roots of Mexican marigolds (*Tagetes minuta*) secrete a substance which inhibits weeds and other plants. However, in a less specific way, ground-covering plants will inhibit weeds and in a closely-planted cottage garden where there are few bare patches of earth, weeds are rarely a problem and can be pulled out by hand.

USING GREEN MANURES

The idea of plants actually being good for the soil (rather than the other way round) is something organic gardeners have always taken for granted. Legumes (peas, beans and so on) are well known for being 'nitrogen gatherers'. This means they gather nitrogen from the soil while they are growing and when they are dug back into the soil they make this nitrogen available to the next crop. The most decorative 'green manure' plant is the annual lupin and old cottage gardeners often gave one bed over to lupins each year. Sow lupin seed any time between mid-spring and midsummer and grow on for two to three months until just before the flowers open. Then, dig the stems and roots back into the soil ready for a new crop of vegetables. The stems can be cut down with shears first to make it easier to dig them in.

GOOD COMPANIONS

Roses, chives and garlic
This is one of the best known companion plant groupings. The aroma of the chives and garlic is said to deter aphids from the roses and also to reduce the risk of blackspot. If the chives are allowed to flower, the combination of pink or white roses surrounded by clumps of chive flowers is very pleasing. By using garlic and chives, you get the best of both worlds – the stronger scent from the garlic, but prettier flowers on the chives.

Cabbages and broad beans
Research by a leading organic gardening organization has shown that growing members of the cabbage family (Brassicas) in among members of the bean family (Legumes) misleads and confuses cabbage root fly and aphids. For the best results, plant alternate rows of cabbage and broad or French beans, making sure that the outer rows are beans and

that the plants are all of a similar size at planting time. For further details contact the Henry Doubleday Research Association (address on p.142).

Poached egg plant and gooseberries

The ability of *Limnanthes douglasii* to attract beneficial insects makes it a useful plant to grow alongside or beneath fruit bushes. It is low-growing and therefore does not interfere with the bushes and the cheerful white and yellow flowers enliven a predominantly green area. In a decorative kitchen garden, standard gooseberries, underplanted with *Limnanthes* look very effective.

Wallflowers and apple trees

Wallflowers planted at the base of apple trees are said to be beneficial, possibly because the early flowers bring in pollinators to work on the apple blossom. Nasturtiums are also said to be good companions to apples, no doubt because they attract hoverflies which can feed on aphids.

ATTRACTING BENEFICIAL INSECTS

Wildlife and organic gardeners know that the best pest-eaters are the natural ones – ladybirds, lacewings, hoverflies and parasitic wasps. It is a well-established practice to edge vegetable borders with clumps of marigolds

(*Calendula officinalis*) or poached egg plants (*Limnanthes douglasii*), which attract these beneficial insects. Wire netting stretched between two wooden posts at either end of the vegetable plot can support climbing nasturtiums (*Tropaeolum majus*) or *Convolvulus tricolor*, both of which are excellent for hoverflies. These climbing plants can also be trained up wigwams of canes or wooden trellis for a more decorative effect. All these plants are annuals and can be grown from seed each spring (see p.40).

REPELLING INSECT PESTS

Certain plants seems to be able to deter pests like aphids by their strong aromatic smell. Wormwood (*Artemisia absinthium*) is a good example of this and it also exudes a poisonous, antiseptic substance into the soil. Some gardeners say that the area round a wormwood bush is rarely effected by slugs or snails and the dried leaves of wormwood have long been known as an antidote to fleas in the house. Tansy (*Tanacetum vulgare*), another plant with a distinctive smell, is said to repel ants and, as a dried herb, has been used indoors to deter moths and flies. Perhaps the best known insect repellents are the members of the onion family – chives, garlic and onions themselves. Research has shown that interplanting rows of carrots with onions will deter carrot root fly. Chives are traditionally planted around rose bushes to deter aphids; even if it is not a complete success, the plants look good together. Catnip (*Nepeta cataria*) has been shown to be effective in driving away aphids and flea beetles (which attack the cabbage family) but it will of course attract cats which, to some people, are the most annoying of all garden pests.

THE POWER OF PLANTS

If gardeners doubt the chemical properties of plants, we only have to remind ourselves of the many commercially-produced plant-based pesticides. 'Derris' is made from the roots of plants from the Derris species and is a powerful insecticide against red spider mite, caterpillars and aphids. 'Pyrethrum' made from the flowers of Chrysanthemum cinerariaefolium, is also an effective contact pesticide killing aphids, caterpillars and flea beetles. The leaves of rhubarb, which contain oxalic acid, have also been used to make a spray against aphids, red spider mite and against blackspot on roses. However, although these products are 'organic', they are not safe to all forms of life. Derris is poisonous to fish and kills adult ladybirds. Pyrethrum is also poisonous to fish and, in commercial production, is often mixed with other, non-organic chemicals. All chemicals, whether plant-based or artificial have some dangers associated with them and should be used with caution.

AUGUST

Here's flowers for you;
Hot Lavender, Mints, Savory, Marjoram'
WILLIAM SHAKESPEARE: A WINTER'S TALE

This month, a heat haze seems to hang over the borders, and the purples and blues come into their own. Waves of lavender, salvias, love-in-a-mist, Nepeta *and larkspur create a shimmering artist's impression of a garden in late summer.*

This is one of the most relaxing times of the year. Summer is not yet over and the frenetic activity of autumn lies sometime ahead. Weeds seem to be temporarily halted in their growth by lack of water or heat exhaustion and there is little to do but sit back and contemplate the summer scene. Complete idleness is not quite possible, of course – certain tasks beckon. The cottage gardener's favourite lily (the Madonna lily) is traditionally planted this month, and as many summer flowers start to fade, it is time to collect the seed. Collecting seed is one of the most delightful gardening activities, allowing the gardener to take a part in the plant's natural cycle of growth and reproduction.

Fruit and vegetable gardeners will find this is a busier month than those who just grow flowers. Produce needs to be harvested while it is young and fresh, runner beans need to be watered and fed, and trained espalier apples and pears get their summer pruning. Herbs can be gathered for drying this month. They should be tied together in bundles, lightly washed and hung in a warm, airy place to dry. Less industrious gardeners can leave their marjoram and mint to flower – the flowers are surprisingly pretty and very attractive to bees.

tasks
FOR THE
month

**COTTAGE GARDEN
SHRUBS FOR CUTTINGS**
E = Evergreen

Firethorn (*Pyracantha*) E
Holly (*Ilex aquifolium*) E
**Hydrangea (*Hydrangea
macrophylla*)**
Lavender (*Lavandula*) E
Lilac (*Syringa vulgaris*)
**Mexican orange blossom
(*Choisya ternata*) E**
Mezereon (*Daphne mezereum*)
**Mock orange (*Philadelphus
microphyllus*)**
Rosemary (*Rosmarinus*) E
Rue (*Ruta graveolens*) E*
**Santolina (*Santolina
chamaecyparissus*) E**
**Southernwood (*Artemisia
abrotanum*) Semi-E**
**Winter jasmine (*Jasminum
nudiflorum*)**
**Wormwood (*Artemisia
absinthium*)**
* Care should be taken when
propagating rue as the sap can
cause skin irritation

CHECKLIST

☐ Take semi-ripe cuttings
☐ Collect perennial seed
☐ Cut down foxgloves and hollyhocks
☐ Sow mignonette for winter-flowering
 indoors
☐ Clip holly trees to shape
☐ Plant Madonna lilies
☐ Gather lavender

TAKING SEMI-RIPE CUTTINGS

Many cottage garden shrubs
can be propagated from semi-
ripe cuttings at this time of
year. Although they require a
little more care than
hardwood cuttings taken in
the autumn (see p.110), for
many species, particularly the
evergreens, this is the best
way to produce new plants.
Semi-ripe or 'semi-hard'
cuttings are taken from this
year's growth, which is still
growing actively (so the tops
of the shoots are soft), but has
become woody towards the
base. It is a good idea to take
a 'batch' of cuttings from each
shrub – five cuttings will fit
into a 13cm (5in) pot.

■ Take the cutting using a
sharp knife or secateurs.
Choose a side-shoot about
15–20cm (6–8in) long and cut
it off close to the main stem.
■ Trim the cutting just below
the leaf joint at the base and
remove the bottom leaves.

Take off the tip to leave a
cutting about 10cm (4in) long.
■ Fill each pot with a
proprietary cuttings compost.
Make a hole for the cuttings
with your finger or a dibber
and insert them so that one
third of the cutting is beneath
the compost. Firm in gently
with your fingers. Spray with a
fine mist of water.
■ Place the pots into a
coldframe. If you do not have
a coldframe, put them into a
wooden box, drape a piece of
polythene over the top and
weight it down with bricks.
Place the box in a warm place
but out of the midday sun
which can burn the cuttings. It
is a wise precaution to paint
the panes of the coldframe
with greenhouse shading
paint.

TIP

■ *Cuttings need to be kept
warm and moist but in
particularly hot spells, prop
open the lid of the frame for
an hour or two in the middle
of the day to allow air to
circulate* ■

Aftercare
The cuttings should be rooted
in about three weeks and then
it is time to begin the process
of 'hardening off'– that is,
getting them used to the

climate outside the frame.
Start by lifting the lid (or the
polythene) for progressively
longer periods during the day.
A week or two later, remove
the polythene altogether (or
prop open the lid of the
frame). One week after this
repot the cuttings into
individual pots.

Repotting
■ Tap the pot and remove the
clump of cuttings. Carefully
separate each one with its
root system and repot
individually into 10cm (4in)
pots using a general-purpose
potting compost.

■ Place the plants back in the
open coldframe and keep
them well watered. Pot on
into larger pots as necessary
in autumn and again the
following spring. The young
plants should be ready to put
out into the garden by the
second spring.

COLLECTING AND SAVING
PERENNIAL SEED

This month or next, many of
the summer-flowering
perennials will have ripe seed,
ready for collection and
propagation. Aquilegia
(*Aquilegia vulgaris*),
heartsease (*Viola tricolor*),
Acanthus mollis, perennial
poppies (*Papaver orientale*),
and lupins (*Lupinus
polyphyllus*) can be collected
as they ripen. Cut off the seed
heads and place them in
paper bags to dry. Shake the
bags to release the seed,

separate it from the other plant material, put it in airtight glass jars and store them in a cool dark place for sowing next spring. Remember to label the seeds before storing, and to make a note of the date they were collected. If stored correctly, seed can remain viable for several years.

NOTE

■ *Named varieties of a particular species will not come true from seed – the seedlings will be different from their parents. However, in a cottage garden, this genetic variation is something to be valued and self-sown seedlings that spring up in unexpected places are often a source of surprise* ■

CUTTING DOWN FOXGLOVES AND HOLLYHOCKS

After collecting seed as needed from the biennial foxgloves and hollyhocks (see July Tasks p.76), the spires that have finished flowering can be cut down to ground level: cut off the stems with secateurs just above the basal rosette of leaves. Although both are biennial, if treated in this way they will go on to give an extra one or two years' flowering. Even if the

plant does not regenerate, cutting away the stems will leave more space for other late summer and autumn plants to display their flowers.

SOW MIGNONETTE FOR WINTER FLOWERING INDOORS

Mignonette (*Reseda odorata*), one of the oldest and best-loved cottage garden annuals, was also traditionally grown as an indoor pot plant so that its unmistakable perfume could fill the cottage in winter. For winter-flowering, sow the seed this month in 15cm (6in) pots of seed compost. Water well and keep the pots in a coldframe or greenhouse. Thin out the seedlings to leave three in each pot. Pinch out the growing tips to encourage bushy growth and bring the plants indoors from late autumn onwards.

CLIPPING HOLLIES TO SHAPE

Holly trees grown as standards or as shaped trees can be clipped this month. For best results use hand shears as electric trimmers can tear the leaves and wood too roughly. Clip off the straggly

new shoots, following the outline of the dense growth. Traditionally, cottagers often grew one holly tree in a cone or bell-shape.

PLANTING MADONNA LILIES

The Madonna lily (*Lilium candidum*) differs from other lilies in that it forms basal leaves soon after the flowering stem dies back in autumn. It is important to plant or move the bulbs before the lily grows its winter rosette of leaves. (Other lilies are planted in late autumn.) *Lilium candidum* is bulb-rooting so it needs to be planted shallowly.

■ Dig a wide, shallow hole, about 10cm (4in) deep and wide enough to take three or five bulbs, and sprinkle a layer of sand or horticultural grit in the bottom to help drainage.
■ Place the bulbs in the hole, 15cm (6in) apart, spreading the roots out. Cover the bulbs with 5cm (2in) of soil and water lightly.
■ Remember to mark the position of lilies otherwise it is easy to disturb them when planting perennials and shrubs in the autumn.

GATHERING LAVENDER

Lavender flowers can be cut for drying at any stage of their development, but for the best colour, cut the stems just before the flowers open. If fragrance is more important than colour, leave them on the plant as long as possible, as the sun will bring out the best perfume.

■ Cut the stems as near the base as possible, remove the leaves and tie into bunches with a rubber band, raffia or ribbon. Hang them upside down in a warm, airy place to dry. To retain the best colour, dry them in a dark place. The flowers will keep their scent for several years.

TAKING CUTTINGS WITH A HEEL
Taking semi-ripe cuttings with a 'heel' at the bottom is a useful way to ensure rooting success. Some shrubs, particularly pyracantha, lilac and holly, do better if the cutting includes a sliver of wood from the main stem. When taking the cutting, make two cuts with the knife, one slanting downwards into the main stem and then one upwards to sever the cutting.

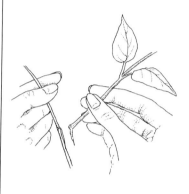

plants
OF THE
month
1

Lavender

LAVENDER
(Lavandula angustifolia)

Lavender was brought into English gardens from the Mediterranean, and was already an essential herb by the 1400s. The strongly scented flowers and aromatic leaves were strewn on floors to discourage lice and fleas, sprinkled among linen to ward off moths and dried in bunches to sweeten the air. In the garden, it is an excellent bee plant, delicately flavouring the honey. It is a very versatile shrub, offering all year round foliage and a long flowering season, with wonderful wafts of summer perfume, and it is ideal for edging pathways and beds or for giving winter structure to otherwise herbaceous borders. The only drawback is its tendency to get woody and leggy after a few years, but replacement plants are easily grown from cuttings. For an unusual two-tiered effect, plant a row of full-sized lavender such as *Lavendula angustifolia* 'Hidcote' behind a row of dwarf lavender.

type	Evergreen shrub
flowers	Grey-blue flowers, borne in spikes; midsummer to early autumn
foliage	Narrow, silver-grey
height	1–1.2m (3–4ft)
spread	1m (3ft)
site	In full sun; in borders, as path edging or at the base of a sunny wall
soil	Light, well-drained soil – ideally a dry, chalky or sandy soil
planting	Plant in autumn or early spring, setting the plants 1m (3ft) apart. (For hedges, plant 40–45cm (15–18in) apart.) If soil is heavy, add sand and gravel before planting, to improve drainage
care	Trim over the plants in early autumn, removing the spent flower heads. Clip lavender hedges in spring. Plants that have grown leggy should be replaced with new plants grown from cuttings
propagation	Take 10cm (4in) cuttings from new shoots in spring and insert into pots of sandy soil in a coldframe. Semi-ripe cuttings can be taken in late summer
varieties	*L. angustifolia* 'Grappenhall' has been a cottage garden favourite since its introduction in 1799. It has a deep colour and grows to about 1m (3ft). *L. angustifolia* 'Hidcote' is one of the best varieties for a low hedge, being compact (60 x 60cm/ 24 x 24in) with masses of deep

purple flower spikes. Also good for edging is *L. angustifolia* 'Munstead Dwarf', which will not grow much above 30cm (12in) and has blue-purple flowers. *L. angustifolia* 'Loddon Pink' is a reliable pink variety

related species	*Lavandula stoechas*, the French lavender, has unusual tufted flower spikes. It may not be hardy in exposed gardens, but can be grown in a pot to be bought into a frost-free porch for winter
cottage garden value	Cut the flower spikes for drying indoors (see p.68). Both leaves and flowers can be added to pot pourri or herb sachets. Old remedies suggest sowing the dried flowers into the lining of a cap to cure a head cold and soothe the brain

LOVE-IN-A-MIST
(Nigella damascena)

Nigella must rank as one of the prettiest annual cottage garden plants, with its misty-blue flowers and froth of feathery foliage. The first species to be grown in England, *Nigella sativa* was recorded at Syon House in Middlesex in the early 1500s. The seeds of this species were used as a spice, known as black cumin. However, it was *Nigella damascena* – said to have been brought to England from Damascus – that seems to have become the more popular garden plant, with double varieties already in cultivation by the end of the sixteenth century. It has taken a range of local names, including fennel-flower (a reference to the foliage) and St. Catherine's flower, but love-in-a-mist is by far the most poetic.

type	Annual
flowers	Blue; mid- to late summer
foliage	Bright green, finely cut
height	30–60cm (12–24in)
spread	30cm (12in)
site	In full sun; borders
soil	Any, well-cultivated
planting	Grown from seed, sown in flowering position
care	Deadhead to encourage larger flowers
propagation	Nigella will self-seed if the ground around the plants is left undisturbed. Alternatively, sow seed in spring in flowering position. Cover lightly with soil and thin out seedlings to 23cm (9in) apart
varieties	*N. damascena* 'Miss Jekyll Blue' is one of the most popular, having bright blue, semi-double flowers

related species *N. sativa* is rarely grown these days, but was a species grown in early Tudor times for its aromatic black seeds. These were used rather like nutmeg, to flavour cakes and drinks and also ground up for use in variety of medical remedies

cottage garden value Apart from looking stunning in the border, the flowers are good for cutting and the seedheads dry well

SOAPWORT
(Saponaria officinalis)

Soapwort is a very pretty plant for larger cottage gardens, where its natural tendency to spread can be forgiven. It has a blowsy, unkempt appearance and is not for those who like their gardens neat and tidy. The juice from the leaves was well known to countrywomen as a cleaning agent, which according to Gerard *'scoureth almost as well as sope'*. The leaves were also used to make a poultice for cuts and grazes. It was thought to be an important enough plant to accompany the early settlers from Britain to North America, where it became naturalized. In western Britain and in the USA it is known by the name of 'bouncing Bet'. The single pink flowers of the species were soon superseded by cultivated doubles which make more interesting border plants.

type Spreading herbaceous perennial
flowers Pink, 2.5–5cm (1–2in) across, scented; midsummer to early autumn
foliage Pale green, elliptical
height 60cm (24in)
spread 30cm (12in)
site Sun or partial shade; borders
soil Any, fertile soil
planting Plant out any time between mid-autumn and early spring when the ground is not frozen or waterlogged, setting the plants 60cm (24in) apart
care Support tall plants with twiggy sticks if necessary. Cut down stems to ground level in late autumn. To prevent them from spreading too much, cut around the plants with a spade and remove the outward runners
propagation Remove underground runners in late autumn or winter (as above) and replant immediately
varieties Double varieties are very popular, especially *S. officinalis* 'Alba Plena' the white form, 'Rosea Plena' the frothy pink double and 'Rubra

Plena', a dark rose-pink
cottage garden value The crushed leaves, boiled up in water and strained, produce a liquid that will lather and can be used for washing clothes.

MIGNONETTE
(Reseda odorata)

A cottage garden is not complete without a patch of mignonette, and yet when you look at the plant itself, with its unsensational brownish flowers, it is hard to imagine why. The answer of course lies in the wonderful scent that drifts from the plant on summer evenings. Despite many attempts to breed brighter and more showy plants, the perfume of the original has not been bettered. *Reseda* arrived in France in the eighteenth century and immediately caught the imagination of romantic gardeners, who are believed to have given it the common name of 'mignonette' or little darling. In Britain, its heyday was the Victorian era, when the plant could be seen spilling out of country gardens and city windowboxes alike. It looks well in a border, surrounded by more colourful plants, but it is particularly good under windows where after a shower of rain, the evening perfume is tremendous.

type Annual
flowers Buff-yellow, scented; early summer to mid-autumn
foliage Mid-green, smooth
height 30–60cm (12–24in)
spread 23–30cm (9–12in)
site In full sun; borders and containers
soil Well-drained, fertile, alkaline; add lime if soil is acid
planting Sow in position in mid-spring
care No special care needed
propagation Sow seeds on a well-prepared bed (with added lime if necessary) in mid-spring. Scatter the seed thinly, covering lightly with soil. Thin out the seedlings as they appear to 15–23cm (6–9in)
varieties *R. odorata* 'Goliath' has striking, double red flowers. *R. odorata* 'Machet' is a paler red
cottage garden value Mignonette has one of the sweetest scents of all cottage garden plants. It fills the garden all through the summer and well into autumn. The flower spikes can be cut and brought indoors where, in a cool room they will give off their perfume for weeks. Mignonette is also attractive to bees

Top to bottom: love-in-a-mist, soapwort and mignonette

practical project 1

GROWING COTTAGE GARDEN HERBS

It is clear from many of the old gardening books that cottage gardeners did not distinguish herbs from other garden plants. Plants were grown either because they were good for medicinal and household uses, or they were useful in the kitchen, or because they were pretty and attracted bees. Botanically, the term 'herb' actually covers most plants except trees and shrubs although we tend to think only – in the words of a famous song – of parsley, sage, rosemary and thyme.

Early cottage gardeners were not restricted by such a narrow definition of kitchen herbs. This is clearly illustrated by one of the first lists of garden plants compiled by Thomas Tusser in 1557. His list of herbs and seeds for the kitchen included marigolds, primroses and violets, and for 'strewing' he recommended hops, lavender, santolina and chamomile; the list of 'physic' herbs includes archangel, saxifrage, mandrake and woodbine. Although in grander houses, separate herb parterres, knot gardens and physic gardens would have featured, it is clear that a huge range of plants would have been grown in mixed borders in a cottage garden with the average cottager probably not designating a special area for herbs.

SIX ESSENTIAL CULINARY HERBS

Whether grown informally in the flower beds or formally in a herb garden (see p.99) there are a handful of kitchen herbs that no cottage garden should be without. They all thrive in an open sunny position on well-drained soil and require a minimum of care.

Prepare the ground by removing any perennial weeds and adding horticultural grit if the drainage is poor. The planting plan here is designed for the smallest garden and only one plant of each of the essential herbs is included. Larger beds could repeat the planting pattern, introducing variegated and coloured varieties, such as purple sage, golden thyme or the pink-flowered rosemary. However, in most cases, the species have a better flavour for cooking than the varieties.

HERB BORDER

Key

1 Basil (*Ocimum basilicum*) – half-hardy annual, grow from seed or buy new plants each year. Do not plant out until after danger of frosts is passed

2 Sweet Marjoram (*Origanum marjorana*) – perennial

3 Parsley (*Petroselinum crispum*) – hardy annual, grow from seed each year

4 Rosemary (*Rosmarinus officinalis*) – evergreen shrub

5 Sage (*Salvia officinalis*) – evergreen sub-shrub

6 Thyme (*Thymus vulgaris*) – evergreen sub-shrub

TEN MEDIEVAL HERBS

The following chart illustrates some of the herbs commonly grown and used in medieval times. They are all listed in a document dated around 1400 and many have histories stretching back to Anglo-Saxon times. The traditional remedies and uses are included for interest and are *not* recommended in practice. Many of the plants are still grown in gardens today.

Key: P = perennial, A = annual, S-S = sub-shrub

Name	Ht x Sp	Flowers	Foliage	Uses
AGRIMONY (P) *(Agrimonia eupatoria)*	45x30cm (18x12in)	Yellow spires; summer	Basal rosette; toothed	Highly valued for its astringent qualities. The flowers were made into a tea to alleviate cold symptoms
CALAMINT (P) *(Calamintha nepeta)*	30x23cm (12x9in)	Pale lilac spikes; late summer	Small, oval	Closely related to wild marjoram and basil, it has aromatic leaves which were used to make a stomach-soothing tea. Attractive to bees
COMFREY (P) *(Symphytum officinalis)*	60x60cm (24x24in)	Purple pink clusters; summer	Large, coarse	An essential wound herb for the medieval physician, it was also supposed to knit bones together and cure consumption. Can be invasive. Toxic, not to be taken internally
CORIANDER (A) *(Coriandrum sativum)*	60x20cm (24x8in)	Pink-white flat heads; summer	Feathery	The seed, harvested in late summer, is aromatic and spicy, highly prized in exotic cookery
ELECAMPANE (P) *(Inula helenium)*	90x60cm (36x24in)	Yellow, large, daisy-like; summer	Large, hairy	The preserved root was used for medicinal purposes – as a tonic, a cough medicine and a diuretic. Attractive to bees
HYSSOP (S-S) *(Hyssopus officinalis)*	60x30cm (24x12in)	Blue clusters; late summer	Semi-evergreen; narrow	An ancient medicinal and strewing herb. The leaves are used to flavour salads; and the flowers are added to pot pourri. Attractive to bees
SUMMER SAVORY (A) *(Satureja hortensis)*	30x15cm (12x6in)	Purple clusters; midsummer	Small, narrow	Leaves have a strong peppery flavour when added to meat dishes and stuffings
TANSY (P) *(Tanacetum vulgare)*	90x90cm (36x36in)	Yellow buttons; late summer	Ferny	Long valued for its insecticidal and disinfectant properties, the leaves were also baked into 'tansy pudding' at Easter
VALERIAN (P) *(Valeriana officinalis)*	90x60cm (36x24in)	Purple-white clusters; summer	Divided	A valuable medicinal plant, used to make tinctures and teas to cure headaches and hysteria
VERVAIN (P) *(Verbena officinalis)*	45x23cm (18x9in)	Pale pink spikes; summer	Deeply divided	Considered to be a very powerful herb against the demons of disease, plague and witchcraft

ANCIENT HERBS FOR A SHADY PLACE

If the only place available for herb growing is a shady corner of the garden, there are one or two plants that will flourish:

Woodruff (*Galium odoratum*) Sometimes known as the 'hay plant' because when dried, it scents the air with the smell of new-mown hay, woodruff was stuffed into beds, tied into bundles and hung in the sleeping rooms, and made into a tea to cure headaches and colds. It is a spreading, mat-forming perennial which bears small, fragrant white flowers in early summer

Balm (*Melissa officinalis*) Melissa has a long association with beekeeping and therefore was an essential cottage garden plant. The leaves were rubbed on the inside of the hives and the aroma was believed to attract new bees to the hive and to help resident bees to find their way home. They have a lemon fragrance and can be made into a cordial or tea. It is a very easy-to-grow plant, even in deep shade, although the small white or pale yellow flowers are unexceptional.

Sweet Cicely (*Myrrhis odorata*) A tall easy-to-grow perennial, rather like a cow parsley in appearance, although less coarse. The leaves, roots and seeds of sweet Cicely are sweetly scented with a faint flavour of aniseed and all parts of the plant have been used at one time or another in cookery and medicine.

plants
OF THE
month
2
DECORATIVE
HERBS

Southernwood

SOUTHERNWOOD
(Artemisia abrotanum)

This shrubby plant is one of three garden artemesias which have been grown since medieval times for their aromatic foliage. In the sixteenth century *The Art of Gardening* by Thomas Hyll decreed that *'No adder will come into a garden in which grow wormwood, mugwort and southernwood'* (*A. absinthium, A. vulgaris* and *A. abrotanum* respectively). Of the three, southernwood has the strongest aroma and was an essential plant for the cottage garden, used for nosegays, strewing and a host of medicinal remedies. It is also tough and resilient and was much in demand in late eighteenth century London as it could withstand smoke and lack of light. For best results, though, plant in a sunny spot. Wormwood (*A. absinthium*) was best known to cottages as an antidote to fleas. A sixteenth-century verse suggests: *'Where chamber is sweeped, and wormwood is strowne No flea for his life dare abide to be knowne'*

type	Semi-evergreen shrub
flowers	Dull yellow; midsummer to early autumn
foliage	Grey-green, downy
height	1m (3ft)
spread	60cm (24in)
site	Full sun; herb bed or borders
soil	Any, well-drained
planting	Plant in mid-spring
care	Cut back leggy growths in spring to keep a compact shape. Snip off flower heads if grown for foliage
propagation	Take semi-ripe cuttings in late summer. Grow on in a coldframe for planting out the following autumn
related species	Mugwort (*A. vulgaris*) is rarely grown in gardens these days although it can still be seen growing wild in hedgerows. Although it is not attractive, it was an important herb: travellers would pick it from the roadside and lay the leaves inside their shoes to alleviate weariness. It was also used to flavour beer, a leaf being placed in a mug of ale to steep for a few minutes before drinking – hence the common name
cottage garden value	The dried leaves of southernwood can be incorporated into insect-repellent sachets or pot pourri and are said to repel moths. In a mixed border, it makes a good mound of feathery foliage, which can be clipped to shape or grown as a low hedge

ALEXANDERS
(Smyrnium olusatrum)

Alexanders is one of the oldest cultivated garden herbs, certainly grown in Chaucer's day in England and probably before. It takes its name from the Mediterranean area of Alexandria from where it may have originated. It has been found in the vicinity of a number of monasteries and ruined castles: presumably it was grown in the kitchen gardens and escaped into the countryside and became naturalized, especially near the coast. For centuries it was a highly valued pot vegetable, the leaves and upper root being added to broth, rather like celery – its other name is black lovage and lovage also has a celery-like flavour. It makes a bold garden plant, best planted at the back of the border where the yellow flower heads can be appreciated.

type	Biennial
flowers	Yellow, large umbels; spring to early summer
foliage	Dark green, shiny, lobed
height	90cm (36in)
spread	60cm (24in)
planting	Set out young plants in spring, 60cm (24in) apart
site	Sun or light shade; herb garden or flower border
soil	Any, well-drained
care	No special care needed
propagation	Alexanders self-seeds freely. New plants can be grown from seed sown in pots in autumn, overwintered in a coldframe and planted out in spring
related species	The perfoliate Alexanders (*S. perfoliatum*) is similar to *S. olusatrum* but has very decorative, heart-shaped, yellow-green leaves
cottage garden value	The reason Alexanders is not more widely grown as a garden vegetable or herb is partly fashion and partly due to the fact that the shoots have to be blanched otherwise they leave a bitter aftertaste, even when cooked. However, even if not used in the kitchen Alexanders is worth growing for its good looks and ancient pedigree

FENNEL
(Foeniculum vulgare)

As a herb that is both decorative and useful, fennel is hard to beat. The plant grows to a striking 2m (6ft) in height, bearing a haze of bluey-green foliage and flat umbels of yellow flowers in midsummer. The bronze fennel is a real beauty, with dark, burnished foliage – the perfect backdrop to pastel-coloured perennials. The whole plant can be used in the kitchen; the fresh leaves are added to sauces or cooked with fish, the stems can be braised like celery or grated raw into salad, and the seeds, which have a strong aniseed flavour, are used to decorate cakes and breads. The plant had hundreds of medicinal uses for the traditional cottager, but in particular the seed was thought to allay hunger. In America, Puritan churchgoers would carry a handkerchief full of seeds to nibble during long services and it acquired the name of 'meetin' seed'.

type	Herbaceous perennial
flowers	Golden-yellow; mid- to late summer
foliage	Blue-green, feathery
height	1.2-2m (4-6ft)
spread	60cm (24in)
site	Full sun; herb garden or flower border
soil	Any, well-drained
planting	Put out young plants in mid- to late spring, or sow seed 1.5cm (½in) deep in early spring and thin out to 30cm (12in) apart
care	Water young plants until established
propagation	Collect seed in early autumn, dry and store for sowing in spring. Established plants can be lifted and divided as soon as the new foliage starts to appear in early spring
harvesting	Snip off fresh foliage as needed through the summer and early autumn. For seeds, choose a dry day in early autumn and cut off the seed heads. Hang them upside down in a warm place for 1-2 weeks. Place a tray underneath to catch the ripe seeds as they fall. When dry, store in airtight containers
varieties	*F. vulgare* 'Purpureum' has purple foliage when young, turning bronze as the season progresses
cottage garden value	Decorative foliage, an interesting aroma and a host of culinary uses.

CLARY
(*Salvia sclarea*)

Clary has long been associated with clear sight and was used to make an eyewash that reduced inflammation and brightened the eyes. The plant originates from southern Europe and has pungent strongly aromatic leaves. Oil of clary has long been used in the commercial production of perfume and the leaves are used to flavour meat dishes and soups. Although not often grown these days, it makes a good plant for the mixed border where the tall flower stems create a haze of purple-blue in the late summer months. The foliage is quite coarse, but not unattractive.

type	Biennial, often grown as an annual
flowers	Pale blue with purple bracts; late summer
foliage	Dark green, hairy, triangular leaves
height	60–90cm (24–36in)
spread	45cm (18in)
site	Full sun; herb garden or flower borders
soil	Any, well-drained
planting	Set out container-grown plants in autumn or spring. Otherwise, sow seed in mid-spring, thinning out the seedlings to 30cm (12in) apart
care	No special care needed
propagation	Sow seed in mid-spring (see planting)
harvesting	Use fresh leaves to flavour soups and casseroles
related species	Most salvias make good cottage garden plants, including the culinary sage (*S. officinalis*) and the annual *S. horminum* which has pale pink or purple flower spikes
cottage garden value	A substantial foliage plant with decorative flower spikes and aromatic leaves

Top to bottom: Alexanders, clary and fennel

practical project 2

INFORMAL AND FORMAL HERB GARDENS

Herbs are as much a part of cottage gardening as pinks and hollyhocks. Although historically they were grown informally, mixed in with the other flowers, many people like to keep their herbs separate, or to recreate the decorative knot gardens and parterre traditions of the sixteenth and seventeenth centuries. In a cottage garden, simplicity is the key so complicated ground plans are rarely in keeping with its relaxed style. Here are two suggestions for using herbs in the garden: the first is to make a series of informal, colour-themed borders where herbs are the predominant, but not the only, plants. The second is a formal plan, but based on the four-quarters design which was at the heart of some of the first cottage gardens.

INFORMAL COLOUR-THEMED BORDERS

Using perennial and biennial plants, these borders can be planted to create permanent and relatively low-maintenance features in the garden. They include one or two mainstay foliage plants, such as melissa and rosemary, which form substantial clumps, plus self-seeders like borage and feverfew, which add an air of spontaneity: if the seedlings prove too intrusive, they can be weeded out by hand in spring. To avoid confusion, it is safer to assume that these borders are non-edible, although some of the plants, like rosemary, can be used in the kitchen.

YELLOW BORDER KEY

1 Angelica (*Angelica archangelica*) 2m (6ft)
2 Agrimony (*Agrimonia eupatoria*) 45cm (18in)
3 Golden feverfew (*Chrysanthemum parthenium* 'Aureum', syn. *Tanacetum parthenium* 'Aureum') 30cm (12in)
4 Achillea (*Achillea* 'Cloth of Gold') 1.8m (5ft)
5 Balm (*Melissa officinalis*) 75cm (30in)
6 Lady's mantle (*Alchemilla mollis*) 30cm (12in)
7 Dyer's chamomile (*Anthemis tinctoria* 'E.C. Buxton') 60cm (24in)

BLUE BORDER KEY

1 Clary (*Salvia sclarea*) 60cm (24in)
2 Borage (*Borago officinalis*) 45cm (18in)
3 Hyssop (*Hyssopus officinalis*) 60cm (24in)
4 Rosemary (*Rosmarinus officinalis* 'Miss Jessop's Upright') 1.2m (4ft)
5 Winter savory (*Saturea montana*) 15cm (6in)
6 Salvia (*Salvia farinacea* 'Victoria') 45cm (18in)

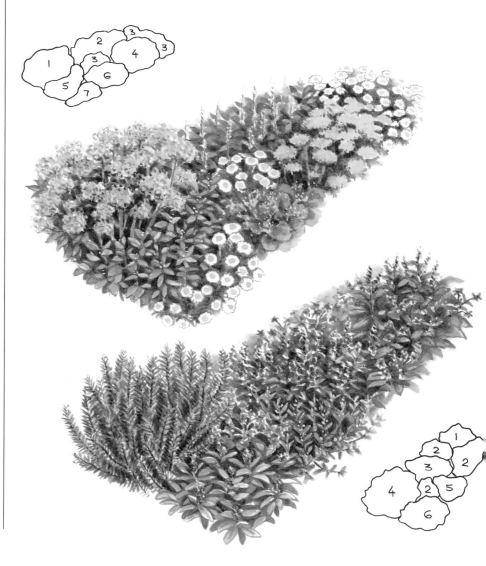

FOUR QUARTERS HERB GARDEN

BETWEEN THE PAVING STONES:
Creeping thyme (*Thymus serpyllus coccineus*)
Golden creeping thyme (*Thymus serpyllus* 'Goldstream')
Cretan mint (*Calamintha cretica*)
Spanish mint (*Mentha requienii*)
Lawn chamomile (*Anthemis nobilis*)
Pennyroyal (*Mentha pulegium*)

FOR HEDGING:
Box (*Buxus sempervirens* 'Suffruticosa') 20cm (8in)
Santolina (*Santolina chamaecyparissus* var. *nana*) 23cm (9in)
Lavender (*Lavandula officinalis* 'Munstead Dwarf') 30–45cm (12–18in)
Artemisia (*Artemisia schmidtiana* 'Nana') 15cm (6in)

KEY TO BEDS:
A
Chives (*Allium schoenoprasum*) 30cm (12in)
Sweet marjoram (*Origanum marjorana*) 45cm (18in)
Purple sage (*Salvia officinalis* 'Purpurascens') 45cm (18in)
French tarragon (*Artemisia dracunculus*) 45cm (18in)

B
Italian flat-leaved parsley (*Petroselinum crispum* var. *neapolitanum*) 45cm (18in)
Coriander (*Coriandrum sativum*) 45cm (18in)
Golden marjoram (*Origanum vulgare* 'Aureum') 23cm (9in)
Chervil (*Anthriscus cerefolium*) 30cm (12in)

C
Dill (*Anethum graveolens*) 1m (3ft)
3-colour sage (*Salvia officinalis* 'Tricolor') 45cm (18in)
Lemon-scented thyme (*Thymus* x *citriodorus* 'Golden King') 23cm (9in)
Caraway (Carum carvi) 60cm (24in)

D
Bronze fennel (*Foeniculum vulgare* 'Purpureum') 2m (6ft)
Purple basil (*Ocimum basilicum* var. *purpurascens*) 45cm (18in)
Summer savory (*Saturea hortensis*) 45cm (18in)
Cumin (*Cuminum cyminum*) 15cm (6in)

FOUR QUARTERS HERB GARDEN

Here, the garden is divided into four herb beds, each one edged with a low-growing hedge of lavender, box or santolina. The cross-shaped path is softened by creeping thymes and chamomile. Each bed is filled with a selection of the most frequently used herbs, all chosen so as not to outgrow their allotted space. Mints have been deliberately left out of the plan as their underground runners allow them to spread too freely. Instead they are planted in pots placed around the hard paving. In the centre of the cross a sundial or bird bath makes a focal point, although this could be replaced with a container of herbs.

Constructing and planting
■ Dig over the ground thoroughly, removing perennial weeds. Add horticultural grit to improve the drainage and incorporate plenty of organic matter (garden compost is ideal).
■ Lay paths (see pp.24–5).
■ Mark out the lines of the hedging 'squares' using string and pegs.
■ Plant small hedging plants in spring or autumn (see p.28).
■ Plant perennial herbs in autumn, adding the annuals in late spring.

Mint pots
■ Choose long 'toms' terracotta pots and cover the base with stone chippings.
■ Fill with a multipurpose compost and pot up one root of mint in each. (It will soon spread and fill the pot.) Choose four different types – pineapple mint, ginger, spearmint and eau de cologne, for example, would give a good variety of leaf colour and form.
■ Keep well watered and pinch out the young leaves for adding to new potatoes and summer drinks.
■ Each spring, renew the pots. Discard the old roots and start afresh with a new piece.

SEPTEMBER

Autumn glows with the colours of gold and other precious metals: late sunflowers and montbretia, burnt orange Helenium *and golden-yellow* Rudbeckia. *Hydrangeas fade to the colour of oak and the yellow flowers of* Clematis tangutica *shine out from their climbing frames. Day lilies (*Hemerocallis*) may last into the beginning of the month in shades of yellow, orange and chestnut-pink, as will asters and Shasta daisies (*Chrysanthemum maximum*), ensuring that the cottage borders are as vibrant now as they are at any other time of the year.*

*Other predominant colours are from the purple-pink end of the spectrum. Purple cone flowers (*Echinacea purpurea*), salvias, sedums and Japanese anemones offer an alternative scheme. Most of these plants were introduced into Europe from America and Asia, so they do not have a long cottage garden history; nevertheless, the ability to create a flowering border in late summer and autumn more than compensates for their lack of pedigree.*

This is the traditional time for planting spring bulbs. New gardeners have the chance to stock their gardens inexpensively and old hands have a yearly opportunity to increase their range of plants. Daffodils, tulips and crocuses, of course, are the garden mainstays, but exciting cottage effects can be obtained with less common bulbs such as Scilla, Iris reticulata, Chionodoxa *and alliums. Bulbs look their best when combined in mixed borders rather than grown apart in separate beds. This is particularly true of alliums which produce pom-pom flowers on leggy stems; by combining them with clump-forming perennials, the stems are hidden and the effect is effortlessly 'cottagey'.*

tasks

FOR THE

month

UNUSUAL COTTAGE GARDEN BULBS

***Narcissus* 'Irene Copeland'** – Double, creamy-yellow flowers with alternate long and short petals

***Tulipa* 'Angelique'** – peony-flowered tulip with apple-blossom pink petals that deepen with age

***Tulipa* 'Estella Rynveld'** – parrot tulip with frothy petals in raspberry ripple colours

Fritillaria persica – tall fritillary with dark plum-coloured bell-shaped flowers

***Muscari* 'Blue Spike'** – a double-flowered blue scented variety, giving a softer effect than the tightly packed flower heads of the single grape hyacinths

---

CHECKLIST

- Plant out biennials raised from seed
- Plant spring bulbs
- Layer winter-flowering shrubs

LAYERING WINTER SHRUBS

New plants of winter jasmine (*Jasminum nudiflorum*), witch hazel (*Hamamelis mollis*) winter sweet (*Chimonanthus praecox*), laurustinus (*Viburnum tinus*) and forsythia (*Forsythia* x *intermedia*) can be produced by layering this month. Layering is a very simple way to increase your stock of shrubs without the need for any special propagating equipment. It is particularly useful for shrubs with long flexible stems that can easily be bent down to ground level.

- Lightly fork over the ground around the shrub.

- Choose a young, flexible stem that has borne no flowers.

- Bend the stem down to the ground, about 23cm (9in) from the tip.

- Make a small hole (10cm/4in deep) with a trowel and fill with seed or cuttings compost.

- At the point where it will touch the soil, remove all the leaves from the stem and make a shallow cut in its surface (on the underside, nearest the soil).

- Bend the tip of the plant so that it stands upright and place the cut into the compost hole. Secure with a loop of heavy-duty garden wire.

- Fill the hole with compost and water thoroughly.

Aftercare
The stem should produce roots in one or two years. Check the following autumn by scraping away the soil. If there are no roots, but the shoot is still healthy, replace the soil and leave until the spring. If the roots are well grown, cut the stem to leave the new plant growing independently and transplant to a new position.

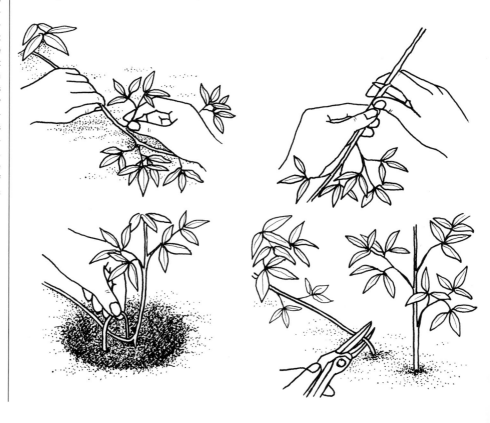

BULB PLANTING DEPTHS

plant	height	planting depth
Aconite (Eranthis)	10cm (4in)	5cm (2in)
Allium moly	25cm (10in)	5cm (2in)
Crocus	15cm (6in)	5cm (2in)
Cyclamen	10cm (4in)	5cm (2in)
Fritillary (Fritillaria)	20–25cm (8–10in)	5cm (2in)
Glory-of-the-snow (Chionodoxa)	10cm (4in)	5cm (2in)
Snowdrop (Galanthus)	15–20cm (6–8in)	5cm (2in)
Bluebell (Scilla)	23cm (9in)	8cm (3in)
Grape hyacinth (Muscari)	15–20cm (6–8in)	8cm (3in)
Tulip (Tulipa sp.)	20–30cm (8–12in)	8cm (3in)
Allium giganteum	1.2m (4ft)	12cm (5in)
Narcissus	23–45cm (9–18in)	15cm (6in)
Crown imperial (Fritillaria imperialis)	20cm (8in)	20cm (8in)
Tulip (full-sized)	35–40cm (14–16in)	15–20cm (6–8in)

PLANTING OUT BIENNIALS

Spring-flowering biennials like wallflowers, Brompton stocks, forget-me-nots and sweet William, grown from seed earlier in the year should be ready to plant out into the garden. Bear in mind that the plants are going to be quite short-lived – one or two years at the most – and therefore plant them where they can be easily pulled out and replaced. Some gardeners have particular borders for spring-flowering biennials, which they replace with bedding plants or hardy annuals in early summer. This is quite a time-consuming method of gardening, but the rewards are beds that are always colourful and scented. For extra effect, spring biennials can be combined with narcissus, tulips or other spring-flowering bulbs.

The biennials will need to be transplanted from their nursery beds or pots (See July Tasks, p.76). If you have not grown any from seed, garden centres will be stocking young biennial plants at this time of year.

Water the plants before transplanting. Use a trowel to make the planting holes and firm it well.

PLANTING SPRING BULBS

This is A simple garden task and one which brings almost guaranteed success. The spring garden would be a dreary place without the addition of bulbs and corms.

Choosing bulbs

Cottage gardeners have always been adventurous in their choice of bulbs and for centuries have grown crown imperials, hyacinths, fritillaries, cyclamen, tulips, snowdrops and lilies. Narcissus and crocus were taken for granted and, when available, the cottage gardener would try the latest double, frilled and unusual coloured forms. Today, the range is almost endless and includes some that the old cottage gardener would not have known such as decorative alliums, *Chionodoxa*, *Camassia* and *Muscari*.

Planting

All the bulbs mentioned above can be planted this month or next, with the exception of lilies (see p.90 and 123.). The planting instructions are simple:

■ Use a bulb planter or trowel and put the bulb in at the correct depth, pointed end upwards, and cover with soil. In cottage gardens without lawns, bulbs can be planted in any border, or in pots and window boxes. Check the height of each species and plant accordingly.

MONTHLY REMINDERS

■ *This is the last chance to plant evergreen shrubs until next spring. Plant box and privet for hedging and edging and holly as a specimen shrub (see p.132)* ■

■ *Plant bulbs for indoor flowering (hyacinths and miniature narcissi). Set the bulbs in bowls or pots of bulb fibre and keep in a cool dark place for 8 weeks. When the shoots are 2.5cm (1in) high bring the bowls into the light and warmth* ■

■ *Evergreen hedges can be given a final light trim to remove any straggly growth and to keep them looking shapely through the winter* ■

GOOD COMPANIONS

Spring-flowering bulbs can be combined with biennials and perennials to give a variety of colour effects:

Pink and blue – the classic combination of pink tulips and blue forget-me-nots looks effective in narrow borders, against the wall of the house or as a path edging. Plant the tulips behind the forget-me-nots. Try *Tulipa* 'Hermione' or 'Angelique' (height 45cm/18in) with *Myosotis* 'Ultramarine' or 'Blue Ball' (height 15cm/6in) in front.

Yellow and red – for a hot colour combination of brilliant yellows, burnt oranges and velvety reds, plant daffodils with wallflowers. Try dwarf *Narcissus* such as 'Tête-à-Tête' or the double 'Rip van Winkle' (height 15cm/6in), among *Cherianthus* 'Tom Thumb' (height 15–23cm/6–9in). The same colour combination can also be achieved with full-sized daffodils and wallflowers. Set out the plants and bulbs in a random pattern for an informal effect.

Burgundy and cream – the deep wine-coloured *Allium sphaerocephalon* looks particularly good planted with creamy *Astrantia major* or the feathery-leafed sweet Cicely (*Myrrhis odorata*).

plants
OF THE
month
1

SUNFLOWER
(Helianthus annuus)

Perhaps the romantic recreation of a cottage garden demands only soft, tasteful pinks and blues, but the gaudy sunflower is proof that in reality, cottage gardeners grew whatever took their fancy. Victorian paintings of cottage gardens show sunflowers quite clearly, peeping over the hedge or leaning against an open casement window. And it is not difficult to imagine why they were grown, being the simplest of all annual flowers to cultivate and loved by children for their sunny faces. Originally from America, the plant has been grown in cottage gardens for centuries. Gerard, the sixteenth-century gardener, claimed that a sunflower in his garden grew to a height of 14 feet – although this might have been a slight exaggeration.

type	Annual
flowers	Bright yellow with a large brown central disc; 30cm (12in) across; late summer to early autumn
foliage	Mid-green, heart-shaped, toothed
height	Up to 3m (10ft)
spread	30–45cm (12–18in)
site	In full sun; borders
soil	Well-drained
planting	Sow in position in mid-spring
care	Keep well watered and support stems with sturdy canes as they grow
propagation	Sow two or three seeds together, 45cm (18in) apart, in mid-spring. As the seedlings grow, remove the weakest, leaving one to make a strong plant
varieties	The flowers of the double form *H. annuus* 'Flore Pleno' more closely resemble a chrysanthemum and do not have the central disc
related value	*H. decapetalus* is perennial and is more compact than the sunflower (although still reaching 2m/6ft). It bears a crown of small yellow flowers from late summer onwards and makes a good autumn border plant
cottage garden value	Apart from the obvious joys of the flower itself, the plant is also worth growing for the honeycombed seedheads. They contain up to 2000 seeds per head and provide a ready-made food store for finches

GOLDEN ROD
(Solidago hybrids*)*

The first golden rod in cottage gardens was probably the native *Solidago virgaurea*, which was renowned for its wound-healing properties, but was a coarse, unattractive plant. It was supplanted by a North American species, *S. canadensis*, introduced by Tradescant in the mid-seventeenth century but found no favour with gardeners as it was reputed to impoverish the soil and exterminate other plants. In the twentieth century, breeders produced a range of hybrids which suit the cottage garden very well, being non-invasive, late flowering and good for bees. These hybrids vary considerably in height, but they all make good border plants with their arching plumes of soft, golden-yellow flowers.

type	Herbaceous perennial
flowers	Pale lemon or golden-yellow; late summer to mid-autumn
foliage	Yellow-green
height	30cm–2m (1–6ft) depending on variety
spread	30–60cm (12–24in)
site	In full sun or partial shade; borders
soil	Any
planting	Plant out in late autumn, late winter or early spring, 30–60cm (12–24in) apart, depending on variety
care	Taller varieties might need staking. Set the stakes to reach half way up the stems. Cut down stems after flowering in late autumn. *Solidago* can exhaust the soil, so should be divided regularly
propagation	Divide and replant the roots in mid-autumn or in late winter/early spring
varieties	*S.* 'Goldenmosa' is 1m (3ft) high with yellow-green foliage and 23cm (9in) sprays of fluffy flowers in late summer. One of the most compact forms is *S.* 'Golden Thumb' ('Queenie'), which is only 30cm (12in) high and forms a neat rounded plant
related species	The wild golden rod (*S. virgaurea*) was an important medicinal herb in Elizabethan times and was sold at the famous Bucklersbury market in London. It was taken as a drink to heal internal wounds and the dried plant was in great demand. It was replaced in gardens by more compact hybrids
cottage garden value	Golden rod is attractive to bees and butterflies and provides invaluable splashes of colour in autumn borders. The flower plumes are good for cutting. *Solidago* species can be toxic and should not be used internally

BLACK-EYED SUSAN
(Rudbeckia hirta)

This late-flowering plant originates from North America and arrived in Britain in the early 1700s. It is not difficult to see why it became a cottage garden favourite, being hardy, free-flowering and providing colour in autumn when many other flowers are over. Like many autumnal flowers it is golden-yellow. somehow reminiscent of long 'Indian summer' days. The 'black' eye is actually a deep purple or brown cone in the centre of the plant, very noticeable against the ray of petals. The plant can hardly be described as dainty, standing up to 1m (3ft) tall with branching stems, but the flowers are favoured for cutting. Although actually a short-lived perennial, the best plants are grown fresh from seed each year.

type	Short-lived perennial, treated as an annual
flowers	Golden-yellow, 8cm (3in) across with a dark centre; late summer to mid-autumn
foliage	Mid-green, oblong
height	30–90cm (12–36in)
spread	45cm (18in)
site	Full sun; borders
soil	Any, well-drained
planting	Young plants are set out in late spring, 30–45cm (12–18in) apart
care	Cut down stems after first flowers and apply a liquid tomato feed to encourage a second flush
propagation	Sow seeds in pots in early to mid-spring and plant out into flowering positions in late spring
varieties	The Gloriosa daisy (*R. hirta* Tetra 'Gloriosa') has even larger flowers (up to 13cm/5in across) which are particularly good for cutting. Dwarf rudbeckias are available for hanging baskets and pots
related species	*R. fulgida* is the perennial version of the black-eyed Susan and an equally popular border plant. *R. fulgida* 'Goldsturm' is one of the most successful varieties with golden-yellow flowers that last well into autumn
cottage garden value	All the rudbeckias – and the related coneflowers (*Echinacea purpurea*) – flower late and over a long period, a valuable asset in any garden. The perennial coneflower is ideal towards the back of the border, although it will need to be divided every few years, in autumn. The stems are 1–1.2m (3–4ft) high and carry purple-crimson flowers from late summer to early autumn. Both are good for cutting

BETONY
(Stachys officinalis)

This plant, found growing wild on the heaths and open woodlands of Europe, has an ancient association with man. The Romans used the leaves as a blood purifier and medieval herbalists believed it held all kinds of magical properties. Dried leaves were used as a substitute for snuff and as a herbal tea and it was reputed to bring relief for no less than 47 ailments. Culpeper called it *'a very precious herb, that's certain and most fitting be kept in a man's house both in syrup, conserve, oil, ointment and plaister'*. The local name of 'bishop's wort' is perhaps a reference to the cathedral or monastery physic garden. But in cottage gardens too, it found a niche and stayed there. Most gardeners find the species too coarse and variable to be used with much success, but the named varieties are reliably compact and free-flowering.

type	Herbaceous perennial
flowers	Bright pinkish-purple flower spikes; late summer to mid-autumn
foliage	Mid- to dark green, oval, toothed leaves in a basal rosette
height	23–30cm (9–12in)
spread	30cm (12in)
site	Sun or partial shade; front of borders or path edging
soil	Any, well-drained
planting	Plant out in autumn or spring, setting the plants 30cm (12in) apart
care	Cut down flower spikes in late autumn
propagation	Divide and replant the roots in early spring
varieties	The two best garden varieties are *S. officinalis* 'Alba, the white-flowered form and *S. officinalis* 'Rosea Superba' which has lilac-pink flower spikes
related species	The woolly-leaved *S. lanata* or lamb's tongue is widely planted but is less 'cottagey' than betony
cottage garden value	Betony has such a long history of being grown close to man that it surely deserves a place in the cottage garden. The purple flower spikes appear at the end of summer and last well into autumn, attracting bees and late flying insects

Top to bottom: golden rod, black-eyed Susan and betony

practical project

THE FLORIST'S GARDEN

SHOW VARIETIES

Not all the old varieties listed here are available – many have been replaced by modern hybrids.

PANSY
'Alice Rutherford' – pure yellow
'James Thom' – yellow ground with chocolate-violet upper petals

AURICULA
'Old Yellow Dusty Miller' – powerful scent, deep golden-yellow flowers
'Old Red Dusty Miller' – dark crimson-brown, 'dusty' appearance
'Old Suffolk Bronze' – golden-bronze with a strong perfume

RANUNCULUS
'Turban Dore' – scarlet, marked with gold, the most sought after show ranunculus

Compare the flower shape of the show pansy (left) with that of the simple heartsease

In the seventeenth century, cottage gardening took a new turn. From being the comparatively haphazard cultivation of flowers, fruit, herbs and vegetables, it became, for some, a much more serious activity. Artisans and other craftsmen began to develop an interest in the breeding of flowers to produce perfect specimens. These specialists were known as 'florists' – gardeners who wanted to breed and exhibit plants for show.

Growing for show was most popular in the industrial areas of northern England and Scotland, where the practice of floristry allowed manufacturing workers – particularly weavers – to exercise their artistic skills outside the workplace. The range of 'florist's flowers' was broad and included violets, narcissus, roses, clematis, marigolds and many others, but, by the end of the eighteenth century, only eight flowers were deemed worthy: anemone, auricula, carnation, hyacinth, pink, polyanthus, ranunculus and tulip. In the nineteenth century the definition was widened again to include pansies, pelargoniums and dahlias and the movement reached its peak. Workers in different regions became famous for their skills with particular plants: the miners of Derbyshire, Yorkshire and the Black Country with pansies; the textile workers of Paisley in Scotland with laced pinks; the Lancashire weavers with auriculas and the potters of Staffordshire with polyanthus. Artisans working from their own cottages or in small workshops had time to tend their plants between work, but as they began to travel further to the larger factories they had little time for floristry.

Although largely an historical idea rather than a practical one, today's cottage gardens often incorporate an area that is dedicated to one type of plant grown to exhibition standard. In the heyday of floristry, each flower may have had as many as five hundred named varieties whereas today most are numbered in tens. Yet there is still a band of dedicated specialists for whom a flower is not a flower unless it meets the exacting criteria of the show judge.

PANSY

The first Pansy Society, formed in 1841, aimed to produce a perfectly circular flower, with five rounded petals, a far cry from the simple heartsease (see p.55) from which it was bred.

Pansies are short-lived perennials but are usually grown like biennials – sown in mid- to late summer, planted out in autumn for flowering the following spring and summer. Pansies like moist soil and a sunny or partly shaded position. Flowers should be snipped off as they fade to prolong flowering.

Attributes of the show pansy
- May be self-coloured (plain) or bicoloured.
- Should have smooth, velvet-like appearance.
- Two centre petals must meet above the 'eye'.
- The whole bloom must be balanced.

AURICULA

Introduced in 1575, auricula primulas were prized by cottagers and more wealthy gardeners alike. They were the most demanding of the florist's flowers requiring rich feeding and careful nurturing but, with their powerful scent and 'old masters' colouring, the plants were thought to be well worth the trouble. Special staging was constructed to display them to perfection and they were sometimes viewed through a picture frame to look like a work of art.

Plant perennial auriculas in spring or autumn in a sunny spot. They like a moist soil and an annual mulch to conserve moisture.

Attributes of the show auricula
- Creamy 'paste' centre.
- Velvety blooms.
- Rich colourings.

RANUNCULUS

Ranunculus asiaticus arrived in Britain in Elizabethan times. Not a hardy plant, it had to be nurtured under glass and taken indoors in cold winters. It was immensely popular in the eighteenth century when 800 named varieties are recorded, but, by the end of the Victorian era only a few dozen remained. It was considered to be time-consuming and its popularity decreased. Today, only mixed, plain colour ranunculus are available as multi-coloured forms have disappeared.

Ranunculus asiaticus is not fully hardy and tubers must be lifted and brought indoors in winter. Store in a cool, airy place until replanting in the spring. They prefer a rich soil, with added manure or compost, and sunny position.

Show-worthy ranunculus
- A black ranunculus was highly prized.
- White or yellow varieties with red stripes were the most prestigious.
- Plain colours were not thought to be show-worthy unless very unusual.

TULIPOMANIA

- *By 1796, one catalogue listed 700 varieties*
- *A virus disease that attacks the bulbs, causes the colour to 'break', that is form streaks, feathering and stripes. These forms known as Bizarres, Edgers and Bybloemens, were highly sought after and as they could only be propagated by offsets, bulb values soared. Single bulbs sold for hundreds of pounds; buying tulips became like buying a work of art*
- *Cottagers were never in the 'art' market and when the tulip trade finally crashed, it was the 'English' tulips – plain coloured, simple flowers – that became highly sought after*
- *In 1836, The Wakefield and North of England Tulip Society was formed as part of the nineteenth-century revival of interest in tulips. Cottage tulips (self-coloured singles and doubles) formed the basis of a sustainable movement that has lasted until the present day*

TULIP

The name *Tulipa* is taken from the Persian word for turban, which the flowers are said to resemble in shape. It reached England from Turkey in the sixteenth century and many double and single varieties were soon available.

Tulips like a hot, sunny spot and well-drained soil. Bulbs are planted in mid- to late autumn, 15–20cm (6–8in) deep.

COTTAGE TULIPS
Single or double, self-coloured flowers are the hallmark of cottage garden tulips. Examples that survive in cottage gardens include:
'Schoonard' – double white scented
'Queen of the Night' – single, very dark purple

PARROT TULIPS
Frilled petals tulips, introduced about 1620, never found favour with 'florists'. However, they are enjoying something of a revival and several varieties suit the relaxed cottage style.
'Black Parrot' – fringed deep wine petals
'Estella Rynveld' – raspberry and white frills

PEONY-FLOWERED TULIPS
Peony tulips do not have a long pedigree, but they have a suitably soft, relaxed appearance for the cottage garden.
'Hermione' – ice-cream pink, loose petals
'Angelique' – apple-blossom pink

'Estella Rynveld'

'Queen of the Night'

'Hermione'

OCTOBER

This is a very satisfying time of year, when growth slows down and there is time to reflect on past successes and failures. As the majority of plants in a cottage garden are perennial, this is a good month for considering how well they have worked and perhaps lifting and transplanting some of them to a new position. It is also an excellent time to plant new perennials as the warmth of the soil and the autumn rains will help them to become established before the cold weather. Climbers like to be planted now, too, and as the garden loses its coat of foliage, it is much easier to erect and maintain trellises and arches.

Increasing the stock of plants is probably the cottage gardener's raison d'être. No self-respecting, thrifty cottager goes out and buys plants – he collects seed, takes cuttings, and acquires plants from any source.

Taking snippets of plant material from other people's gardens – private or public – without asking is an increasing and worrying phenomenon. But, friendly swapping of cuttings between neighbours, sharing divided plants and rhizomes and growing more plants than you need from seed to give some away is in the true spirit of cottage gardening. This month is the time for taking hardwood cuttings, a simple way to propagate a whole range of deciduous shrubs and one of the most fail-safe methods for beginners. There may still be a little seed to be collected and division of clump-forming perennials can continue until the hard frosts.

Among the copper colours of autumn, two pink bulbous flowers deserve mention: nerines and Amaryllis. Nerines, from South Africa are not always hardy, but they are worth growing close to a sunny wall where they will produce rich pink flowers. The belladonna lily (Amaryllis), with its pale pink lily-like trumpets makes a good autumn companion for Nerine bowdenii.

tasks
FOR THE
month

EVERGREEN CUTTINGS

Evergreen cuttings sometimes fail to root because of water loss through their leaves. For cuttings of large-leafed evergreens like ivy, cut the leaves in half (using sharp scissors) before planting to reduce their surface area. This month take cuttings from:

Buddleia (*Buddleia davidii*)
Elder (*Sambucus nigra*)
Flowering currant (*Ribes sanguineum*)
Forsythia (*Forsythia* x *intermedia*)
Grape vine (*Vitis vinifera*)
Honeysuckle (*Lonicera periclymenum*)
Ivy (*Hedera helix*)
Mock orange (*Philadelphus microphyllus*)
Privet (*Ligustrum ovalifolium*)
Virginia creeper (*Parthenocissus*)
Weigela (*Weigela florida*)

CHECKLIST

- Take hardwood cuttings
- Plant spring-flowering perennials
- Plant lily-of-the-valley and irises
- Collect and sow seed from berry-bearing shrubs
- Divide perennials (Reminder)

TAKING HARDWOOD CUTTINGS

The simplest way to increase your stock of hardy shrubs and climbers is to take cuttings this month, just as the shrubs are beginning their period of winter dormancy. It is a good idea to take a range of cuttings, from different shrubs, and grow them together in a nursery bed outdoors. If there is not room for this, they can be grown in pots, individually or in batches. Hardwood cuttings do not need the protection of a coldframe or a propagator.

Preparing and planting

■ Choose vigorous stems that are hard and woody with healthy buds all along the stem.

■ Cut the stem near its base using secateurs.
■ With a knife or secateurs, trim the stem to about 25cm (10in) long, cutting just below

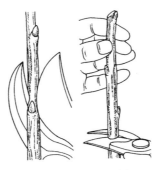

a joint at the bottom and just above a joint at the top. (For evergreens, cut just below and above a leaf and remove all the leaves from the lower half of the cutting.)
■ To increase the chances of rooting, slice off a thin piece of bark from the base of the cutting.
■ Make a trench in well-dug soil by inserting a spade to its full depth and pulling forwards several inches to make a V-shape. Add a 5cm (2in) layer of coarse sand to the bottom of the trench to improve drainage.

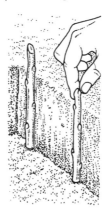

■ Plant the cuttings so that two thirds of their length is underground. Set them about 10cm (4in) apart and refill with soil. Firm down.

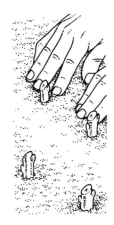

Aftercare

In hard frosts, the cuttings may be 'lifted' out of the ground. If this happens, just firm them in again using your foot. Keep the area free of weeds and water in dry spells in the summer. The cuttings should have rooted by the following autumn and be ready to plant out. If not, leave them in position for a second year.

NOTE

■ *If growing cuttings in pots, use 13cm (9in) deep pots filled with a cuttings compost* ■

PLANTING SPRING-FLOWERING PERENNIALS

Spring-flowering perennials such as primulas, periwinkle (*Vinca*), Pasque flower (*Pulsatilla vulgaris*), cuckoo flower (*Cardamine pratensis*), hellebores, and peonies should be planted this month. This gives them the best possible start: the soil is still warm and there is usually plenty of rain in autumn, both of which will encourage the plants to build up a good root system before the spring.

■ To prepare the soil, dig over a week or two before planting and add garden compost or well-rotted manure. Leave the soil to settle and then rake level.

■ Water the plants in their containers before planting. Use a trowel or spade to make the holes according to the size of the plant.

■ Take account of the final height and spread of the plant and plant the bed accordingly. It is a good idea to plant in groups of three or more, rather than individually, as the plants will soon grow together to make a mass of colour or foliage. Also take into account any special growing conditions the plants prefer — hellebores, for example, need a humus-rich soil and some shade, while peonies can tolerate a poorer soil and full sun. (For more detailed growing requirements see Plant Profiles.)

PLANTING LILY-OF-THE-VALLEY AND IRISES

Perennials with rhizomes rather than conventional roots are also planted this month, but they need to be planted more shallowly than other plants.

Lily-of-the-valley (Convallaria majalis)
Choose a partly shaded

position and work plenty of humus (leafmould or garden compost) into the soil to retain moisture around the plant's roots. The ideal position for lily-of-the-valley is under not-too-dense deciduous shrubs.

■ Plant the crowns pointed end upwards, so that the points are just below the surface of the soil.
■ If the crowns are single, set them 8cm (3in) apart; if they are in a clump, set the clumps 15cm (6in) apart.
■ Water well and cover the area with a layer of leafmould or garden compost.

Planting irises
Rhizomatous irises — which includes the flag iris (*I. pseudacorus*), *I. germanica*, *I. pallida* and all the bearded hybrids — need to be shallow planted in an open, sunny position. They like a neutral soil (not too acid) which should be well dug with added manure and compost.

■ Plant the rhizomes firmly, so that the tops are just visible through the soil.
■ Water well and do not allow the plants to dry out for two to three weeks.

COLLECTING SEED FROM SHRUBS

Fruit or berry-bearing shrubs can be propagated from seed in mid- to late autumn. New plants can be grown from honeysuckle, Japanese quince (*Chaenomeles*) cotoneaster, species roses, hawthorn, witch hazel (*Hamamelis mollis*) and *Viburnum opulus*. Leave the berries on the shrub until completely ripe and then pick them, remove all the flesh around the seeds and sow immediately.

■ Fill 10cm (4in) diameter pots with moist seed compost and level the surface. Sow the seed thinly (if possible, one seed to a pot) and cover with

a thin (2cm/1in) layer of compost.
■ Stand the pots in a coldframe (p.126) or in a sheltered position outdoors (protected from wind and rain). Most will germinate the following spring but if not, leave the pots outdoors for a second winter so that they can be exposed to a period of cold and frost — this sometimes encourages germination in seeds that prove stubborn.

In mid- to late autumn the berries of hawthorn and cotoneaster, and the hips of species roses, can be picked to collect the seed

MONTHLY REMINDER

Mid-autumn is a good time to divide overgrown clumps of perennials. It is sometimes easier to divide and replant herbaceous species (like Aquilegia) now, rather than in late winter when the foliage may not be visible. (For full instructions see p.20.)

Divide:
Alchemilla mollis
Achillea species
Aquilegia
Campanula
Coneflowers (*Echinacea*)
Geraniums
Globeflowers (*Troillus*)
Heleniums
Lungwort (*Pulmonaria*)
Rudbeckias

plants
OF THE
month
1

*Japanese anemone
and saffron crocus*

*'Let me see…what am I to buy for
our sheep-shearing feast? …
I must have saffron to colour the
warden pies.'*
the clown
in shakespeare's a winter's tale

JAPANESE ANEMONE

(*Anemone japonica*, syn. *Anemone* x *hybrida*)

Perhaps this is a strange choice for the cottage garden, as it is an introduction from Asia, but one which sits well in western gardens. It is actually a native of China but, because it spread into Japan and naturalized there, nineteenth century botanists believed Japan to be its country of origin. The tall plants, bearing delicate pink or white flowers late in the year, are excellent in borders where they will soon form substantial clumps.

type	Herbaceous perennial
flowers	White, pink, crimson; late summer to mid-autumn
foliage	Mid-green, divided
height	60–90cm (24–36in)
spread	60cm (24in)
site	Partial shade
soil	Any fertile, well-drained
planting	Put out young plants in mid-autumn or early spring, 45–60cm (18–24in) apart
care	Cut stems down to ground level after flowering has finished. Once established, Japanese anemones prefer to remain undisturbed although clumps that spread too rapidly can be checked by lifting and dividing
propagation	Take root cuttings in winter and grow on in a coldframe
varieties	One of the nineteenth century favourites was *A.* x *hybrida* 'Honorine Jobert', a white, tall-growing, 1.2m (4ft) variety, still grown today. *A.* x *hybrida* 'Lady Gilmour' has semi-double, slightly shaggy, pink flowers
cottage garden value	Once established, Japanese anemones will provide long-lasting flowers from late summer to late autumn. They can spread exuberantly if not checked, so are not recommended for small gardens

SAFFRON CROCUS

(*Crocus sativus*)

The history of saffron is closely linked with the town of Saffron Walden in Essex, where a single corm was supposed to have been imported secretly by a returning medieval pilgrim. Whatever the truth, a thriving industry grew up in the area and the flowers were cultivated for their precious stigmas which, when dried, produce the vibrant yellow saffron powder. As it takes over four thousand flowers to produce one ounce of saffron, it would not have been a viable crop for the average cottage gardener, but the plant did find its way into gardens, and small quantities may have been harvested for colouring cakes and pastry.

type	Corm
flowers	Deep purple flowers with blood-red stigmas, mid-autumn
foliage	Narrow, grey-green leaves appear before the flowers
height	10cm (4in)
spread	10cm (4in)
planting	Plant corms 8–10cm (3–4in) apart and 5–8cm (2–3in) deep in summer
site	Full sun
soil	Well-drained
care	No special care needed, but plants may fail if ground is waterlogged, or in cold, wet summers. May be grown in pots with a gritty compost and can then be given shelter from the worst weather. Needs warmth in summer to ripen the corms
propagation	Lift the corms every three years after flowering and detach and replant the offsets
varieties	There is a pure white form, *C. sativus cartwrightianus* 'Albus'
related species	The true autumn-flowering crocus, *C. speciosus* has large bright violet blue flowers with orange stigmas. It is easy to grow and is a good alternative if the saffron crocus is proving difficult to establish

NERINE

(*Nerine bowdenii*)

Nerine bowdenii is perfectly hardy in all but the wettest, coldest winters: the flowers themselves will survive any amount of frost, but the bulbs may be lost if the ground is continually sodden or frozen. The species was discovered by an English surveyor, Mr Cornish Bowden, who was working in South Africa. He sent it home to his mother's garden in Newton Abbot, Devon in 1889. It is not a difficult plant to grow and once planted will produce its umbels of pink flowers for five years or more before it needs attention. The flowers are so welcome towards the end of autumn, somehow holding back the inevitability of winter.

type	Bulb
flowers	Rich pink; early to late autumn

foliage	Mid-green, strap-shaped leaves appear after the flowers
height	60cm (24in)
spread	15cm (6in)
site	Full sun; against a wall or towards the back of a border
soil	Well-drained
planting	Plant bulbs in late summer, 10cm (4in) deep. In areas where winters are particularly harsh, plant in mid-spring
care	Leave undisturbed until clumps become overcrowded and start to produce fewer flower stems (usually after five years). The bulbs will gradually work their way to the surface of the soil as they increase. In severe winters, cover with a layer of bracken or straw
propagation	Lift, divide and replant the bulbs (see care) in late summer
varieties	*N. bowdenii* 'Mark Fenwick' is taller than the species, with larger, deeper pink flowers. *N. bowdenii* 'Pink Triumph' has silvery-pink flowers which appear in late autumn

AUTUMN-FLOWERING CLEMATIS

Although the large-flowered, summer clematis are more well-known to gardeners because of their showy blooms, there is a group of autumn-flowering clematis that deserve closer attention. The flowers may be smaller, but as they fade the real stars appear – stunning, silvery seed heads that shimmer in the autumn sunlight. Clematis are shrubby climbers that use their leafstalks to hoist themselves up into the light. They look best grown with an evergreen climber such as ivy or planted to grow through a tall shrub, where the stems disappear and only the flowers and seed heads are visible.

CULTIVATION
of autumn-flowering clematis

site	Sun or light shade; ideally with the top growth in sun, but with shade around the roots. Avoid a heavily-shaded aspect when planting *C. flammula*
soil	Any fertile soil
planting	Plant in autumn or spring, adding

well-rotted manure to the planting hole

care	Mulch around the base of the plant in spring, with well-rotted manure or garden compost
propagation	Take semi-ripe cuttings in late summer or layer in early spring

Clematis orientalis

A native of the Himalayas, *C. orientalis* has pretty, nodding, star-shaped flowers, followed by decorative, feathery seed heads.

type	Deciduous climber
flowers	Yellow; 5cm (2in) across, scented; late summer to mid-autumn
seed heads	Silky, silver-grey; early to late autumn
foliage	Light green, fern-like
height	To 6m (20ft)
spread	60–90cm (24–36in), depends on training

Clematis flammula

C. flammula (Fragrant virgin's bower) originates from southern Europe and is another good late flowerer. It has tiny white, meadow-scented flowers followed by the characteristic fluffy seed heads. It arrived in Britain from Spain in the seventeenth century and has been a cottage garden favourite ever since.

type	Deciduous climber
flowers	White, scented; late summer to mid-autumn
seed heads	Silky, silver-grey; early to late autumn
foliage	Bright green
height	To 3m (10ft)
spread	60–90cm (24–36in), depends on training

Clematis tangutica

Very like *C. orientalis*, this has similar yellow flowers and silvery seed heads. It looks best when allowed to ramble freely.

type	Deciduous climber
flowers	Bright yellow lantern-shaped flowers; late summer to mid-autumn
seed heads	Conspicuous silky heads; early to late autumn
foliage	Grey-green, divided
height	To 6m (20ft)
spread	60–90cm (24–36in), depends on training

Top to bottom: clematis tangutica, C. flammula and C. orientalis

practical project

GROWING FRUIT IN THE COTTAGE GARDEN 1: BUSHES AND CORDONS

If we go back to the basic function of a cottage garden – to provide food for the cottager's family – then fruit must have a place in even the smallest plot. Fruit appeared in gardens in the middle ages, even before vegetables. The plum, apple or pear tree would have been a necessity, along with herbs and a beehive, to supplement the predominantly meat-based diet. Bees would work the blossom and pollinate the trees, so beekeeping and fruit growing often went hand in hand. By Elizabethan times the range grown had extended to include soft fruits like strawberries and gooseberries along with rhubarb and grapes. Gooseberries became the Victorian's favourite crop. Cultivated for show and for eating, they were frequently grown in a hedge to maximize space.

TRAINING FRUIT TREES

In a small garden, fruit trees can be trained in a number of different ways to make the best of the available space. If your garden already contains a full-sized standard apple or pear tree, retain it and use walls and fences to grow other fruits. Garden and house walls can be fitted with wires to take an espalier or fan-trained tree (see p.118). Cordons (single-stemmed plants, usually grown at an angle) can be grown against fences, walls or trained with wires and posts to make a free-standing row.

PLANTING A BUSH TREE

The best time for planting apple, pear, plum or cherry trees is late autumn, but they can be planted any time between autumn and early spring, as long as the soil is not waterlogged or frozen. Choose an open sunny position, away from the house and clear of any existing garden features such as ponds or sheds.

■ Dig a hole large enough to take the roots when fully spread out. The depth will depend on the tree itself: the aim is to plant it at the same level as it was planted at the nursery (shown by the soil mark on the stem).
■ Break up the earth at the bottom of the hole with a fork and add a spadeful of well-rotted manure. Work this into the loose soil.
■ Place a stake firmly in the centre of the hole. The stake should reach the point at which the trunk forks to form the upper branches. Place the tree beside the stake and hold in position while the loose soil is shovelled into the hole. (Two people are useful for this task.) Shake the tree occasionally to settle the soil around the roots. Firm down and water thoroughly.
■ Attach the trunk of the tree to the stake, using a rubber tree tie. Make sure the buffer comes between the bark and the stake.

PLANTING A LINE OF CORDONS

Cordon training is suitable for apples, pears, gooseberries and red- or white-currants. Choose one-year-old plants (maidens) with a single stem.

■ Set posts about 2m (6ft) apart and attach vine eyes, with straining bolts, at heights of 30cm (12in), 1m (3ft), 1.5m (5ft) and 2.2m (7ft). Stretch lengths of wire between the vine eyes, adjusting the nut at the back of the post to ensure the wire is taut.
■ Dig a trench 30–45cm (12–18in) wide in front of the wire and posts. Loosen the soil at the base with a fork and work in a few spadefuls of well-rotted manure.
■ Set the plants 1m (3ft) apart, refill the trench and firm down.
■ Insert a 2m (6ft) cane behind each plant and wire it to the horizontal wires at the same angle as the plant. Using soft string, tie each cordon to the cane.

Aftercare
Cordons can be grown vertically or at an oblique angle. The usual angle is 45 degrees. As the cordon reaches the top of the wire, the cane is used to lower the stem to the desired angle. Once the cordon is at the correct angle and growing strongly, the cane can be removed. Be careful not to force the cordon so that it breaks – it is better to lower it gradually, a few inches at a time.

Pruning a cordon
In the first year after planting, cut back the laterals (the side shoots off the main stem) in late

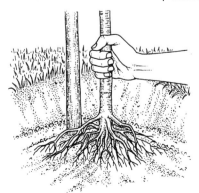

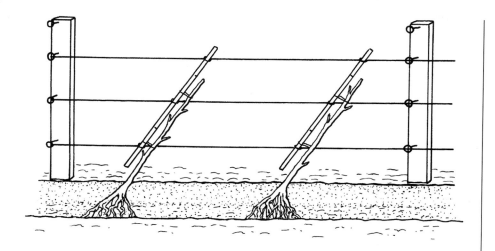

summer. Any that are over 23cm (9in) long should be cut back to three leaves from the joint with the main stem. Repeat this in subsequent years.

When the main stem reaches the top of the wires and cannot be lowered any further (probably in the second or third year) cut the growing tip (leader) in late spring. Make the cut just above a bud so that the stem is just beyond the last wire. Repeat this each year.

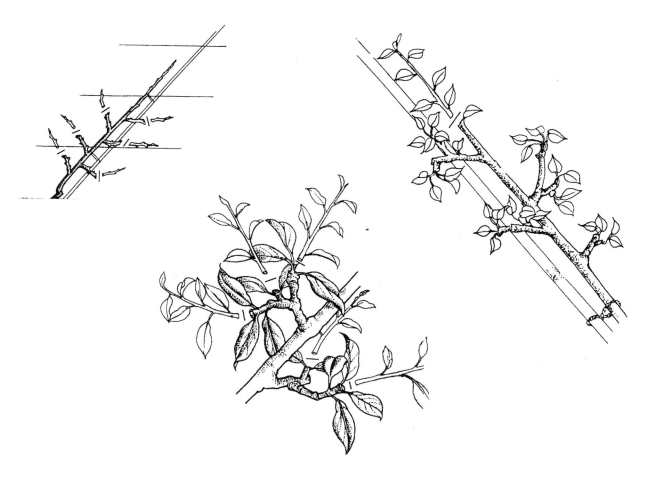

plants
OF THE
month
2

FRUIT FOR THE
COTTAGE GARDEN

Strawberry

STRAWBERRY
(Fragaria x *ananassa)*

The first cottage garden strawberries would have been dug up from the hedgerows, more for the curiosity value of the occasional sweet berry than to provide a serious food supply. By Elizabethan times, however, strawberries were being grown in greater quantities, not only for the berries, but for the leaves which were dried and infused into a tea. As bedding plants, they are space consuming and need quite a lot of care, but most gardeners undertake this gladly in return for their summer crop. The single-crop varieties such as 'Cambridge Favourite' are the best choice because, although there is a summer glut, the excess fruit can be bottled or made into jam.

type	Perennial
fruit	Red berries; early to midsummer
height	20–30cm (8–12in)
spread	Up to 30cm (12in)
site	Open, sunny
soil	Rich, well-drained
planting	Plant out in late summer or early autumn, setting the plants at 45cm (12in) intervals. Dig in plenty of well-rotted manure before planting
care	Water well after planting. In late spring surround the plants with straw (or proprietary strawberry mats) to keep the berries off the ground. After harvesting, remove and burn the straw and any plant debris; this cuts down the risk of disease and pests. Discard and replace plants after four or five years
harvesting	Pick fruits when they are large and fully coloured but still firm, from early summer onwards
propagation	From runners in late summer. Choose the strongest runners from each plant and peg them down directly into the soil or into a pot of compost, set into the ground. Sever the new plant approximately 4–6 weeks later and plant into its permanent position
varieties	'Cambridge Favourite' is a heavy cropper producing its fruits in early summer. 'Redgauntlet' is hardy enough for cold regions. It fruits in midsummer

APPLE
(Malus domestica)

If there is room for only one tree in the garden, then most people would go for an apple. It has the oldest cottage garden pedigree and is one of the most adaptable fruits: it can be grown as a bush tree, pyramid tree, cordon or espalier. There are so many varieties and the choice depends on personal taste and whether you want cooking or eating apples. 'Cox's Orange Pippin' is one of the most popular eaters, while 'Bramley' is hard to better as a cooker.

type	Deciduous tree
fruit	Green, yellow or red; early autumn to early winter
height	Depends on rootstock. Approximate heights: dwarf – 1.2m (4ft), M9 – 2m (6ft), M27 – 2.5m (8ft)
spread	Depends on training
site	Open, full sun; free-standing or trained against a sunny wall or fence. Apples can also be grown on wire and posts
soil	Any, as long as it is not waterlogged or very dry
planting	Plant any time between late autumn and early spring. Plant cordons at 1m (3ft) intervals and espaliers 4–5m (12–15ft) apart.
care	Mulch around the plants after planting with garden compost or well-rotted manure. (For pruning trees and espaliers see p. x., for cordons see p.x)
harvesting	Thinning is usually only necessary on full-sized trees (not on cordons or espaliers): when there is heavy crop, thin out some of the misshapen or small fruit in early summer. To check when apples are ripe, lift the fruit in the palm of the hand and give a slight twist. If the stalk comes away easily from the spur it is ready to pick. Apples are harvested from early to late autumn, depending on the variety
propagation	By expert grafting
varieties	Early autumn: 'Egremont Russet' (eater), 'James Grieve' (eater); mid-autumn: 'Cox's Orange Pippin' (eater); late autumn: 'Bramley's Seedling' (cooker), 'Lane's Prince Albert' (cooker)

PLUMS AND GAGES
(Prunus domestica)

The plums and gages now grown in gardens owe their parentage to the wild bullaces and sloes that the early cottage gardeners 'stole' from the hedgerows and nurtured in their sheltered plots. As a general rule, plums are hardier and less demanding, while gages need a little more attention. Both are suitable for growing as pyramid or bush trees and for training as fans against a warm wall.

type	Deciduous tree
fruit	Green or purple fruit; late summer
height	Trees 5–6m (15–20ft); fans 2.5–3m (8–10ft)
spread	4–5m (12–15ft)
site	Open, sunny; wall that faces the sun
soil	Good loam soil
planting	Plant trees from late autumn to late winter. Allow a space of 5m (15ft) for wall training
care	Mulch with well-rotted compost in winter. Plum trees are pruned in spring, cutting the leaders back by a half or one third for the first five years of growth. After that, only dead and crossing branches need to be removed each year, straight after harvesting. For fan-training see p.118.
harvesting	If necessary thin out the fruit in early summer to leave the plums 8cm (3in) apart. Pick fruits when they are ripe in late summer. Eating plums should be left on the tree until needed
propagation	By expert grafting
varieties	Small gardens with only room for one tree need a self-fertile variety such as 'Victoria', which can be used for dessert and for jams. 'Golden Transparent Gage' which has large, dessert fruit is also self-fertile but it needs the protection of a sunny wall

GOOSEBERRY

(Ribes)

Gooseberries have been popular with cottage gardeners since Elizabethan times when they were first made into delicious tarts, crumbles and fools. It is one of the easiest fruits for the beginner to cultivate and will give a good crop with the minimum of fuss. It can be grown as a low-growing bush, as a cordon, or in a row as a hedge. The gooseberry reached the pinnacle of its popularity in the mid-nineteenth century, particularly around the industrial towns in the north of England, where it was raised to an almost god-like status with annual gooseberry shows and contests forming part of the quest for the largest and most perfect berries. There are sweet dessert varieties and more acidic ones for cooking, although several varieties are good to eat both raw and cooked.

type	Deciduous bush
fruit	White, green or red berries; early to late summer
height	Depending on pruning: bushes 60cm (24in), hedges 1m (3ft), cordons 1.2m (4ft)
spread	1m (3ft); cordons 30cm (12in)
site	Open, full sun; free-standing or against a sunny wall, fence, or posts and wires
soil	Any, as long as it is not waterlogged or very sandy and dry. Heavy clay soils can be opened up by adding garden compost, light soils can be boosted with well-rotted manure
planting	Plant out in autumn or early winter, setting the plants at 30cm (12in) intervals for cordons, 1m (3ft) apart for bushes and hedges. Before planting, dig in plenty of well-rotted manure or garden compost
care	Mulch around the plants in winter with garden compost or well-rotted manure. To protect the buds from birds in the spring, cover the area with a fruit cage or netting or, if this is not possible, weave lengths of black cotton sowing thread between the bushes. (For pruning bushes see p.XXX and for cordons see p.115.)
harvesting	Thin out the fruit in late spring, picking off the small berries and leaving the remaining ones at least 5cm (2in) apart so that they can grow larger. These early thinnings can be used in cooking. Harvest the fruit from early summer onwards as the berries become ripe and start to change colour
propagation	Take 25cm (10in) hardwood cuttings in mid-autumn. Plant outside in a V-shaped trench, burying the cuttings so that two thirds of the wood is underground. The cuttings should have rooted by the following autumn
varieties	'Invicta' is a modern disease-resistant variety with green fruit for cooking; 'Whinham's Industry' is an old-fashioned variety with red berries for eating or cooking; 'Leveller' is one of the old prize-winning gooseberries which is still grown. Its yellow fruit can be used for dessert or cooking

Top to bottom: apple, plum and gooseberry

practical project

GROWING FRUIT IN THE COTTAGE GARDEN 2: ESPALIERS AND FANS

The need to fit fruit trees into small spaces has led to the development of some very inventive ways of training. Fan training, where the branches are spread out like the ribs of a fan, is suitable for peaches, apricots, nectarines and plums and works best against a wall or sturdy fence. Apples, pears and grapes can be grown as espaliers and trained against a wall, a fence or on wires and posts. Modern day methods of growing espaliers have been heavily influenced by French gardeners, who grow many different types of espalier including the very intricate *arcure*, which needs expert pruning and training. The simplest form, with a central vertical stem and horizontal branches, is known in French as *cordon ferraguti* and this is the method most commonly used in British gardens.

FAN TRAINING A PEACH TREE

Peaches are not the exotic fruit they might seem and were among the first fruits grown in cottage gardens. They are self-fertile, so do not need another nearby to produce a good crop, and are ideal for smaller gardens where it is possible to grow only one fruit. Peaches are generally hardy outdoors in Britain but they do best when trained against a wall that faces the sun, where the reflected warmth helps to ripen the fruits. For a fan-trained tree, you will need a wall space of at least 3.5m (12ft) wide and 2m (6ft) high.

Buy your peach tree from a good fruit nursery who will provide a two-year old tree with at least two side branches. Set up the wire and vine framework (see illustration) and plant the tree as described on p.114.

■ After planting, cut back the two branches to 45cm (18in) making the cut just above a bud. Tie two canes to the support wires at an angle of 45 degrees and tie the branches to them .

■ During the growing season, identify three shoots on each branch to develop into the 'ribs' of the fan. Two of these should be on the upper side of the branch and one on the lower. Rub out all the other shoots and tie in the selected ones to new canes.

DECORATIVE ESPALIERS

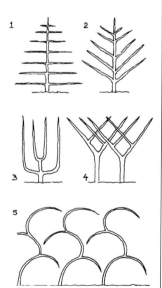

1 Cordon ferraguti
2 Palmette oblique
3 Palmette verrier
4 Losange (or Croissant)
5 Arcure

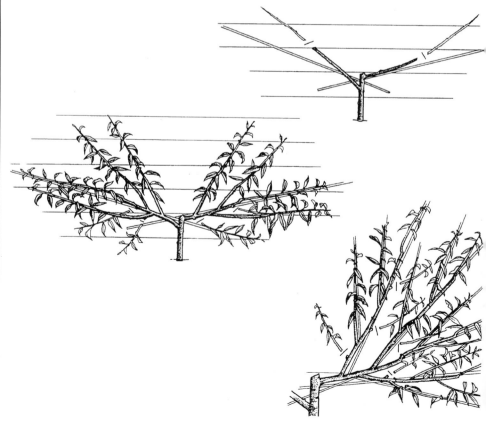

- During the winter, prune each of the eight branches (or ribs) to 75cm (30in). Cut back to just above a 'triple bud' – a cluster of buds with two blossom buds (round) and one growth bud (pointed).

- In the following summer, train in new ribs as needed to fill the wall space, removing any shoots that spoil the fan shape

GROWING AN ESPALIER PEAR

Pears like to be grown against a sunny wall, but if no wall is available, wires and posts can be set up in a suitable position. The first wire should be inserted at the level of the first dividing branch of the main stem. The horizontal wires should be set 30cm (12in) apart (NOTE: not 60cm (24in) apart as you normally would for wires and posts, see p.48) as pears are heavy croppers and will appreciate the extra support. It is advisable to grow at least two different varieties to ensure pollination – 'Conference', 'Louise Bonne of Jersey' and 'Williams' Bon Chrétien' are good mid-season varieties that all flower at about the same time.

- Plant pear trees in autumn. Choose a part-

ly trained espalier (two-year-old) from a specialist fruit nursery.

- Dig in plenty of organic matter (garden compost or well-rotted manure) to improve the soil. This is particularly important for trees to be grown next to a wall where the soil is likely to be poor and to dry out quickly. Allow a space of 4–5m (12–15ft) between trees.

- After planting, prune the central stem back to 5cm (2in) above the second wire, cutting just above a bud. Choose two buds to form the second tier of branches (these will be just below where you have made the cut) and rub out all the other buds on the central stem. Tie in the horizontal branches to the first wires and cut back by about one third.

- The following year in midsummer, tie two canes to the new second tier branches at an angle of 45 degrees. Cut back the mature laterals on the first tier (that is, those shoots which have grown to 23cm (9in) or longer) to three leaves from the basal cluster.
- In winter, tie in the second tier branches and cut the central stem to 5cm (2in) above the third wire. As before, select two buds to make the third tier of branches.

Correct

Incorrect

ARTIFICIAL POLLINATION

The main cause of failure of the peach crop is cold weather in spring which means there are not enough insects about to ensure pollination. If this seems to be the case, use an artist's paintbrush and dab it into the flowers each day during the flowering period. Frost can also damage the flowers and if a spell of heavy frost is likely, drape the tree overnight with sheets of insulating fleece.

OUTDOOR PEACH VARIETIES
'Peregrine' – late summer, large, crimson-skinned fruit (introduced 1906)
'Rochester' – late summer, hardy and reliable (introduced 1912)

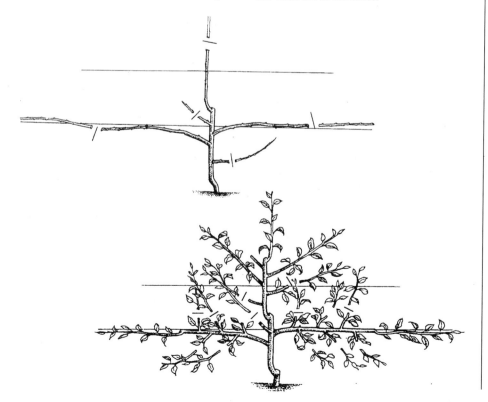

NOVEMBER

Few gardens look their best in late autumn, but the cottage garden has a number of seasonal charms. The misty air clothes everything with a veil of moisture, making the leaves of evergreens sparkle. It is at this time of year that we rely on the silver-leafed plants for much-needed definition in the borders and at path edges. Santolinas, artemisias, lavender and rue add form and patches of welcome soft bluey-grey colour. There are more vivid splashes as well – from the fiery red berries of Pyracantha *and* Berberis *and from the purple foliage of the decorative grape vine* Vitis vinifera *'Purpurea'. Flowers are not completely absent and there may be blossom on the winter-flowering cherry (*Prunus subhirtella *'Autumnalis'), as well as early shows on* Vibernum tinus *and* Viburnum x bodnantense. *It also the time for woodland plants to come into their own – evergreen ferns, the first leaves of the hellebores and the silver-splashed foliage of* Cyclamen hederiifolium. *The sweet violet (*Viola odorata) *sometimes flowers this month, producing a rare and precious hint of perfume.*

The flowers that gave so much pleasure earlier in the autumn can now provide for the garden's birds if they are left uncut. Sedum spectabile, *globe thistle, teasels, fennel and the late-flowering clematis (*Clematis vitalba *and* Clematis tangutica) *will provide seeds for finches and sparrows while the stems are convenient cover for overwintering insects. Cottage gardeners knew the importance of encouraging their pest-eating friends and would have left at least parts of the garden untidied. Spare a thought for hedgehogs just starting hibernation and prone to making their bed under piles of leaves or prunings. If the piles are not obtrusive, leave them undisturbed until the spring when they will do just as much good on the compost heap. Use milder days for digging over new patches of ground that are to be brought into cultivation. It is not too late to plant spring bulbs, while perennial plants will get a head start in the warmth of the autumn soil.*

tasks
FOR THE
month

MONTHLY REMINDERS

■ **Check pots of bulbs planted and kept in the dark for indoor flowering. Water occasionally to keep bulb fibre just moist. Once the shoots are over 2.5cm (1in) high, bring the pots into a light position indoors, but avoid extreme heat**

■ **Any seedlings or cuttings in pots standing outdoors (from late summer propagation) should be bought into the shelter of a porch or put into the cold frame to protect them from frost**

■ **For a supply of fresh mint through the winter, lift some roots from the garden, cut them into short 10cm (4in) sections and lay them in wide, shallow pots (or trays) of compost. Water lightly and keep on the windowsill where they will soon shoot and produce leaves for cutting**

CHECKLIST

☐ Cut down perennial plant stems
☐ Make leafmould (and compost see p.127)
☐ Plant lilies
☐ Move seedlings to cold frame

CUTTING DOWN PERENNIAL PLANTS

Some gardeners are naturally tidy and feel better for doing an autumn clear-up. Stems of Japanese anemones, golden rod and peonies may look a bit dishevelled at the tail end of the year and can be cut down to ground level. However, it is equally acceptable to leave them *in situ* and some gardeners like the rather ethereal effect of frost and snow on old plant stems. Overwintering insects will make their cold-weather quarters in hollow stems and late seed heads can be useful to birds. If you do decide to leave the stems then trim off any remaining in late winter or early spring just as the new foliage is starting to appear.

MAKING LEAFMOULD

Home-made garden compost is one of the mainstays of the cottage garden, providing a nutrient-rich growing medium and a place to store prunings and garden debris. This is a good month to start compost as there is usually plenty of material around. (For a choice of bins and detailed instructions see Practical Project p.126.)
If you have several large deciduous trees in the garden, and a lot of leaves, then leafmould is a very valuable and worthwhile substance to make; otherwise simply add the fallen leaves to the compost heap. Leafmould is used to open up the structure of heavy soils and to make poor, sandy soils more moisture retentive.

Traditionally, leaves are stored in any convenient 'pen' usually made from wire mesh, and left to rot down for two years or more. For quicker results, collect the leaves in black plastic bin bags and sprinkle with water before sealing up the bags. (You can use a leafmould activator to speed up the process; it should be diluted and watered on to the leaves before sealing the bag.) After a few weeks, pierce the bags with a garden fork to release any liquid and to allow air in. With the activator, the leafmould should be ready for use next spring. Without the activator, the leaves will still rot down in less time than when stored in the open.

Deciduous leaves such as oak or beech make the best leafmould. Evergreens take longer to rot down and are best added in only small quantities to either the leafmould pile or the compost heap.

PLANTING LILIES

Lilies (with the exception of *L. candidum* see p.91) can be planted this month in pots or in the borders. Most lilies need to be planted deeply because they are 'stem-rooting': that is they produce roots from the lower part of the stem which therefore needs to be underground. Ensure the bulbs have 15cm (6in) of soil above them. The exceptions are *Lilium* x *testaceum*, the martagon lily (*Lilium martagon*), the Pyrenean lily (*Lilium pyrenaicum*) and the Madonna lily (*Lilium candidum*); these root from the bottom of the bulb and should be shallow-planted with 2.5–5cm (1–2in) of soil above them.

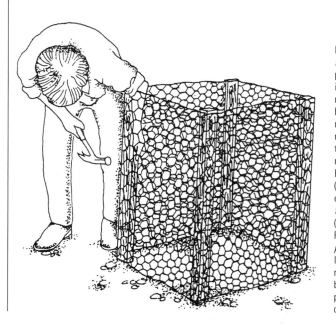

turk's cap

bowl

star

cup

open trumpet

trumpet

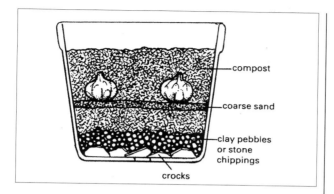

- compost
- coarse sand
- clay pebbles or stone chippings
- crocks

Deep planting lilies

■ Dig over the soil well before planting. Add compost or leafmould if necessary to improve the soil, which should be friable and well-drained. Make a hole 23cm (9in) deep and wide enough to take three or five lily bulbs, spaced 8cm (3in) apart.

■ Add a layer of coarse sand to improve drainage and set the bulbs, pointed end up, on this.

■ Fill the hole with soil and firm gently. Mark the position of the lilies with labels bearing their species name and variety as it is easy to forget they are there in the spring.

GROWING LILIES IN POTS

Most lilies can be grown in pots, although those that grow over 1.2m (4ft) do tend to look too leggy. The new dwarf varieties such as 'Apollo' are particularly suitable; also good is *Lilium regale* 'Album', which stays a reasonably compact 1m (3ft). The slightly tender florist's lily (*Lilium longiflorum*), with its long, highly scented white trumpets, can be grown in pots and kept indoors in a cool conservatory or greenhouse until the danger of frost is past next spring.

■ Choose terracotta, pottery or stone pots as they will be more stable than plastic ones,

which are liable to topple over with the top weight of the stems. Pots must be at least 30cm (12in) deep and preferably more. As in the garden, lilies look best when grown in groups of three or five, rather than singly or in twos. Use a loam-based or a multipurpose compost.

■ Stand the pots in a sheltered position where they will not receive too much direct rain which may waterlog the pots and cause the bulbs to rot.

LILIES FOR THE BORDER

■ Lilium regale – *scented white trumpets, flushed with deep pink, 1.2–1.5m (4–5ft) tall*

■ *Golden-rayed lily (Lilium auratum) – very fragrant, trumpet flowers with golden 'rays' or bands and deep purple spotting, 1.5m (5ft) tall*

■ *Martagon lily (Lilium martagon) – purple-pink 'turk's-cap' flowers, prefers partial shade, 1–1.2m (3–4ft) tall*

■ Lilium cernuum – *very fragrant, small lilac-pink 'turk's-cap' flowers, on slender stems 60cm (24in) tall*

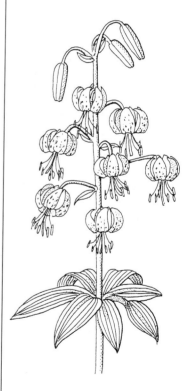

Lilium martagon

plants
OF THE
month

Winter jasmine

WINTER JASMINE
(*Jasminum nudiflorum*)

Winter jasmine has only found its way into cottage gardens in the last hundred years or so, but has become a favourite for its primrose-yellow blossom appearing on naked stems from late autumn onwards. It does not have the scent of the summer white jasmine, but the two grown together, entwined around an arch or trained against the house wall, make good companions. The flexible, arching stems need some support and it can be coaxed to grow over banks, low stone walls and fences. Winter jasmine is very hardy and will bloom in just about any position, even on a shady wall.

type	Deciduous shrub
flowers	Bright yellow, on bare stems; late autumn to late winter
foliage	Dark green, small leaves; spring onwards
height	To 3m (10ft)
spread	1m (3ft) depending on how it is trained
site	Sun or shade; trained against a wall, fence, arch or pergola
soil	Any, well drained
planting	Plant in autumn or spring
care	Cut back all shoots that have just flowered to within 8cm (3in) of the base, in mid-spring. Cut out any dead or damaged shoots. Tie in new shoots to the support as they grow
propagation	Layer shoots in early to mid-autumn. Alternatively, take semi-ripe cuttings in late summer
varieties	There is a variegated form, *J. nudiflorum* 'Aureum', which looks the same as the species in winter, but in summer has green foliage splashed with yellow. *J. officinale* has fragrant white flowers from early summer into autumn. It can reach 10m (30ft) but is easily tamed by twining the growths around a pergola or arbour
cottage garden value	Any plant that flowers so freely through the bleakest months of the year deserves a place in the cottage garden. The bare stems with their star-shaped, shining flowers can also be cut for indoor arrangements, without fear of spoiling the plant

FIRETHORN
(*Pyracantha* spp. and hybrids*)*

It is easy to see how the firethorn got its name with its heavy autumn crop of vivid orange-red berries. It has been grown in cottage gardens for several centuries, as a hedge, as a free-standing shrub and most commonly as a wall shrub. In early summer, the frothy, hawthorn-like blossom is covered with foraging bees and hoverflies. In fact, this is one of the best all-round shrubs for garden wildlife, with the berries providing a long-lasting food source for winter-visiting birds. Firethorn is very easy to grow, even on a cold, shady wall and only needs the lightest pruning. Shrubs to be grown against a wall or fence will need to be tied in to a framework of wires.

type	Evergreen shrub
flowers	Creamy-white; early summer
foliage	Dark green, small, narrow
height	2.5m (8ft)
spread	2.5m (8ft)
site	Sun, partial sun or shade; as a hedge, shrub or wall shrub
soil	Well-drained, fertile
planting	Put out young plants in autumn or spring. For hedging, set them 45–60cm (18–24in) apart
care	Shrubs need no pruning. Wall shrubs can be kept to size by pruning after flowering (in midsummer). Hedges should be clipped in late spring or early summer
propagation	From semi-ripe cuttings taken in late summer. Alternatively, sow seed in late winter in a greenhouse or coldframe
hybrids	Most garden firethorns are hybrids such as *P.* 'Mohave', an early berrying form, and *P.* 'Orange Glow', which has masses of long-lasting orange berries
related species	The best known species are *P. rogersiana*, which is good for hedging, and *P. coccinea*, which has vivid scarlet berries
cottage garden value	The thorny stems and evergreen leaves make *Pyracantha* an effective hedge, although regular trimming means there will be few or no berries. As a wall shrub it can brighten a gloomy corner on the darkest of winter days

RUE
(*Ruta graveolens*)

The winter border is greatly enhanced by a clump or two of rue with its constant blue-green foliage. The foliage looks its best with a dusting of light frost and the autumn mists do nothing but enhance its dusky colour. Its one drawback is that some people find touching the plant causes an allergic skin reaction, so it is not advisable for gardens where children may brush against it. Nevertheless, it was a highly-prized herb in ancient times, and perhaps by homeopathic association, it was recommended for inflammations of the skin, such as bee, wasp and hornet stings. There is an old superstition that if a rue plant is to thrive, it must have been stolen – a throwback to the days when judges on prison duty carried it in their nosegays, to protect against contagious diseases. It has a powerful, pungent smell and was widely used as a strewing herb in law courts, workhouses and prisons. Rue can grow leggy and out of shape and should be replaced regularly.

type	Evergreen sub-shrub
flowers	Sulphur-yellow, 1cm ($\frac{1}{2}$in) across; midsummer
foliage	Blue-green, deeply-divided
height	60–90cm (24–36in)
spread	45–60cm (18–24in)
site	Open, full sun; borders, as edging
soil	Light, well-drained
planting	Plant in autumn or spring. For edging, set the plants 40cm (16in) apart
care	Trim the plants in mid-spring to maintain a compact shape
propagation	Take cuttings in late summer and grow on in a cold frame. Plant into permanent positions the following autumn
varieties	*R. graveolens* 'Jackman's Blue' is the most widely-grown variety, being compact (maximum height 60cm (24in) with bright foliage. There is also a variegated form *R. graveolens* 'Variegata' with creamy-yellow leaves
cottage garden value	The leaves of rue can be dried and used in insect-repellent herb sachets Great care should be taken with the fresh foliage to avoid skin irritations

SWEET VIOLET
(Viola odorata)

Technically, the sweet violet is a spring flower, but in mild areas it begins to flower in late autumn and continues through the winter until the end of spring. Perhaps no one would have noticed the flowers if they had not been so beautifully scented, but this fact alone ensured the violet a place in the annals of history. Few flowers were grown so prolifically by the Ancient Greeks, the Turks, the Syrians and the Romans. Napoleon, its most famous advocate, always offered violets to Josephine on their wedding anniversary. When he was banished to Elba, his last words were '*I will return with the violets in the Spring*'. The sweet violet is a British native and, as such, was probably one of the first plants to be adopted by gardeners. It was held to have many medicinal properties, to be cooling and soothing, and was thus made into ointments, syrups and oils. Candied violets and oil of violets were used as a sweetener and cure for fevers. Many cultivated forms have improved the original flower.

type	Spreading herbaceous perennial
flowers	Purple, mauve; late autumn to late spring
foliage	Mid-green, heart-shaped
height	15cm (6in)
spread	30cm (12in)
site	Partial shade; under hedges, deciduous trees or shrubs
soil	Humus-rich, moisture-retentive
planting	Plant in autumn or spring, setting the plants 30cm (12in) apart. Add manure or compost to poor soils before planting
care	Mulch around the plants in spring to help prevent the soil from drying out in the summer
propagation	Lift overcrowded clumps and divide rhizomes in late spring, discarding any old parts of the plant
varieties	Many of the old single varieties are are still in cultivation including *V.* 'Coeur d'Alsace', a rich pink, *V.* 'Norah Church' with scented dusky-pink flowers and *V.* 'Sulphurea', the only yellow violet (actually a creamy-apricot colour) but unfortunately unscented. Very few double violets are still available, but specialist nurseries do have stocks occasionally
cottage garden value	Violets can be collected for bringing indoors for posies, where the scent from just a few flowers will fill the room. In Elizabethan times they were used as a substitute for sugar, cooked with meat and, when dried, were strewn on the floor to combat household smells. Their use as a cure for insomnia is suggested in *A Little Herbal* of 1525: '*For they that may not sleep, seep this herb in water and at even' let him soak well his feet in water to the ankles, and when he goeth to bed, bind of this herb both temples and he shall sleep well, by the Grace of God.*'

Top to bottom: firethorn, rue and sweet violet

practical project

ORGANIZING A UTILITY AREA

BASIC TOOL KIT

D-handled fork – for digging
D-handled spade – for lifting and cultivating
Wooden-handled trowel – for planting
Dutch hoe – for weeding
Draw hoe – for making seed drills (optional) for vegetable plots only
Secateurs – for pruning and dead heading
Wheelbarrow – for weeding and transporting soil
Watering can – for watering containers and seedlings

Late autumn is a good time to be thinking about the practical aspects of the garden. Every garden needs a utility area – somewhere to keep tools and store pots and a site for the compost bin and cold frame. In a cottage garden, particularly one with a limited amount of space, the decision about where to site the 'business end' of the garden might be dictated by the fact that there is already a permanent feature such as a shed or greenhouse. If there is a choice, the first instinct might be to hide everything from sight, but this is not necessarily the only option. By choosing traditional materials, like wood, terracotta and glass instead of aluminium and plastic, and following styles that are in keeping with the cottage garden, the utility area can be integrated into the design rather than excluded: utility objects become as much a part of the working garden as the shrubs and borders. In the past, this was nearly always the case: gardeners did not hide their cloches, terracotta pots and rhubarb forcers – they valued them and bought the best they could afford.

THE BASIC TOOL KIT

It goes without saying that you should buy the best tools you can afford and look upon them as investments; beautiful objects that can be cherished for years to come. Cottage gardening often takes less equipment than other types of gardening (you may not even need a lawn mower) so the few pieces you buy should be chosen carefully (see list in margin). Stick to tried and trusted designs in traditional materials and avoid gimmicks. The exception to this is a stainless steel spade – a long-lasting, non-rusting, once-in-a-lifetime purchase – if you can afford it.

THE COLDFRAME

If the cottage gardener has only one substantial piece of 'technology' then it must be a coldframe. This simple device for protecting seeds, cuttings and young plants is absolutely indispensable for any gardener who wants to increase his own stock of plants each year and is a lot less costly than a greenhouse.

The average coldframe is basically a wooden box with a sloping hinged lid, usually made of glass lights. The solid sides of the box protect the plants from wind and cold, while the see-through lid allows light in. Although it is unheated, so is not absolutely frost-proof, the coldframe allows a range of young plants to be protected from the worst of the winter weather. In spring, it can be used to bring on seedlings which might otherwise be set back by snow, rain or winds in an open bed. The roof is hinged so it can be propped open from time to time to allow air to circulate and to stop condensation building up.

Site the coldframe in a position that has shade from the midday sun in summer. A home-made coldframe can be made using old timber and discarded window frames.

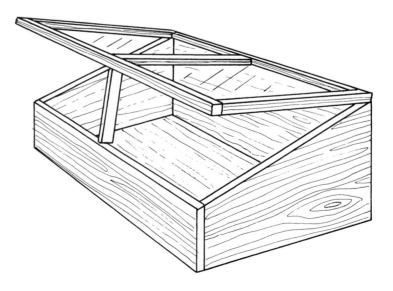

*NB cover not shown
(see text)*

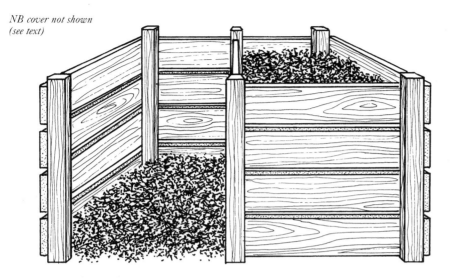

THE POTTING SHED

No self-respecting cottage gardener would be without a potting shed – a simple wooden hut with a bench and some shelving where compost, pots and tools can be stored, seeds can be sown and cuttings taken. The simpler the construction the better: it needs to be tall enough to stand up in, it should have an adequate entrance and a good-sized window to allow light in for working. Cedar sheds will last a lifetime but are very expensive. Other models are made from pressure-treated softwood and are often a bright orange colour; if this is too glaring, tone it down with a dark brown wood stain. Unstained wood could also be stained dark green. The wooden walls make it easy to fit hooks and shelves inside to keep all the tools neat and tidy. The only requirement for fitting a shed in your garden is a clear space (approximately 3 × 3m/10 × 10ft) on level ground.

COMPOST BIN

In a cottage garden, the traditional wooden slatted compost bin is the best choice. It fits in with the low-tech style, recycles organic materials, thus keeping the garden tidy, and provides free compost. If there is room, a double bin is recommended, so that after turning the heap from the first bin into the second, the first bin is free again for new compost.

Key to compost success
■ Collect enough material to fill the bin at least two thirds full. If necessary collect material over several months in black plastic bin bags and store until you have enough to fill the bin. Half-filled bins will not generate enough heat to compost.
■ Add the material in 23cm (9in) layers and sprinkle each layer with water if the material is very dry.
■ Add a high nitrogen activator between each layer. Fresh stable manure or urine is good. Or use a proprietary compost activator.
■ Turn all the material into the second bin after six weeks. If you only have one bin, turn the material out on to a large waterproof ground sheet and fork it back into the bin.
■ Keep the compost covered with a lid or piece of old carpet. This will help to retain heat and moisture.
■ Compost should be ready after about twelve weeks – although it rots down much more slowly in winter.

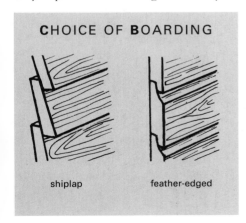

CHOICE OF BOARDING

shiplap   feather-edged

WHAT TO COMPOST

Dead flowers, stems and foliage
Bedding plants
Grass clippings (in small quantities)
Fallen leaves
Raw vegetable peelings
Tea leaves and tea bags
Weeds (except problem perennials)
Soft prunings

WHAT NOT TO COMPOST

Perennial weeds (like ground elder, couch grass)
Woody prunings
Cooked food
Diseased plants

DECEMBER

'For no new flowers shall be born
Save hellebore on Christmas morn,
And bare gold jasmine on the wall'

VITA SACKVILLE-WEST: THE LAND

Winter and its lack of flowers holds no sadness for the cottage gardener, who enjoys the chance to review the garden structure and make plans for the year ahead. Without the pressure to sow, dig or mow, the mind is left free to conjure up pictures of the flower-filled summer ahead.

Wintertime is filled with festivities that demand a good stock of plant material for wreaths, garlands and table centres. Holly, winter jasmine, ivy, winter sweet and viburnum provide cuttings for every kind of indoor decoration. Mistletoe is a precious commodity at this time of year and cottage gardeners should be delighted to find it on the boughs of their old apple or pear tree. Because old trees have gnarled, crevice-ridden bark, mistletoe seeds lodge easily and tend to germinate.

In Herefordshire and other parts of western England, it was customary for cottagers to hang a bough of mistletoe above the fireplace throughout the year. They would ceremonially replace it with a new one on the stroke of midnight on New Year's Eve: having the plant indoors was supposed to bring luck and to aid fertility.

Strangely, midsummer and midwinter are the two best times to think about cottage garden roses. A few, repeat-flowering climbers are hanging on to their blooms tenuously, despite the icy cold and snow. There are few sights more cheering than a rose, dusted with frost on Christmas day. It is a timely reminder to order and plant bare-root roses and a good excuse to dream ahead to midsummer days when the roses will truly be in bloom.

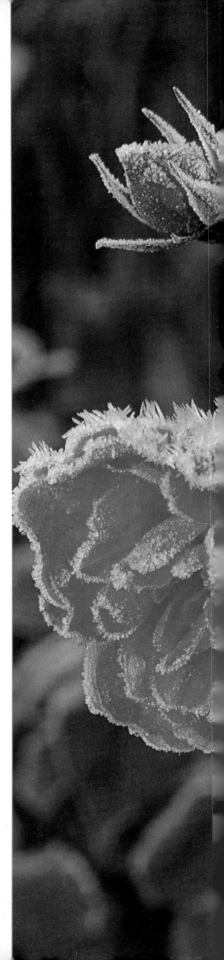

tasks

FOR THE

month

TAKING ROOT CUTTINGS OF PERENNIALS

Perennials like Japanese anemones (*Anemone japonica*), oriental poppies (*Papaver orientale*), bear's breeches (*Acanthus mollis*), phlox, verbascum, globe thistles (*Echinops*), soapwort (*Saponaria*) and bleeding heart (*Dicentra*) can be increased by taking root cuttings between now and late winter. This is a particularly useful way of making new plants from those that are not yet ready to be divided, or ones which you don't wish to divide because they are required to fill up a particular space.

Preparation and procedure

■ Scrape away the soil from around the plant with a trowel, taking care not to dislodge or damage the main crown.
■ Use a sharp knife to cut off pieces of healthy root.
■ Cut the root section into 5–8cm (2–3in) pieces. It is important to know which was the top end of the root and which was the bottom, so make a slanting cut at the lower end to distinguish it.
■ Prepare trays and pots of cutting compost. Slender cuttings (such as those from phlox) should be laid in rows on the surface and covered with 1cm (¹/₂in) of compost. Thicker pieces should be inserted vertically, and the right way up into pots of compost. (Hence the need to know which is the top and

bottom.) Push the cuttings into the compost so that their tops are just beneath the surface.
■ Water the pots and trays with a fine rose and place in a cold frame and keep the lid closed.

Aftercare

Check the cuttings in spring. When they are growing strongly and have produced several healthy shoots with leaves, transfer each cutting to a single 8cm (3in) pot. Stand the pots outdoors and put into new planting positions in the autumn.

PRUNING A NEGLECTED APPLE TREE

Many cottage gardens have just one tree, often an old fruit tree, that is well-loved by its owner, but has seen better days when it comes to bearing fruit. Winter is the best time to set about restoring an old apple, pear or plum tree to its former glory, as it is easy to see the shape and branches clearly. If the tree is very large, it might be better to call in a tree surgeon. However, small trees can be tackled by gardeners who are experienced in using saws and tree loppers.

5-step renovation plan

■ Cut out any damaged, dead or diseased wood.
■ 'Open up' the centre of the tree by taking out some of the large branches.
■ Cut out any crossing or distorted branches.

■ If the tree has got too tall, cut back the highest branches to a lateral (side branch).
■ Thin out the spurs to leave them approximately 23cm (9in) apart. Do this gradually over a couple of years, otherwise no fruit will be produced.

Caution

When making pruning cuts on any tree or shrub, take care to make the cuts cleanly: do not tear the bark. On large branches, seal the cut with a wound sealant (available from good garden centres).

WINTER PRUNING OF ESPALIER TREES

Partly trained two-year-old espalier fruit trees (apple, pear, cherry, and so on) are available from nurseries now and will need to be pruned immediately after planting (see p.119). Established espalier trees also need to be winter-pruned this month.

Two-year-old espaliers

Cut back the central leader to a bud, 5cm (2in) above the second wire. The two buds just below this will shoot to form the next tier. Also cut back the horizontal branches by about half their length. If

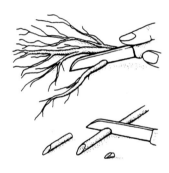

Taking root cuttings

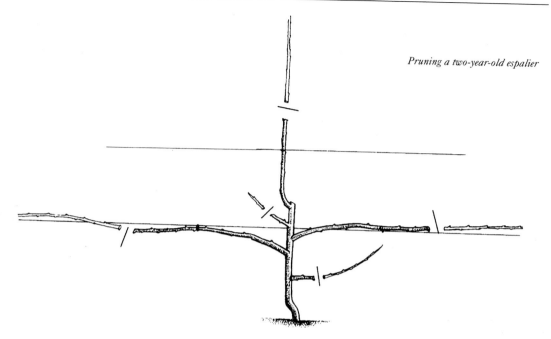

Pruning a two-year-old espalier

the branches seem weak cut them back further than halfway; if they are growing strongly, cut back by only one third.

Established espalier trees

Established trees are pruned to shorten the latest upward-growing shoots. Cut back the laterals to within two or three buds from the main horizontal branches.

FORCING CHICORY

Chicory roots grown in the vegetable garden can be lifted this month to produce blanched 'chicons' for cooking and winter salads. The characteristic white growth is produced by keeping the roots in warmth and darkness.

■ Lift clumps of chicory roots with a garden fork. Cut off the top leaves, leaving a tuft of 5cm (2in).
■ Trim the roots to about 15–20cm (6–8in) long and rub off any side shoots.
■ Use terracotta pots, 23cm (9in) deep and put a layer of compost at the base. Put four or five roots in each pot and fill around them with compost. Water them thoroughly.
■ Cover the pots with another pot of the same size (to exclude the light) and place them in a warm place such as a greenhouse or a kitchen that does not get too hot. They need a temperature of no more than 16°C (60°F) and no less than 7°C (45°F).

Aftercare

The chicons will shoot upwards from the roots and will be ready to cut when they are 15cm (6in) high, in about one month. Cut with a sharp knife at the base and use immediately in the kitchen. The chicon can be chopped or grated into salads or braised whole as a vegetable.

MONTHLY REMINDER

■ **Late seed sowings outdoors in the beds should be covered with cloches. Cloches are also useful for protecting show plants such as the Christmas rose *(Helleborus niger)*, which can get damaged by heavy rain or snow**
■ **Any deciduous trees, shrubs or hedging plants can be planted if the ground is workable and there is no frost or waterlogging**

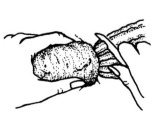

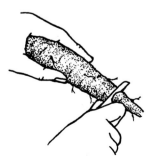

plants
OF THE
month
1

Holly

HOLLY
(*Ilex aquifolium*)

Look over any cottage garden hedge and – if the hedge itself is not holly – then there is almost certainly a holly bush or tree somewhere in the garden. Holly is so entwined in the culture and folklore of Britain that it often goes without mention. It stands for protection against evil and was believed to hold such power against goblins, demons and witches that no house would be without a few decorative branches from Christmas Eve to Candlemas. Naturally then, it was encouraged to grow outside the back door, where its powers were within easy reach. Superstition aside, holly is an integral part of the winter garden. Dark, strong and brightened by berries twinkling like lights on a Christmas tree, it holds a place in every gardener's heart. As a hedge it is impenetrable (if slow growing) and as a specimen shrub it can be clipped and cajoled into topiary-like shapes. Its only requirement is permanency; it is best to buy young plants and be patient with their growth, as mature shrubs do not like to be disturbed. For berries, you need to have a male and a female plant in close proximity or grow one of the hermaphrodite varieties that produce berries on their own.

type	Evergreen shrub or tree
flowers	White, tinged with pink or green, inconspicuous; mid- to late spring
foliage	Dark green, glossy, spiny
fruit	Bright red berries; late autumn to late winter
height	To 5m (15ft)
spread	3m (10ft)
site	Sun or shade (variegated forms may lose their colouring in deep shade); as hedging, informal shrubs, or clipped bushes
soil	Moist, loamy
planting	Put out young plants in late spring. For hedging choose plants 45cm (18in) high and plant 60cm (24in) apart
care	Water new plants frequently in dry weather. After a year of growth, the growing shoots of hedging plants should be pinched out in spring. Clip mature hedges in mid-spring; clip specimen bushes to shape in late summer. Informal shrubs need no pruning
propagation	By layering in mid-autumn. Alternatively take semi-ripe cuttings in late summer

varieties	*I. aquifolium* 'J.C. van Tol' bears berries without another tree nearby and the virtually spineless leaves make it good for hedging. The male hedgehog holly *I. aquifolium* 'Ferox' has densely spined leaves and produces a compact bush; there is a variegated version 'Ferox Argentea' which has creamy edges and spines. One of the most stunning garden hollies is *I. aquifolium* 'Argentea Marginata Pendula', a female form with long, weeping branches, silver-edged leaves and a good crop of berries
related species	*I. crenata* 'Golden Gem' is a dwarf, small-leafed, non-berrying shrub, quite unlike the native holly. The leaves are golden-yellow and as it grows no more than 60cm (24in) high it makes an excellent low hedge

WINTER SWEET
(*Chimonanthus praecox*)

Winter sweet is one of the handful of shrubs that were not available to early cottagers, but surely merit an inclusion in the contemporary cottage garden. Its flowers appear on bare stems at the beginning of winter, perfuming the air with their heavy, spicy scent and providing architectural stems for the flower arranger. The leaves appear later and clothe the shrub through the spring and summer. The shrub stays a manageable size and, as long as it is given a sheltered position, should flower reliably year after year.

type	Deciduous shrub
flowers	Yellow outer petals, with dark purple inner petals, scented; early to late winter
foliage	Mid-green, shiny, willow-like
height	To 3m (10ft)
spread	2.5m (8ft)
site	In full sun; ideally trained against a sunny wall or as a free-standing bush in a sheltered border
soil	Any fertile soil
planting	From mid-autumn to early spring
care	If grown as a bush, thin out old wood after flowering, in early spring. If trained against a wall, cut back all the shoots that have just flowered to within a few inches of the base, in early spring
propagation	By layering in early autumn. Alternatively, seed can be collected

when ripe in mid-autumn and sown in a coldframe. The plants will take five years or more to reach flowering size

varieties The two most widely available varieties are *C. praecox* 'Grandiflora', which has flowers that are larger than the species with deep red centres, and *C. praecox* 'Luteus' which is pure yellow

LAURUSTINUS
(Viburnum tinus)

Once quite a common cottage garden shrub, the evergreen laurustinus has largely been superseded by other more fragrant winter-flowering viburnums. However, it flowers for such a long period and fits so well into a traditional cottage garden, that it is still worth growing. Growing no more than 2.2m (7ft) high, it can be easily clipped into a hedge.

type Evergreen shrub
flowers Pink in bud, opening white; late autumn to late spring
foliage Mid-green, oval
height 2.2m (7ft)
spread 2.2m (7ft)
site In full sun; ideally sheltered from cold winds
soil Moist, fertile soil
planting Plant out in late spring (60cm/24in apart for hedging)
care Thin out old or damaged wood in late spring. Trim hedge after flowering, in late spring
propagation Take semi-ripe cuttings in late summer. Alternatively, layer shoots in early autumn
varieties *V. tinus* 'Eve Price' has particularly dense foliage and deep pink flowers
related species The most popular winter viburnum is *V.* x *bodnantense* 'Dawn', which produces its scented flowers on bare wood and is very frost resistant. It is a larger shrub than *V. tinus*, growing up to 4m (12ft). Also popular is *V. fragrans*, a large, deciduous shrub with richly scented, pendent flowers. Both flower from early to late winter
cottage garden value *V. tinus* is a good choice for the new cottage garden as it makes a quick growing hedge with all-year round foliage and long-lasting flowers

CHRISTMAS ROSE
(Helleborus niger)

The 'black hellebore' takes its name from the colour of its roots, once held in great reverence as they were said to cure madness. They were ground to a powder and taken like snuff to relieve headaches and melancholy. The common name 'Christmas rose' is simply explained by its ability to bloom at Christmas time, although in reality it is often later. There is a medieval tale of a country girl who attended the birth of Christ and was dismayed to find no flowers to present to the Holy child. An angel led her outside and touched the earth from which the Christmas rose sprang up and blossomed. It was traditionally planted at the cottage door to prevent evil spirits from crossing the threshold. *Helleborus niger* is not difficult to grow, given the right conditions – a cool, shaded spot, well-manured ground and minimum disturbance. Cottagers often used to cover the plant with a bell cloche in late autumn to protect the flowers from rain, earth and wind. There are records of plants which have been nurtured through fifty or more winters.

type Partly evergreen perennial
flowers White with yellow anthers, 5cm (2in) across; early to late winter
foliage Dark green, leathery, multi-lobed
height 30–45cm (12–18in)
spread 30cm (12in)
site Partial shade; sheltered from winds
soil Moist, improved with well-rotted manure
planting Set out in mid-autumn, 30–45cm (12–18in) apart
care Protect blooms with cloches in early winter if desired. Top dress with well-rotted manure in mid-autumn
propagation Divide roots in early spring
varieties *H. niger* 'Potters Wheel' has the largest flowers – up to 13cm (5in) across – is widely available. *H. niger* 'Saint Brigid' is an old form with bright green foliage only sold by specialist nurseries
related species The Lenten rose (*Helleborus orientalis*) was introduced into Britain in the nineteenth century and proved very popular with cottage gardeners. The flowers are predominantly pink, purple or rose-coloured. They bloom, as the name suggests, during Lent – from late winter to early spring. Nurseries stock named varieties in many colours including dark browns, purples and a range of speckled forms

Top to bottom: wintersweet, laurustinus and Christmas rose

practical project

PLANTING AND GROWING COTTAGE GARDEN ROSES

In the depths of winter there is nothing more cheering than planning next year's show of roses. It is easy to forget how briefly they bloom, yet most gardeners gladly wait patiently all year for that burst of midsummer colour and perfume.

There are no rules about which roses you can and cannot grow in a cottage garden – the only stipulation is that you have at least one. However, old-fashioned roses and those with a softer, less formal appearance do seem more appropriate than the highly-sculptured blooms of the hybrid teas, which are cultivated for cutting. Perhaps more important is the way they are grown – in mixed borders with other flowering shrubs and perennials or scrambling over arches and doorways, rather than singly in rose 'beds'.

Cottage garden roses seem to divide themselves into two groups: those used for height – climbers and ramblers (see p.45) and those used in borders – old-fashioned shrub roses and the twentieth-century 'English' bush roses. These English bush roses, bred specially for borders, are an exciting introduction, aiming to combine the best of old and modern roses. They have the long-flowering period and range of colours we expect from a modern rose but the softer form and fragrance valued in an old-fashioned type.

PLANTING BARE-ROOT ROSES

Prepare the ground before planting by digging it over well. Cover the ground with an 8cm (3in) layer of organic material (garden compost, well-rotted manure, old potting compost or leafmould, as available) and work this into the earth. The aim is to make the soil friable and open to allow air to circulate. Prepare a separate pile of 'planting soil' made up of one part garden soil and two parts organic matter.

■ Dig a hole wide enough to take the roots when they are spread out. It should be deep enough so that the 'union' of the rose (where the rootstock meets the stem) will be at or only just below soil level. The roots of roses often spread out in one direction so that the rose itself will sit to one side of the hole.

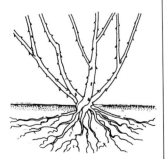

■ Spread the roots out in the hole as much as possible, so that they are not crossing over one another. Fill the hole with the 'planting soil' shaking the plant gently to ensure that the soil fills the spaces between the roots.

■ Firm down the soil by treading it lightly. Fill the hole with ordinary soil, but do not tread down a second time. If the ground seems dry, water directly around the roots, using a watering can with a spout (not a sprinkler rose).

A BRIEF HISTORY OF THE ROSE

■ *The first roses in cottage gardens were probably grown from cuttings, suckers or hips taken from the wild hedgerow roses,* Rosa arvensis *(field rose) and* Rosa canina *(dog rose) or* Rosa rubiginosa *(sweet briar). Grander gardens had, of course, been cultivating roses for thousands of years. The Romans grew roses for scenting their baths and* Rosa gallica *'Officinalis', the oldest rose still in cultivation, was being grown in Europe in the thirteenth century. Known as the 'apothecary's rose', it formed the basis of a perfume industry around Provins in France. Gallica roses were a mainstay of many medieval gardens and were subsequently joined by damask roses from the Mediterranean countries, centifolias bred in Holland and moss roses from France.* ■

■ *Well-to-do gardeners joined in the eighteenth- and nineteenth-century passion for rose breeding, although how far this filtered down to ordinary cottage gardeners is not clear. It is possible that cuttings and hips were purloined from the squire's garden or a nearby monastery and planted around the door as a status symbol, in much the same way as people nowadays adorn their houses with carriage lamps and cast iron signs. The Edwardian fad was for bedding roses and the soft crimsons and pinks gave way to scarlet, bright yellow and orange. Hybrid tea roses, which are robust and perpetual flowering, fitted the bill perfectly by filling formal long borders with summer colour. But something of the spontaneity of the rose was lost: its unexpectedness and relaxed form. Now we have a return in popularity of the old-fashioned roses and cottage gardens are the perfect setting in which to grow them* ■

CHOOSING AND ORDERING ROSES

For the best range of old-fashioned roses, consult the catalogues of specialist nurseries. Not only will the choice be wider than in a garden centre, but the catalogues themselves are full of interesting information and growing tips. Most roses – particularly those from nurseries – are sold bare-rooted and must be planted in winter while the plant is dormant. Try to plant roses before the onslaught of snow and frost, but if the ground is very hard or waterlogged, delay ordering until late winter.

When the plants arrive, take them out of their packaging and examine the roots. Cut off any that are damaged and trim the whole root system to about 25cm (10in). Also check the branches and cut off any that have been damaged in transit. Make sure all the stems are cut to an outward-facing bud. If the weather is unsuitable for planting straight away it is important that the roots are kept moist until they can be planted: stand them in a bucket of potting compost or peat substitute in a shed or outhouse.

COMPANIONS FOR ROSES

These are some suggestions for combining with roses:

Chives (*Allium schoenoprasum*)
Marjoram (*Origanum marjorana*)
Nepeta (*Nepeta* 'Six Hills Giant')
Purple-leaved sage (*Salvia officinalis* 'Purpurascens')
Santolina (*Santolina chamaecyparissus*)
Senecio (*Senecio cineraria*)

OLD ROSES

Gallicas (*R. gallica* and varieties)
Mainly 1.2×1.2m (4×4ft), gallicas have heavily perfumed, pale pink to deep crimson flowers in summer. *R.* 'Gloire de France' is 1m (3ft) high with full, mauve-pink flowers
Damasks
Mainly 1.5×1.2m (5×4ft), damasks have full, perfumed flowers in white and pink shades, usually in summer. (Portlands may flower into autumn.) *R.* 'Omar Khayyam' is 1×1m (3×3ft) with downy, grey foliage and pink flowers.
Centifolias (Cabbage roses)
These floppy shrubs bear large, very double, white, or pink to crimson flowers with a lovely scent. *R.* 'Fantin Latour' is 1.5×1.2m (5×4ft), full-petalled and blush-pink.
Bourbons
Upright, slender roses (max 2.2m/7ft high); taller varieties, like *R.* 'Madame Isaac Pereire', can be trained on a post. Delicate, perfumed flowers in pink, lilac and carmine shades are borne from summer to autumn.
Albas (*R. alba* and varieties)
Up to 2m (6ft) high, these upright shrubs have single or double, white or palest pink flowers in early summer. *R.* 'Felicité Parmentier' is pale pink and 1×1m (3×3ft).

Gallica

Damask

Bourbon

Centifolia

Alba

plants
OF THE
month
2

ESSENTIAL ROSES
FOR THE
COTTAGE GARDEN

Sweet briar

SWEET BRIAR
(*Rosa rubiginosa*)

No cottage was complete without a sweet briar – or eglantine – twining around the porch or over a garden seat. It has a wonderful fresh fragrance which comes mainly from the leaves and tends to be strongest in spring, particularly after a shower of rain; the single, clear pink flowers in summer also have a delicate scent. The arching branches can be trained over arches and pergolas, although they are very thorny, and the shrubs are equally at home in the border or grown as an informal hedge. The sweet briar is native to Britain and northern Europe and can be found growing in hedgerows and on chalk downland. It was one of the first roses grown in cottage gardens from at least the sixteenth century onwards.

type	Deciduous shrub with arching stems
flowers	Single, pink, delicate scent, 4cm (1½in) across; early summer
foliage	Mid-green, scented
hips	Bright red; autumn to winter
height	To 3m (10ft)
spread	2.5m (8ft)
site	In sun or shade
soil	Tolerates poor soils but will do best on fertile ground
planting	Plant bare-root specimens from late autumn to early spring, adding plenty of organic matter to the planting hole
care	Water new plants during first summer and train around arches or pillars while stems are still young and pliable. Mulch around the base of the plants with well-rotted manure annually in spring. Sweet briars need little pruning, but any weak or old stems should be cut out at ground level in early spring. Remove any straggly growth from hedges
propagation	Remove seeds from hips when ripe (usually mid-autumn) and sow in pots of seed compost. Place in a coldframe. When the seedlings are large enough to handle, plant them outdoors in a nursery bed to grow on for one or two years. Alternatively, take semi-ripe cuttings with a heel in late summer (see p.91)
hybrids	The Penzance hybrids, bred by Lord Penzance at the end of the nineteenth century, have the same aromatic foliage as the original but the flowers are available in a wider colour range. *R.* 'Flora McIvor' has rose-pink flowers with white centres; *R.* 'Amy Robsart' is deep pink
cottage garden value	Sweet briars are vigorous shrubs with a long season of interest. The foliage is best in spring, the flowers in summer and the hips in autumn. The thorny stems make it a good plant for an informal hedge

THE APOTHECARY'S ROSE
(*Rosa gallica* 'Officinalis')

Perhaps no other rose has a history as rich and authentic as *Rosa gallica* 'Officinalis'. It is certainly the oldest gallica rose in cultivation and although at first it was only grown in monasteries and physic gardens, it soon found its way into cottage gardens. It has been grown in Europe since the thirteenth century, and was known as the 'Rose of Provins' because the monks of Provins, near Paris, made a famous conserve from the hips. This was the rose adopted as the symbol of the House of Lancaster in the Wars of the Roses. The light crimson petals of the semi-double flowers keep their fragrance longer than most other roses and are essential ingredients of pot pourri. In the garden, it makes a medium-sized shrub for the cottage border.

type	Deciduous shrub
flowers	Semi-double, crimson to pink, scented, 6cm (2½in) across; early summer
foliage	Mid-green
hips	Bright red; autumn to winter
height	1–1.2m (3–4ft)
spread	1–1.2m (3–4ft)
site	In sun or shade; in borders or as a low hedge
soil	Tolerates poor soils but will do best on fertile ground
planting	Plant bare-root specimens from late autumn to early spring, adding plenty of organic matter to the planting hole
care	Water new plants during first summer. Mulch around the base of the plants with well-rotted manure annually in spring. Little pruning needed. Cut out any weak or old stems at ground level in early spring if necessary. If grown as a hedge, remove any straggly growth in early spring

propagation Take semi-ripe cuttings with a heel in late summer (see p.91)

other varieties The best known sport of *R. gallica* 'Officinalis' is *R. mundi* (*R. gallica* 'Versicolor'), the crimson- and white-striped rose. Legend tells that it was named 'fair Rosamund's rose' after the mistress of Henry II, but others claim it was not discovered until the sixteenth century. It has the same compact habit as *R. gallica* 'Officinalis' and makes a striking hedge

cottage garden value All gallica roses have a good perfume and their petals are highly prized for making pot pourri. As a garden shrub they are hardy and compact, and although the flowers are short lived, the hips extend the season of interest

OLD MOSS ROSE
(*Rosa centifolia* 'Muscosa')

The 'old moss rose' has been known in gardens since the seventeenth century and is a sport of *R. centifolia*. Moss roses are all sports (or mutations) of other roses, the 'moss' actually being green hairs on the stems, leaves and calyx which give the plant a soft, mossy appearance. The old pink moss makes an open medium bush with heavily scented flowers which appear over two months of the year.

type Deciduous shrub

flowers Double, clear pink, heavily scented, 10cm (4 in) across; early to mid-summer; repeat flowering

foliage Mid-green, heavily toothed

height 1.2m (4ft)

spread 1.2m (4ft)

site In full sun; in a border

soil Any fertile soil, will tolerate poorer soil

planting Plant bare-root specimens from late autumn to early spring, adding plenty of organic matter to the planting hole

care Water new plants during first summer. Mulch around the base of the plants with well-rotted manure annually in spring. Little pruning needed. Remove dead or straggly stems from the base in early spring

propagation Difficult to propagate except by expert budding

other varieties *R.* 'William Lobb' is an established cottage garden rose, known as the 'old velvet moss'. It makes a tall shrub (2.5m/8ft) with rather lanky stems which need to be supported by a wall or pillar. The dark, magenta blooms are well-scented and, towards the end of the flowering period, they fade to a dusky mauve

cottage garden value The moss roses have a good scent, pretty flowers and the lovely 'moss' covered buds and stems

OLD GLORY ROSE
(*Rosa* 'Gloire de Dijon')

This hybrid rose, introduced into Britain from France in 1853, generated a lot of excitement and went on to become one of the best-loved climbing roses. It is a hardy plant with large, scented flowers which are often the first to open in late spring and often repeat later in the season. The buds are buff-coloured but the flowers open to a full, soft, apricot pink – the warmer the weather, the stronger the pink. 'Gloire de Dijon' is among the best climbers for growing against the wall of a house and is hardy even on a shaded wall.

type Deciduous climber

flowers Double, buff apricot-pink, scented, 10cm (4 in) across; late spring to early summer; often repeats later in the summer

foliage Dull green

height To 5m (15ft)

spread 2.5m (8ft)

planting Plant bare-root specimens from late autumn to early spring, adding plenty of organic matter to the planting hole

site In sun or shade; against a wall, any aspect (a sunny wall will ensure the blooms are earlier and have a strong colour)

soil Any fertile soil

care Water new plants during first summer. Mulch around the base of the plants with well-rotted manure annually in spring. Prune in early spring to retain a good framework, cutting back the laterals (which bear the flowers) to two or three buds

propagation Difficult to propagate except by expert budding

cottage garden value *R.* 'Gloire de Dijon' is an excellent covering plant for a bare wall where the heavy blooms can be fully appreciated. The flowers have a good scent and a relaxed, old-fashioned appearance

Top to bottom: the Apothecary's rose, the Old Glory rose and the Old Moss rose

appendix
1

COTTAGE
GARDENERS AND
WRITERS

An illustration of John Parkinson from the Paradisus

There are several names that crop up time and time again in any history of the cottage garden. These men and women helped to shape our ideas about what plants to grow and, in many cases, played an active part in breeding, developing and distributing the plants. They are the people who, through their study and practice have added greatly to our enjoyment of British native plants, as well as those from other parts of the world. A few are listed here. While these gardeners are assured a place in the history books, we should not forget the thousands of ordinary cottagers who, through their enthusiasm and curiosity, made many unrecorded advances in gardening. We will never know *their* names, but without them, our idea of cottage gardening simply would not exist.

JON THE GARDENER

Jon the Gardener takes credit for writing *The Feate of Gardening* (c1400), the first horticultural work in the English language. Nothing is known about Jon (which was probably an assumed name) except that he wrote in verse, to help those who could not read to remember the advice more easily. He lists almost one hundred, mainly native, plants which are suitable for gardens: there are lots of herbs of course, a limited range of vegetables including leeks and cabbage, some fairly adventurous salad crops including lettuce, garlic, radish and salad burnet, and a basic selection of flowers, such as daffodils, primroses, lilies and lavender. Gardening was still heavily biased towards plants that had a medicinal or household use like chamomile, liverwort and valerian and any decorative effect was purely accidental.

THOMAS TUSSER

By the Elizabethan age, gardening had come on in leaps and bounds. Tusser's *Five Hundred Points of Good Husbandry* (1573), also written in verse, was aimed at the small farmer or husbandman whose wife tended to the gardens as part of the division of labour on an average smallholding.

'Good housewifes in summer will save their own seeds,
Against the next year, as occasion needs'

Tusser may not have penned prize-winning poetry, but he gives us a fascinating insight into what plants were grown and their uses. He divides them into 'Physic herbs' (such as betony, cumin and poppy), 'Flowers for pots' (bay, cornflowers, pinks and French marigolds), 'Strewing herbs' (hops, tansy and violets) and 'Seeds and herbs for the kitchen' (fennel, rosemary, saffron and thyme). The list is surprisingly wide-ranging and readers following Tusser's advice would have a very attractive and well-stocked cottage garden, even by today's standards.

THE AGE OF THE HERBALS

The general renaissance of scholarship in sixteenth- and seventeenth-century Europe, coupled with the invention of printing, which enabled an easier exchange of ideas, encouraged the production of botanical books and a more scientific approach to plants. Several names stand out from this period, although whether these scholars directly influenced the ordinary cottage gardener is debatable. At any rate, the herbals they produced are a valuable resource for gardening historians, confirming the existence of certain plants and their assumed properties.

William Turner

Turner served under Henry VIII and Queen Elizabeth I and his *New Herball* (1551–68) was a breakthrough in British botany. He was the first botanist to record native plants scientifically and use their local names such as 'sneezewort' for *Achillea ptarmica* and 'purple loosestrife' for *Lythrum salicaria*.

John Parkinson

Parkinson began his career as an apothecary and took to gardening in retirement. His garden in Covent Garden, London was the 'laboratory' from where he produced the first illustrated book on ornamental plants (*Paradisi in Sole, Paradisus Terrestris, 1629*). It was so well received that he was appointed as King's botanist to Charles I. The book was intended for well-off people with pleasure gardens, but there was a section on what the 'poor' might grow which included globe artichokes, marrows, peas, onions and turnips.

John Gerard

Gerard supervised the making and care of some major gardens of his time, including his own considerable plot in Holborn, London. It was from here that he drew on his experiences of plants and their habits to compile his *Herball or Histories of Plantes* (1597). Sadly, many of his entries have proved to be inaccurate and he was known to describe plants growing wild in places he had never actually visited. Nevertheless, the lists of plants give a good indication of what were common garden plants of the time.

Nicholas Culpeper (1616–54)

Probably the most popular of the herbalists, Culpeper translated other physicians' work from Latin into English, thereby making it accessible to the common man. He not only described the plants but explained how and why they cured certain ailments, risking the contempt of the medical profession, who no doubt had an interest in keeping their knowledge a secret. Culpeper died tragically young, but despite the fact that his theories were heavily based on astrology, his work is still in print today – in cheap paperback versions – just as it was in the seventeenth century.

Reverend Samuel Gilbert

Samuel Gilbert wrote a book called *The Florist's Vade Mecum* (1683) in which he somewhat snobbishly separated plants into those worthy of the attention of the 'florist' (see. p.106) and those which he thought were only fit for 'countrywomen'. The latter are, of course, the true cottage garden plants of the time and include double hollyhocks, snapdragons, lupins, scabious, foxgloves and mallows.

THE POETS AND WRITERS

Our knowledge of ordinary country gardens would be very much the poorer without the work of some of the great literary figures. Writers like Chaucer, Shakespeare, Wordsworth and Coleridge took an interest in the gardens and dwellings of cottagers and, fortunately for us, described their flowers in poetry, prose and song. But the writer most closely associated with cottage gardens is the early nineteenth-century poet **John Clare**. A labourer himself, John Clare described the cottages and countryside around his home in Northamptonshire in affectionate and authentic detail. It is through him that we know how plants found their way into gardens in the first place:

'The cottager when coming home from plough
Brings home a cowslip root in flower to set...'.

And the range of plants that cottagers grew:

'Fine cabbage roses, painted like her face,
The shining pansy, trimm'd with golden lace,
And tall-topped lark's heels, feather'd thick with flowers,
The woodbine climbing o'er the door in bowers...'.

Clare's keen eye for plants, fills out the picture of the rural cottager's plot and although he wrote with great sentimentality about his home village, there is no reason to believe that his picture is not an accurate one.

TURN-OF-THE-CENTURY REACTIONARIES

Two names stand out from the latter years of the nineteenth and early part of the twentieth century: **Gertrude Jekyll** and **William Robinson**. Neither of them were cottage gardeners in the original sense – they were professional people, not labourers – yet they greatly influenced the style of gardening we now call cottage gardening. Both of them reacted against the late Victorian passion for orderly rows of bedding: Robinson by advocating natural planting (in the *English Flower Garden* 1883), and Jekyll by encouraging her wealthy Edwardian clients to plant herbaceous borders.

Gertrude Jekyll took her inspiration from the small cottage gardens which she made a point of visiting, translating their planting schemes to country house proportions. Her own home at Munstead Wood, Surrey was no cottage, but the garden was planted with a cottage style mix of lilies, delphiniums, pinks, lavender and catmint, all carefully designed to create drifts of harmonious colour. More than any other gardener, she represented the idea that manor house gardens could be enclosed with hedges and filled with cottage plants. In the early 1900s, **Lawrence Johnston** was putting similar ideas into practice at Hidcote in Gloucestershire and, in the 1930s at Sissinghurst Castle, Kent, **Vita Sackville-West** made a cottage garden on a grand scale.

Now, the wheel has turned full circle. Cottage gardening is again enjoying a surge in popularity with owners of plots large and small. Authenticity is less important than preserving the spirit of former ages. Plants are again taking centre stage above landscaping, lawns and 'features', and we are witnessing the dawn of yet another century of cottage gardening in all its myriad interpretations.

Clematis Batica.
The Spanish Trauellers-Ioy.

The sixteenth century plantsman and herbalist, John Gerard, saw the wild clematis (Clematis vitalba) growing in every hedgerow and marvelled at the shade it offered to weary travellers, 'thereupon have I named it Traveller's Joy'. But, it has an older name, 'old man's beard' – clearly a reference to the shaggy seed heads – and a more interesting one, 'poor man's friend' or 'boy's bacca' – a reference to the use of the stems as a substitute for tobacco. Shepherds, gypsies and no doubt local youths smoked lengths of the dry stems in the absence of anything more addictive. It is still found growing in cottage gardens, although the imported species are less rampant and have better flowers and smoother seed heads. All parts of Clematis are slightly toxic. (Illustration from Gerard's Herball)

appendix
2

Buried in the gardening history books are plants that used to be commonplace but are now largely forgotten or overlooked in favour of newer varieties. Many are still available although rarely grown, a few have been lost to cultivation, but flourish in the wild. For interest here are a few, with what is known of them.

Common centaury

CENTAURY
(Centaurium erythraea)

This plant appears in Jon the Gardener's list of c1400, and Culpeper remarked on its bitter taste. The wild common centaury, which is a small wort-like plant with clusters of pink flowers in midsummer, was obviously grown in gardens for hundreds of years, mainly for its medicinal properties against poison and fevers. Centauries are rarely grown these days except as part of a wildflower meadow.

DITTANDER
(Lepidium latifolium)

Dittander, or pepperwort, was widely grown in gardens and was used to flavour food and sauces before the introduction of pepper. It is a tall perennial with bluey-green leaves and panicles of white flowers. Like horseradish, the roots and leaves give the burning taste of pepper. It grows wild in damp, sandy places, often on salt marshes, and is rarely seen in gardens, probably due to the fact that it has a tendency to spread and swamp out more delicate plants.

GROMWELL
(Lithospermum officinale)

A member of the borage family, gromwell is a tall, hairy perennial with insignificant cream flowers followed by shiny white 'nuts' or seeds. It was a common garden plant from 1400 onwards and the seeds were made into a concoction for hastening childbirth. Modern research is investigating a possible contraceptive substance contained in them. Today, gar-

Common gromwell

Tutsan

deners grow the related, mat-forming *Lithodora diffusa* (syn. *Lithospermum diffusum*) from southern Europe.

HENBANE
(Hyoscyamus niger)

This is a poisonous plant which was grown for its narcotic properties, particularly to alleviate toothache. It is tall and coarse-looking, with an unpleasant smell, and can never have been grown for its attractiveness. Culpeper warned against taking the plant internally, but said it was excellent for swellings, gout and chilblains. It can still be found growing wild of Britain.

Henbane

WHITE HOREHOUND
(Marrubium vulgare)

This plant belongs to the germander family and has been grown in Britain for over a thousand years. It is a white downy perennial with a thyme-like scent and small white flowers, which are attractive to bees. It can still be found in cottage gardens where it was valued for use against coughs and chest problems. Pharmacies continued to make lozenges and syrups from it well into the twentieth century.

TUTSAN
(Hypericum androsaemum)

With its sunny yellow flowers, this small evergreen shrub resembles the more commonly grown 'rose of Sharon' (*H. calycinum*) although the flower sepals have distinctive red edges. Tutsan, from the French *toute-saine*, and meaning wholesome, was adored for its aromatic smell and all-round medicinal virtues. The leaves were dried for scent and, because it was also supposed to bring luck, they were pressed between the pages of prayer books and bibles. It has been grown in gardens since the Middle Ages and is still available from nurseries. Tutsan makes a good garden plant, although in cold areas it may lose its leaves in winter.

COTTAGE GARDEN PLANTS

Cottage garden nurseries tend to be small concerns and may not be open all year round. Therefore it is important to write first, requesting a catalogue and to check the opening times and conditions of sale. Those listed here are just a small selection of the many good specialist nurseries found throughout the British Isles.

Bernwode Plants
Ludgershall
Aylesbury
Buckinghamshire

Comprehensive range of cottage garden and unusual plants. Mail order catalogue available from The Thatched Cottage, Duck Lane, Ludgershall, Aylesbury, Buckinghamshire, HP18 9XZ

Bloms Bulbs
Primrose Nursery
Sharnbrook
Bedfordshire
MK44 1LW

Mainstream bulb supplier, but catalogue includes lots of old favourites and unusual new varieties – especially narcissus and tulips

---

Cottage Garden Roses
Woodlands House
Stretton
Near Stafford
ST19 9LG

Old roses – including gallicas, bourbons and damasks – by mail order

---

Foxgrove Plants
Enborne
Newbury
Berkshire
RG14 6RE

Good range of hardy and unusual plants, by mail order and in person

---

Glebe Cottage Plants
Pixie Lane
Warkleigh
Umberleigh
Devon
EX37 9DH

Catalogue of interesting, garden-worthy plants, by mail order and in person

---

King's Seeds
Monks Farm
Coggeshall Road
Kelvedon
Essex
CO5 9PG

Comprehensive catalogue of flower, vegetable, salad and herb seeds

---

The Margery Fish Plant Nursery
East Lambrook Manor
South Petherton
Somerset
TA13 5HL

East Lambrook, created by the great cottage gardener and plant collector, Margery Fish, is very much a plantsman's garden. The nursery stocks plants propagated from the gardens and visitors are welcome in person. There is also a mail order catalogue

---

North Green Snowdrops
North Green Only
Stoven
Beccles
Suffolk
NR34 8DG

The connoisseur's choice for snowdrop bulbs and a specialist selection of flower seeds by mail order only

---

Rupert Bowlby
Gatton
Reigate
Surrey
RH2 OTA

An extensive collection of alliums and other unusual bulbs by mail order

USEFUL ADDRESSES

● SOCIETIES

The Cottage Garden Society
Hurstfield House
244 Edleston Road
Crewe
Cheshire
CW2 7EJ

Members receive regular newsletters on cottage garden plants and their history, plus events and garden visits

Henry Doubleday Research Association
Ryton Organic Services
Ryton-on-Dunsmore
Coventry
CV8 3LG

The National Sweet Pea Society
3 Chalk Farm Road
Stokenchurch
High Wycombe
Buckinghamshire
HP14 3TB

Members receive growing instructions, regular bulletins on seasonal topics and tickets to sweet pea exhibitions and trials

FURTHER READING

For a vivid, readable account of cottage garden history, look no further than Anne Scott-James' *The Cottage Garden* (Penguin 1982). Also of historic interest are: Culpeper's *Complete Herbal* (1653), William Robinson's *The English Flower Garden'* (1883) and writings by Gertrude Jekyll, Margery Fish and Vita Sackville-West – many of which are available as affordable reprints.

For fascinating, although somewhat outdated, descriptions of individual flowers, *Flowers and their Histories* by Alice M. Coats (1956), and Roy Genders' *The Cottage Garden* (1969) are worth dipping into (both out of print). For folklore and plant tales, the standard work is Geoffrey Grigson's *The Englishman's Flora* (1955). For wild flower identification, *The Illustrated Flora of Britain and Northern Europe* by Marjorie Blamey and Christopher Grey-Wilson (Hodder and Stoughton 1989) is indispensable. For garden plant identification, the Pan Garden Plants series by Roger Phillips and Martyn Rix is excellent, especially the volumes on perennials, vegetables and roses. *The Cottage Gardener's Companion* (David & Charles 1993) compiled by the Cottage Garden Society is also a good source of planting ideas and information.

ACKNOWLEDGEMENTS

The historical elements in this book owe a great deal to the work of Anne Scott-James who did the pioneering and very painstaking research into the history of cottage gardens and made it easier for all of us writers who followed her. However, as always I am totally responsible for the book's content – the good bits and the bad bits. My thanks to Anna Mumford for asking me to write the book, to project editor Jo Weeks for her diplomatic and professional approach and to my agents Shelia Watson and Mandy Little for being there.

INDEX

INDEX